Frederic William Farrar, Julia Louisa Matilda Woodruff

Farrar year book

Selections from the writings of the Rev. Frederic W. Farrar

Frederic William Farrar, Julia Louisa Matilda Woodruff

Farrar year book
Selections from the writings of the Rev. Frederic W. Farrar

ISBN/EAN: 9783741190070

Manufactured in Europe, USA, Canada, Australia, Japa

Cover: Foto ©Lupo / pixelio.de

Manufactured and distributed by brebook publishing software (www.brebook.com)

Frederic William Farrar, Julia Louisa Matilda Woodruff

Farrar year book

PREFACE.

ARCHDEACON FARRAR is no stranger to us. As the author of the "Life of Christ," and other works, strong in intellectual inspiration and spiritual influence, he was well known in this country, and his welcome was ready for him when he visited it ten years ago. The words that he then spoke face-to-face with us were shortly afterwards published in a volume entitled "Sermons and Addresses in America," with a preface by Phillips Brooks. Other volumes have since come from his pen; and all have met with such acceptance as to suggest that a Year Book of short selections from them, for the help and enrichment of daily life, would find eager readers. To such a book there can be no more fitting preface than these words from prefaces of his own:

"If the following pages in any measure fulfil the objects for which such a book should be written, they should fill the minds of those who read with solemn and not ignoble thoughts; they should add 'sunlight to daylight by making the happy happier;' they should encourage the toiler; they should console the sorrowful; they should point the weak to the one source of moral strength. . . . And their purpose will not have wholly failed if they impart to but one single soul a deeper conviction of the certainty of those doctrines which were once found competent to regenerate a diseased and perishing society, and which have lost no single element of their power to quicken, in the hearts of all those who faithfully accept them, the desire to spend a noble life, and the ability to bring that desire to good effect."

In making the selections, care has been taken not to misrepresent the author, although the crowded page has sometimes compelled the omission of the signs of excision. But this has been as seldom as possible, and never when such omission might seem to involve even the slightest change of meaning.

And now the little book is sent forth, with an earnest prayer that God may bless it to

> Some souls who daily burdens bear
> Of sin or sorrow, doubt or care,
> And fain would rise on daily wings
> Of holy thought to better things.

W. M. L. JAY.

Messages of the Books	I
Ephatha	II
The Voice from Sinai	III
The Lord's Prayer	IV
Truths to Live By	V
In the Days of thy Youth	VI
Everyday Christian Life	VII
Sermons and Addresses in America	VIII
Sermons	IX
The Silence and the Voices of God	X
The Fall of Man, and Other Sermons	XI
The Witness of History to Christ	XII
Life of Christ	XIII
Eternal Hope	XIV

The Roman numerals at the end of the selections refer to the above list of books used; the Arabic numerals, to the pages where the selections may be found.

JANUARY 1.

The world passeth away. — I. JOHN ii. 17.
I saw a new heaven and a new earth.
REV. xxi. 1.

AND we may still retain that hope of, nay, that sure belief in, a new heaven and a new earth in the eternity which is to be. But now, at the beginning of this new year, the question is, whether it need be *a hope* only? . . . Is it wholly impossible for us, here and now, to spread over our heads some of the azure of that new heaven, and to make the new earth *begin* at least to blossom as the rose? . . . Yes, it is possible; it is in our power, if through the o'er-arching azure we can gaze into clear openings of the empyrean, and there by the eye of faith see Jesus standing at the right hand of God. . . . Yes, it is possible to the sincere, the humble, and the faithful; to all who feel and have experienced that love and duty can make a little heaven even on this sad earth. VII. 15, 23.

  We pause beside this door:
Thy year, O God, how shall we enter in?
   . . . .
  The footsteps of a Child
Sound close beside us. Listen, He will speak!
His birthday bells have hardly rung a week,
Yet has He trod the world's press undefiled.
"Enter through Me," He saith, "nor wander more;
  For lo! I am the Door."
LUCY LARCOM.

JANUARY 2.

LET us [go forth] to-day with conceptions of duty larger and more hopeful; with more yearning both after the sympathy of Christ and after His activity; with more faith to see that the world would not be so utter a ruin but for our perversity; with more hope to be convinced that even we can help to redeem its disorders, and restore its pristine perfectness. . . . Let us see and be thankful for the beauty of the world, the sweet air, the sunshine, the sea, the splendid ornaments of heaven, the ever-recurring circles of the divine beneficence. Let us learn the secrets of the mighty laws which only crush us when we disobey them, and which teach us, with divine inflexibility, that as we sow we reap. . . . Let us believe — for we were saved in Hope — that "Utopia itself is but another word for time;" and that, if our own work seems but infinitesimal, yet "there are mites in science, as well as in charity, and the ultimate results of each are alike important and beneficial." And so the more we share in . . . the toil of the Saviour, the more shall we share in His redeeming gladness, — the more shall we see and share in

>"The joy of God to see a happy world."

II. 188.

JANUARY 3.

He shall drink of the brook in the way.
Ps. cx. 7.

"MAN never is, but always to be blessed," says the poet ; but if we do not wring our happiness out of the fair, peaceful, humble duties of the present, however great its trials, we shall never find it in the weakened forces, in the darkened rays of the future. Our duty lies, not in regrets, not in resolutions, but in thoughts followed by resolves, and resolves carried out in actions. Our life lies, not in retrospect of a vanished past, not in hopes of an ambitious future ; our life is here, to-day ; in our prayers, in our beliefs, in our daily, hourly conduct. . . . If we have learnt this, we are not far from, yea, we are *in* the Kingdom of Heaven. If we have learnt this, we are both looking for, and hasting unto, the coming of our Lord.

I. 204.

Shines the last age, the next with hope is seen,
To-day slinks off unmarked between ;
Future or past no richer secret holds,
O friendless Present! than thy bosom holds.

EMERSON.

JANUARY 4.

God's hand uncounted agencies
Marshals and notes and counts as His.
Susan Coolidge.

IF life be a battle-field, then, like other battle-fields, it is won by the nameless multitudes, by the unrecorded hosts. The great leaders fight and fall, conscious that theirs shall be the glory of the victory; but as the thin red lines advance to battle amid the storm of shells, each peasant-soldier knows well that where he falls the poppy and the violet shall but blossom over a nameless grave, and yet they advance unflinching to the batteries whose cross-fire vomits death upon them, and so — as a generous leader once exclaimed — and so "they die by thousands, those unnamed demi-gods."

. . . And we too — however commonplace, however humble — we too can keep the ranks unbroken; we too can be of "the faithful who were not famous;" we too can make sure that where we stand, there at least, in the great Armageddon, by the grace of God, there shall be no swerving in the line; and thereby shall our little service be, as has well been said, "precious as the continuity of sunbeams is precious, though some of them fall unseen and on barrenness;" precious as the drops of rain are precious, though some of them seem to be wasted in idle dimples upon the shipless main.

VI. 16.

JANUARY 5.

YOU have heard that your bodies are temples of the Holy Ghost; but a temple that is not desecrated must be tended and adorned. The great city of Ephesus was proud to call herself upon her coins the Νεωκόρος, "the temple-sweeper" of her heathen fane; and will you make no effort to cleanse and tend that heart which is the living temple of the one true God? Oh, if not, beware lest the temple of a living God become the tomb of a dead soul, and the lamp which now shines peacefully within it first wane, then glimmer, then expire.

Prayer, effort, watchfulness, penitence for past sin, effort to aid the souls of others: these are the means of grace which are like fresh oil and fragrant in the lighted lamp of a Christian's soul. Each time you kneel beside your beds, . . . each hour of quiet thought in which you go forth to meet your Lord, each Sunday spent in a calm and holy faith, above all, each Holy Sacrament at which you kneel with peace in your penitent cleansed hearts towards God and man, these shall widen around you the circle of heavenly light, these (and God grant they may!) shall so make the lamp beam in the temple of your souls, that even into its darkest recesses soon no evil thing shall dare intrude. Thus shall your care be

"Fixt and zealously attent
To fill your odorous lamps with deeds of light
And hope, that reaps not shame."

VI. 47, 49.

JANUARY 6.

Speak, for Thy servant heareth. — I. SAM. iii. 10.

TO men, to nations, sometimes almost to a whole world, God is silent: there *is* no God. Their eyes are blinded, so that they cannot see; their ears closed, that they cannot hear. Aye, but it is a penal silence, a retributive blindness. They who love the darkness, have it. To those who will not listen, God does not speak. . . . They suffer, and there is no God; they sin, and there is no Redeemer; they despair, and there is no Comforter.

Aye, but on the other hand, to seek God is to find; and to listen is to hear; and to hear is to know and love; so that, to His saints, day unto day uttereth speech and night unto night sheweth knowledge, and "God is a declaratory God, speaking in ten thousand voices, and the whole year is one Epiphany, one day of manifestation." X. 28, 29.

> Lord, visit Thou our souls,
> And teach us by Thy grace
> Each dim revealing of Thyself
> With loving awe to trace;
>
> Till from our darkened sight
> The cloud shall pass away,
> And on the cleansed soul shall burst
> The everlasting day.
> BP. J. R. WOODFORD.

JANUARY 7.

Grace be to you, and peace, from God our Father, and from the Lord Jesus Christ.
Eph. i. 2.

THE ordinary salutation of a Greek letter was "Joy" (χαιρειν); of a Jewish letter "Peace" (Shalôm). The Apostles unite both, and into each they infuse a far deeper meaning. . . . The "grace" is the Greek's bright joy embathed in spiritual blessing; the "peace" is a peace hitherto hardly dreamed of; a peace of which there is scarcely a trace in all the golden realms of heathen literature; a peace which passeth all understanding. And thus, as it were, by one touch, in a single phrase, does the Apostle show, quite incidentally, . . . that Christianity is not only for individuals, not only for nations, even, but for the world;—that in Christ the distinctions of castes and nations are done away; that in Him there is neither Greek, nor Jew, nor barbarian, nor bond, nor free; that for us the several blessings of Hellenism and Hebraism may be severally intensified and mutually combined.
I. 152.

Bring me to see, Lord, bring me yet to see
  Those nations of Thy glory and Thy grace,
  Who, splendid in Thy splendor worship Thee,
Light in all eyes, content in every face,—

. . . .

Great mitred priests, great kings in crowns of gold,
  Patriarchs who head the army of their sons,

. . . .

Home-comers out of every change and chance, . . .
All blessed hungry and athirst sufficed, . . .
Friends, brethren, sisters of Lord Jesus Christ.
CHRISTINA ROSSETTI.

JANUARY 8.

THE Gospel is nothing more or less than the hidden meaning of the world. Without it the life of a man is but as a tale that is told by an idiot — full of sound and fury, signifying nothing. But what is the strength, what is the essence of all that we call the Gospel? . . . Not a far-off Christ, Who having died has delegated His work to others, but Christ — a living Presence, an abiding Influence, an unerring Example, an ever-present Personality — Christ, Who willeth all men to be saved, and to come to a knowledge of the truth, . . . a Christ Who having reconciled us to God by His incarnation and His cross, is with us and may be in us, in every one of us, for evermore by the Spirit Whom He hath given us.

IX. 43, 44.

> So, to the calmly gathered thought
> The innermost of truth is taught,
> The mystery dimly understood,
> That love of God is love of good,
>
> . . . .
>
> That the dear Christ dwells not afar,
> The King of some remoter star,
>
> . . . .
>
> But here among the poor and blind,
> The bound and suffering of our kind,
> In works we do, in prayers we pray,
> Life of our life, He lives to-day.
>
> WHITTIER.

JANUARY 9.

THAT Christ should have passed thirty years of His brief life in the deep obscurity of a provincial village ; that He should have been brought up not only in a conquered land, but in its most despised province ; not only in a despised province, but in its most disregarded valley ; that during all those thirty years the ineffable brightness of His divine nature should have tabernacled among us, "in a tent like ours, and of the same material," unnoticed and unknown ; that during those long years there should have been no flash of splendid circumstance, no outburst of amazing miracle, no "sevenfold chorus of hallelujahs and harping symphonies" to announce and reveal, and glorify the coming King — this is not what we should have expected — not what any one would have been likely to imagine or to invent. . . . But it *was* so ; and therefore the Evangelists leave it so. XIII. 25.

What a lesson of divine humility! We are heady, high-minded, anxious ; we lade ourselves with gilded dross ; we daub ourselves with thick clay ; we live and move and have our being in the very atmosphere of the infinitely little. Not so He whom we are bidden to follow ; for Him the shop of the carpenter sufficed. No fierce ambition agitated His calm soul ; . . . as now in His glory, so then in His humiliation, His soul was where He has bidden us ascend with Him in heavenly places.
XII. 45.

JANUARY 10.

THE world hardly attaches any significance to any life except those of its heroes and benefactors, its mighty intellects, or its splendid conquerors. But these are, and must ever be, the few. One raindrop of myriads falling on moor or desert or mountain — one snowflake out of myriads falling into the immeasurable sea — is, and must be, for most men the symbol of their ordinary lives. . . . A relative insignificance . . . is the lot of the immense majority, and many a man might hence be led to think that, since he fills so small a space, . . . there is nothing better than to eat, and drink, and die. But Christ came to convince us that a relative insignificance may be an absolute importance; . . . that myriads of the beloved of God are to be found among the insignificant and the obscure. . . . The vast majority of us are placed, by God's own appointment, amid those quiet duties of a commonplace and uneventful life routine which are most closely analogous to the thirty years of His retirement; it was during those years that His life is for us the main example of how we are to live. XIII. 38. 43.

> The best men, doing their best,
> Know peradventure least of what they do:
> Men usefullest i' the world are simply used:
> The nail that holds the wood must pierce it first,
> And He alone who wields the hammer, sees
> The work advanced by the earliest blow. Take heart.
> ELIZABETH BARRETT BROWNING.

JANUARY 11.

My Father worketh hitherto, and I work.
JOHN v. 17.

CHRISTIANITY removed from labor, both manual and agricultural, the unworthy brand of shame. . . . Christians never forgot that their Lord and Master had chosen the earthly position of a barbarian and an artisan. . . . *Laborare et orare* became the motto of the Christian life. . . . To teach that blessedness [of toil] has ever been the Church's duty ; nor will that duty cease till she has trained all her sons to the belief that a life of mere amusement is dishonorable and disgraceful ; that "to consume much and produce little, to sit down at the feast of life and to depart without paying the reckoning," is a sin too deeply seated to be successfully gilded over by the mere profession of a Christian faith.
XII. 177, 178.

> Good it is in the beginning
>   Toil for our true friend to know,
> Place in God's grand purpose winning,
>   Deep into His life to grow, —
> Saying by our work, as He,
> Unto light and order, "Be!"
>
> LUCY LARCOM.

JANUARY 12.

ARE all martyrs? are all hermits? are all students? are all missionaries? No; the one body has many members, and all members have not the same office. There are many gems, and one is green as the emerald, and one is red as the ruby, and one is purple as the amethyst: there are many saints, and each of them flashes back his one ray of the same divine and perfect light. We cannot paint soft, holy, pathetic pictures like Fra Angelico; . . . or purify corrupted Churches, like Luther and Wesley. Well, but can we not control our evil tempers? can we not curb our bitter tongues? can we not mortify our corrupt desires? cannot we try day by day to be useful to some one? can we not rejoice with them that do rejoice, and weep with them that weep? can we not try to make the world a little less sinful, and a little less wretched? can we not at least give to the poorest of Christ's little ones a cup of cold water in Christ's name? And thus to live is to abide in Christ, for it is to walk as He walked. VII. 141.

> To Give is better than to See or Know:
> And both are means; and neither is the end:
> Knowing and seeing, if none call thee friend,
> Beauty and knowledge have done naught for thee.
> **OWEN MEREDITH.**

JANUARY 13.

We, according to His promise, look for a new heaven and a new earth, wherein dwelleth righteousness. — II. PETER iii. 13.

WHAT is our conception of the new heaven and the new earth which we desire? Is it a mere absence of annoyances? Is it an egotism expanded to infinitude? Is it a sensual Mohammedan Paradise? Is it a selfish Palace of Art? Is it a city paved with gold, or a pagoda of jewels like the New Jerusalem of St. John in its mere external aspect? Childish must we be indeed if we have not got beyond these symbols; if we do not know that man is in his essence a spiritual being, and that for a spiritual being there can be no felicity save in spiritual conditions — in communion with God, in serenity of mind, in purity of heart.

VII. 24.

> So sometimes comes to soul and sense
> The feeling which is evidence
> That very near about us lies
> The realm of spiritual mysteries;
> . . . . . .
> Then duty leaves to love its task,
> The beggar Self forgets to ask;
> With smile of trust and folded hands
> The passive soul in waiting stands,
> To feel, as flowers the sun and dew,
> The One true Life its life renew.
>
> WHITTIER.

JANUARY 14.

For whosoever hath, to him shall be given, and he shall have more abundance. — MATT. xiii. 12.

EVEN so it is with life, with the temple of the outward world. We talk of human misery; how many of us derive from life one-tenth part of what God meant to be its natural blessedness? How many of us drink the deep draughts of joy which every pure heart may drink out of the river of His pleasures? Sit out in the open air on a summer day, and how many of us have trained ourselves to notice the sweetness and the multiplicity of the influences which are combining for our delight — the song of birds; the breeze beating balm upon the forehead; . . . the play of lovely colors; "the soft eye-music of slow-waving boughs"? How many of us ever watch the pageant of the clouds, or take in the meaning of a starry night, or so much as see the sunrise?

II. 201.

> We cannot say the morning sun fulfils
> Ingloriously his course; nor that the clear
> Strong stars, without significance, insphere
> Our habitation. We, meanwhile, our ills
> Heap up against this good; and lift a cry
> Against this work-day world, this ill-spread feast,
> As if ourselves were better certainly
> Than what we come to. Maker and High Priest,
> I ask Thee not my joys to multiply,
> Only to make me worthier of the least.
>
> ELIZABETH BARRETT BROWNING.

JANUARY 15.

YOU must not suppose that our blessed Saviour had no bright and joyous hours on earth, or that the legend is true which says that men had seen Him weep often, but never smile. I believe that in those long quiet earlier years which "breathed beneath the Syrian blue" in Nazareth, — as a child, as a boy, as a youth, — . . . He drank sweet draughts of joy and sunlight, . . . and once we are told not only that He "was glad," but that He "exulted" in spirit. . . . This joy of Jesus, — deep joy, though noble and subdued, — I touch on . . . lest any of you should fatally imagine that in this world the children of the devil have a monopoly of happiness. . . . Guilty *pleasure* for a moment there is, the sweetness of the cup whose draught is poison, the glitter of the serpent whose bite is death. Guilty *mirth* there is, the laughter of fools, which is as the crackling of thorns under a pot. But guilty *happiness* there never has been in any life, nor can there ever be. True happiness, happiness in the midst of even scorn and persecution, happiness even in the felon's prison and in the martyr's flame, is the high prerogative of the saints alone — of God's saints, and therefore assuredly, even in His earthly life, of Him the King of Saints; since there is in misery but *one* intolerable sting, the sting of iniquity, and He had none.   II. 11.

JANUARY 16.

IS there any one of us all who would not give up, say, half of his remaining time on earth, if only, escaping from the fret, the vulgarity, the littleness of life, he might have one hour — one half-hour, with his Lord?

> If Jesus came to earth again,
>   And walked and talked, in field and street,
> Who would not lay his human pain
>   Low at those heavenly feet?
>
> And leave the loom, and leave the lute,
>   And leave the volume on the shelf,
> To follow Him, unquestioning, mute,
>   If 't were the Lord Himself?
>
> OWEN MEREDITH.

So we say. My friends, is it true? Do we long for it? do we yearn for it so much? Do you say, Oh, that I could pour forth my burdened heart in tears upon His feet! oh, that I could but see Him! oh, that I knew where I might find Him! oh, that I could give Him something to show my love! Ah, but if we long for it, we may have it — here, now. Would you weep at His feet? You may weep like John upon His breast. Do you long to give Him something? You may give Him, if you like, everything that He cares for.

VIII. 147.

> So . . . comes a human voice,
> Saying, "O heart I made, a heart beats here.
> Face My hands fashioned, see it in Myself;
> Thou hast no strength, nor mayst conceive of Mine;
> But love I gave thee, with Myself to love,
> And thou must love Me who have died for thee."
>
> BROWNING.

JANUARY 17.

The Lord searcheth all hearts, and understandeth all . . . the thoughts.
                            I. CHRON. xxviii. 9.

TEST your sincerity by the manner in which you control or resist your evil thoughts. Do you suffer your thoughts to tamper with evil, to dally with wrong-doing? If so you are not sincere.

The tyrant Nero tried to degrade some of the great Roman nobles to as low a level as his own, by making them appear as actors in the arena on the stage. To disobey was death. Florus was bidden thus to appear, and, doubting whether to obey, consulted the virtuous and resolute Agrippinus. "Go, by all means," answered Agrippinus. "Well, but," replied Florus with astonishment, "you yourself refused to obey." "Yes," answered Agrippinus, "because I did not deliberate about it." The categorical imperative, the naked, absolute prohibition of duty must be implicitly, unquestioningly, instantly obeyed. To deliberate about it is to be a secret traitor; and the line which separates the secret traitor from the open rebel is thin as the spider's web.
                                VII. 260, 261.

> The longer on this earth we live,
> And weigh the various qualities of men, . . .
> The more we feel the high, stern-featured beauty
> Of plain devotedness to duty,
> Steadfast and still, nor paid with mortal praise.
>   JAMES RUSSELL LOWELL.

JANUARY 18.

If there be any virtue, and if there be any praise, think on these things. — PHIL. iv. 8.

THOUGHT passes into action. The thought becomes the word, the word the deed, the deed the habit, the habit the character, the character the eternal being of our souls. "The evening air clad in the beauty of a thousand stars" is not lovelier than the character of him whose whole being is passed in the region of eternal realities; who knows the awful reverence which is due from every man to his own soul; who loveth the thing that is just, and doeth the thing that is lawful and right in singleness of heart; who keeps the temple of his soul pure and bright with the Presence of the Holy One; who loves all that is beautiful whether in Nature or in Art; who hates whatever is ignoble and loves his neighbor as himself. What has such a man to fear? The eternal forces are with him. His heart, his hope, his treasure are beyond the grave, and ever and anon in moments of permitted rapture, he sees the heavens open and the angels of God ascending and descending upon the Son of Man. VII. 58.

In such high hour
Of visitation from the living God,
Thought was not; in enjoyment it expired.
No thanks he breathed, he proffered no request;
Rapt into still communion that transcends
Th' imperfect offices of prayer and praise,
His mind was a thanksgiving to the Power
That made him; it was blessedness and love.
WORDSWORTH.

JANUARY 19.

THE first miracle of Moses was, in stern retribution, to turn the river of a guilty nation into blood, the first of Jesus to fill the water-jars of an innocent family with wine. . . . The world gives its best first, and afterwards all the dregs and bitterness; but Christ came to turn the lower into the richer and sweeter, the Mosaic law into the perfect law of liberty, the baptism of John into the baptism with the Holy Ghost and with fire, the self-denials of a painful isolation into the self-denials of a happy home, sorrow and sighing into hope and blessing, and water into wine. And thus the "holy estate" which Christ adorned and beautified with His presence and first miracle . . . foreshadows the mystical union between Christ and His Church; and the common element which He thus miraculously changed becomes a type of our life on earth transfigured and ennobled by the anticipated joys of heaven — a type of that wine which He shall drink new with us in the kingdom of God, at the marriage-supper of the Lamb. XIII. 79.

> Love, Thine own Bride, with all her might
>   Will follow Thee,
>   And till the shadows flee
> Keep Thee in sight.
> CHRISTINA ROSSETTI.

JANUARY 20.

THE ideal of the Christian family, an ideal lovelier and happier than any which the world has ever known, is the direct creation of Christianity. "*Familia*," to the ear of a Roman, . . . meant a despot who could kill his slaves when they were aged, and expose his children when they were born; it meant matrons among whom virtue was rare, divorces frequent, remarriage easy, . . . it meant children spectators from their infancy of insolence and cruelty, servility and sin. But the new faith, while it sanctioned the authority of parents, checked their despotism; . . . it encircled the position of womanhood with all that was pure and divine and tender, in the names of mother and of wife. . . . For families in which, like sheltered flowers, spring up all that is purest and sweetest in human lives; for marriage exalted to an almost sacramental dignity; for all that circle of heavenly blessings which result from a common self-sacrifice; . . . in one word, for all that there is of divinity and sweetness in the one word *Home*; for this — to an extent which we can hardly realize — we are indebted to Christianity alone. XII. 182.

>Thanks for the common blessings first,
> The commonest of all, —
>. . . . . . .
>The daily bread, the daily joy,
> The greeting morn and eve,
>The kiss of love, the kiss of peace,
> Which daily we receive.
>   JOHN W. CHADWICK.

JANUARY 21.

Let them first show piety at home. — I. TIM. v. 4.

A BRITTLE thing is our earthly happiness — brittle as some thin vase of Venetian glass; and yet neither anxiety nor sorrow, nor the dart of death, which is mightier than the oak-cleaving thunderbolt, can shatter a thing even so brittle as the earthly happiness of our poor little homes, if we place that happiness under the care of God. But though neither anguish nor death can break it with all their violence, *sin* can break it at a touch; and selfishness can shatter it, just as there are acids which will shiver the Venetian glass. Sin and selfishness — God's balm does not heal in this world the ravages which they cause!

VII. 26.

>   Some silent laws our hearts will make,
>   Which they shall long obey;
>   We for the year to come may take
>   Our temper from to-day.
>
>   And from the blessed Power that rolls
>   About, below, above,
>   We'll frame the measure of our souls:
>   They shall be tuned to love.
>
>   WORDSWORTH.

JANUARY 22.

A KIND word of praise, of sympathy, of encouragement; it would not cost you much, yet how often does pride, or envy, or indifference prevent you from speaking it? The cup of cold water, the barley loaves, the two farthings, how often are we too mean and too self-absorbed to give even these! And are we not to give them because we cannot endow hospitals, or build cathedrals, or write epics? Ah! if we be in the least sincere, in the least earnest, let us be encouraged. The little gifts of our poverty, the small services of our insignificance, the barley loaves of the Galilean boy on the desert plain, the one talent of poor dull persons like ourselves, are despised by the world, but they are dear to, but they are accepted of, but they will be infinitely rewarded by Him who, though the conies are a feeble folk, gives them their homes in the rocks; without whom no sparrow falls; who numbers the very hairs of our heads; who builds the vast continents by the toil of the coral insect, and by His grains of sand stays the raging of the sea. VII. 280.

"It is so little I can do!
It is so little I can say!"
Nay, but what God demands of you
Is just that little: Hear — obey.
J. L. M. W.

JANUARY 23.

I delight in the law of God after the inward man; but I see another law in my members, warring against the law of my mind, and bringing me into captivity. — ROM. vii. 22, 23.

FORMED out of the dust of the ground, yet made in the image and similitude of God; children of the Most Highest, yet crushed before the moth; — drinking in iniquity like water, yet filled with the inspiration of the Almighty which giveth him understanding; — a worm and a thing of naught, yet with a destiny higher than the sons of light; — there is in man's nature a terrible dualism, "the angel has him by the hand, or the serpent by the heart;" he may rise to the heights of heaven, he may sink to the abyss of hell. Through all literature, ancient and modern, runs the same antithesis, from the "man is a god on earth" of the Roman orator, to the "man is the shadow of a dream" of the Greek tragedians. XI. 90.

Strange, that we creatures of the petty ways,
  Poor prisoners behind these fleshly bars,
Can sometimes think us thoughts with God ablaze,
  Touching the fringes of the outer stars.

And stranger still that, having flown so high,
  And stood unshamed in shining presences,
We can resume our smallness, nor imply
  In mien or gesture what that memory is.
RICHARD E. BURTON.

JANUARY 24.

THERE is nothing high, there is nothing noble, . . . to which you are not clearly summoned, for which you are not naturally fit. And shall *you* descend voluntarily into the defilement and pollution of sin? Nay, reverence yourselves, for you are greater than you know. Oh, surely when you think of the high and holy men, the household and city of God on earth; or when, yet passing upwards, you mingle in thought with the spirits and souls of the righteous, in those

> "Solemn choirs and sweet societies
> That sing, and singing in their glory move; —"

or when, soaring yet higher on the wings of solemn and consecrated thought, you fix your contemplations on the Father who created you, on the Spirit who sheds His light abroad in your hearts, on the great High Priest who stands to intercede for you by the throne of the Majesty on high; . . . surely, I say, in the light of such contemplations, the rank theories of the worldling and the sensualist become hideous and revolting.   XI. 19.

> "Live while you live!" the epicure would say,
> "And seize the pleasures of the passing day!"
> "Live while you live!" the sacred Preacher cries,
> "And give to God each moment as it flies!"
> Lord, in my view let both united be:
> I live in pleasure while I live to Thee!
>   **DODDRIDGE.**

JANUARY 25.

As he journeyed, . . . suddenly there shined round about him a light from heaven. — ACTS ix. 3.

THOUGH the world scoff at them, there *are* such things as instantaneous conversions, supreme crises and movements in the history of life, which, like the shock of an earthquake, cleave a sudden rift deep down between all that a man has been and all he is. . . . "The man indeed is left untouched, but there is added to him the God who created him." All vain, idle, furious passions disappear. All the mere emptiness of life becomes repulsive. Things temporal vanish, things eternal dawn on him. An awful sense of reality comes over him, and joy accompanies it. . . . Before him there may still be barren wastes and icy tempests, but from that moment, as though there were a new heart in him, he fears no danger before him, he forgets every peril and misery behind. VI. 83, 85.

> A death-blow is a life-blow to some,
> Who, till they died, did not alive become;
> Who, had they lived, had died, but when
> They died, vitality begun.
> **EMILY DICKINSON.**

JANUARY 26.

> To-day grows the harvest of heaven.
> LONGFELLOW.

HAVE you an enemy? Then this very day forgive him. Have you wronged, or are you wronging, another? Then this very day make him restitution. Are you a slanderer or a systematic depreciator of your brethren? Then cease to speak evil, and fling your unhallowed pen into the fire. Are you in debt? Live on bread and water rather than continue in that dishonesty. Are you idle? Go home and earn your own bread by the sweat of your brow. . . . Are you getting fond of drink? Then loose the grip upon you of that devil's hand of flame by taking the pledge. Are you living two lives, of which one is a mere self-deceiving hypocrisy? Then tear off your own mask, and in tears before Christ's throne entreat Him to make you true. Are you stained with impurity? Then come with that leprosy to Him whose answer to the leper's cry, "Lord, if thou wilt, thou canst make me clean," came like an echo, "I will, be thou made clean." V. 120.

> "Would a man 'scape the rod?"
> Rabbi Ben Karshook saith,
> "See that he turns to God
> The day before his death."
>
> "Ay, could a man inquire
> When it shall come?" I say.
> The Rabbi's eye shoots fire—
> "Then let him turn to-day."
> BROWNING.

Beloved, be not ignorant of this one thing, that one day is with the Lord as a thousand years, and a thousand years as one day. — II. PETER iii. 8.

WE live in Time; we cannot adequately conceive of timelessness; yet Time is nothing save a finite sequence, a relative conception. There are no mornings or evenings in heaven. The light of God is always in the meridian. There are no lines, no creeping shadows on the dial-plate of heaven; there is no ripple of Time on the shoreless sea of Eternity; no rolling years at the Centre of the changeless calm. God sees all things in the totality of their existence. "As," and "was," and "will be," to Him are but an ever-present "is." Past and present and future are to Him but one eternal NOW.

V. 36

"But time escapes!
Live now or never!"
He said, "What's time? Leave Now for dogs and apes!
Man has Forever!"
BROWNING.

The One remains, the many change and pass;
Heaven's light forever shines, Earth's shadows fly.
SHELLEY.

JANUARY 28.

TWO things are most noticeable about our life here: that it is so brief, and that it is so silent. The young cherish the vain delusion that life is long, but God has only made our days, even for the oldest, a span long. What is our life? It is even as a vapor, so soon passeth it away and we are gone. And it is in deep, unbroken silence that the years allotted to us pass away. They make no noise as they roll over our heads. The stream of time flows on with the profoundest stillness. All that we know is that it has passed us, and we can only wonder that it should so soon have sped.
IV. 245.

O soul of mine, how few and short the years
  Ere thou shalt go the way of all thy kind,
  And here no more thy joy or sorrow find
At any fount of happiness or tears!
Yea, and how soon shall all that thee endears
  To any heart that beats with love for thee
  Be everywhere forgotten utterly,
With all thy loves and joys, and hopes and fears!
But, O my soul, because these things are so,
  Be thou not cheated of to-day's delight.
  When the night cometh, it may well be night;
Now it is Day. See that no minute's glow
  Of all the shining hours unheeded goes,
  No fount of rightful joy by thee untasted flows.
JOHN W. CHADWICK.

Rejoice in hope of the glory of God.
ROM. v. 2.

JANUARY 29.

I joy, and rejoice with you all. For the same cause also do ye joy, and rejoice with me.
                                              PHIL. ii. 18.

PESSIMISM is becoming a popular philosophy. In its luxury and in its struggles, in its sensuality, and in its very successes, the age is sad. We deserve and we receive the punishment of those whom the great Italian poet described as duly punished for this guilt, since

"Once we were sad
In the sweet air made gladsome by the sun;
Now in this murky darkness we are sad."

But the inward joy of the Christian, if brightest in the sunshine, is unquenched even by the storm. The true Christian, . . . the saint of God, can be glad even in adversity, and rich in poverty, and calm in the prospect of death. Why? Because he has a freedom which no fetters can coerce, and a treasure which makes as nothing the loss of all; and because death, which guilty men regard as the most awful of penalties, is to him the sleep which God sends to His beloved when their day's work is done. . . . "Hath he not always treasure, always friends," the holy Christian man? Yes!

"Three treasures, life, and light,
And calm thoughts, regular as an infant's breath,
And three firm friends, more sure than day and night,
Himself, his Maker, and the angel Death."
                                              I. 306.

JANUARY 30.

Let us not always say,
"Spite of this flesh to-day
I strove, made head, gained ground upon the whole!"
As the bird wings and sings,
Let us cry, "All good things
Are ours, nor soul helps flesh more, now, than flesh
  helps soul!"

BROWNING.

THAT is not religion which is not free and manly. Religion has nothing to do with mawkish and feminine sentimentalism. No one can be a true Christian who is not also a true man.

Reason and conscience, illuminated by faith and prayer, these are the torch-bearers of truth. Seek truth, and you will find it, because God is the God of truth. If you desire heaven you must win it; for heaven is a temper, not a place. . . . You must win it by that obedience to God's laws which nothing but the grace of Christ can enable you to render. . . . The errors, effeminacies, and failures of popular religion all spring up because men trouble themselves about the forms of worship rather than the object of worship; because men are more concerned for that which is their own in religion, than that which is God's; and because they want to *make* religion, and *define* religion, and *display* religion, rather than to evidence its reality in meek and loving lives.

IV. 267.

JANUARY 31.

Thou shalt tread upon the lion and adder; the young lion and dragon shalt thou trample under feet. — Ps. xci. 13.

THERE are lions on the path of life which the slothful man will not encounter, but which the brave man fights, and in the long run slays. There are perils which come to us from the world, the flesh, and the devil, perils from the lions of outward and public wickedness, which we have to face in our lives as citizens and as men. In his struggle against the varied forms of sin and vice which are without and around him, the brave man may often be, or seem to be, defeated, though in such cases his very defeat carries in it the germs of future and of certain victory. When the good man seems to be conquered, the powers of evil have still to rue their short-lived triumph, and to say as Pyrrhus said when he defeated the Romans: "Three such victories would utterly ruin me." VIII. 43.

Count not God's plan defeated in the life
  He gave to us, nor all our toil in vain,
Because we are not victors in the strife;
  Who bravely fights and nobly bears his pain,
Wrests victory from defeat. Not what we win,
  But what strive for, doth the Master heed.
If what we sought to be we have not been,
  Our striving may have helped another's need.
LAURA B. BOYCE.

FEBRUARY 1.

Whatsoever things are lovely, . . . think on these things. — PHIL. iv. 8.

IF you think of *such* things, the baser and viler things will have no charm for you. Try, then, above all, "the expulsive power of good affections." Empty by filling; empty of what is mean and impure by filling with what is noble and lovely. When the Argonauts sailed past the treacherous rocks of the Sirens they sailed in perfect safety, because Orpheus was one of them, and the song of Orpheus was sweeter, more delightful, more full of noble witchery than the Sirens' vile, voluptuous strains. Let your souls be filled with the music of Him whom the early Christians delighted to represent as Orpheus charming the wild beasts of bad passions by his harp.

Your souls are a picture-gallery. . . . Let their walls be hung with all things sweet and perfect — the thought of God, the image of Christ, the lives of God's saints, the aspirations of good and great men, the memories of golden deeds. VII. 55.

What a man thinks, he is;
Then let thy thoughts be thoughts of bliss,
  Of heart-hued love and snow-white purity,
Of heaven and heavenly light,
Of all things high and bright,—
  So bright, high, pure, and lovely thou shalt be.
J. L. M. W.

FEBRUARY 2.

Every one that hath this hope set on Him purifieth himself, even as He is pure. — I. JOHN iii. 3.

AND how divine a hope it is! Earthly hope is disappointed in the very fruition, and bursts like a bubble even in the attainment; and though satiated, never is satisfied; . . . but heavenly hope, while her present fruition is ever fresh and verdant, opens also an illimitable prospect beyond the grave.

He, then, that hath this hope on God, purifieth himself; his hope necessarily inspires effort. He purifies himself not only with outward cleansing from guilty deeds, but with the inward sprinkling of the conscience, until, by Christ's presence within, it shrinks from a stain as from a wound; and a shame lies on it like a spark of agonizing fire; and it feels that its past sins are forgiven, and that, as to the present, we know that he who, by His grace, doeth righteousness is born of Him. V. 206.

Lord, make me pure:
Only the pure shall see Thee as Thou art,
And shall endure.
CHRISTINA ROSSETTI.

FEBRUARY 3.

THERE are men who will see no possibility of merit in human nature. If they hear of a noble deed they will at once invent a low motive for it. They sneer at the notion of disinterested tenderness or self-sacrifice. . . . Lepers themselves, they peer about for the spot of leprosy on every other brow. . . . They always fix all doubt on the darker side, . . . they are never so happy as when they are tearing open the bleeding wounds of society; . . . when they are stimulating the appetite of malice with slanderous inventions; and tricking out, for the delectation of the base, every loathly plume from that foul bird of rapine whose prey is man's good name. Man delights them not, no, nor women neither. Christ loved and esteemed our nature, fallen though it was, so much that He took it into His Godhead and died for it. He came to heal those who are broken in heart, and to find a medicine to heal their sickness. V. 141, 143.

Think of thy brother no ill, but throw a veil over his failings;
Guide the erring aright, for the good, the heavenly Shepherd
Took the lost lamb in His arms, and bore it back to its mother.
This is the fruit of love, and it is by its fruits that we know it. LONGFELLOW.

FEBRUARY 4.

If ye fulfil the royal law according to the Scripture, Thou shalt love thy neighbor as thyself, ye do well. — JAMES ii. 8.

LET us look at our lives. Are we living for self? for pleasure? for gold? for ambition? What a misery, what a vanity of vanities, what a failure of failures is such a life! Are we of any use at all in the world, beyond our mere mechanical routine, with its variations of eating and sleeping? "O my God, grant me" (so they are taught to pray in some monasteries in France), "grant me that to-day I may be of some use to some one." If God, for our good, see fit to deny us all else, may He, as His best gift of all, grant us this — to be of some real, of some deep use to our fellow-men, before we go hence and are no more seen.

I. 240.

Feed My hungry brethren for My sake;
  Give them drink, for love of them and Me:
Love them as I loved thee when bread I brake
    In pure love of thee.

Yea, Lord, I will serve them by Thy grace;
  Love Thee, seek Thee, in them; wait and pray;
Yet would I love Thyself, Lord, face to face,
    Heart to heart, one day.

Let to-day fulfil its daily task,
  Fill thy heart and hand to them and Me;
To-morrow thou shalt ask, and shalt not ask
    Half I keep for thee.

CHRISTINA ROSSETTI.

FEBRUARY 5.

"O HAPPY school of Christ," wrote Peter of the Cells to a young disciple. . . . "O happy school of Christ, where He teaches our hearts with the word of power; where the book is not purchased nor the master paid. There life availeth more than learning, and simplicity than science." . . . It was a natural exclamation, but . . . to the true Christian every school will be a school of Christ. On the ample leaf of knowledge, whether it be rich with the secrets of nature or with the spoils of time, he will read no name save the name of God. The great stone pages of the world will have it carved upon them legibly, as on the granite tables of Sinai, and stars will sing of it in their courses. Each Science, each History, each Literature, will be to him but a fresh volume of divine revelation. We were not meant to leave these volumes clasped, or to suffer the book of life to drop out of our hands unread. . . . To seek for knowledge where it is possible is the clear duty of man; to win it is the gift of God. Knowledge apart from wisdom is like a vestibule dissevered from its temple; but it may be on the other hand the worthy vestibule of that sacred shrine.

X. 155.

Let knowledge grow from more to more,
But more of reverence in us dwell.
TENNYSON.

FEBRUARY 6.

Get wisdom. — Prov. iv. 5.

WISELY Scripture reverses the judgment of the world in making mental culture wholly incommensurate in importance with spiritual growth. . . . To exalt genius would have been superfluous, because the world was too prone already to that idolatry. . . . Wisdom, not knowledge; goodness, not genius; moral deliverance, not material discovery; the regeneration of the multitude, not the exalting of the few — these were the aims of Christian teaching. The knowledge of mankind needed to be sacrificed; it needed to be baptized; it needed to be transfigured from a haughty philosophy to a humble wisdom, from impotent self-assertion to fruitful life.   XII. 156.

> Half-grown as yet, a child, and vain,
>   She cannot fight the fear of death.
>   What is she, cut from love and faith,
> But some wild Pallas from the brain
>
> Of Demons? fiery hot to burst
>   All barriers in her onward race
>   For power. Let her know her place;
> She is the second, not the first.
>   . . . .
> For she is earthly, of the mind,
>   But Wisdom heavenly, of the soul.
>
>   TENNYSON.

FEBRUARY 7.

CHRIST does not require of us, and never in any age has required of any, transcendental theories, superfine moralities, heroic self-martyrdoms. All that He requires of us, first and at present, is to be plainly, simply, ordinarily good. With minutiæ, and ceremonies, and ecclesiastical accuracies we may deceive ourselves; they will not deceive Him, nor will they be more in His sight than the small dust of the balance. You will not find in all His teaching one word of praise for them; but you will find in all His teaching and throughout all Scripture, from Genesis to Revelation, the one plain broad truth: "He that doeth righteousness is righteous."

V. 138.

"My way to Christ," said Cleon, "lies
Through deep and fine philosophies."

"As shaven monk or anchorite,
I'll seek His face," said Theodite.

"Narrow and straight before mine eyes,"
Said John, "my path of duty lies,

"And if I fail to find Him there,
I cannot find Him anywhere."

J. L. M. W.

FEBRUARY 8.

Whatsoever thy hand findeth to do, do it with thy might. — Eccl. ix. 10.

LIFE gives you many a golden opportunity of innocent happiness; many a spring and summer day in which the world is "wrapped round with sweet air and bathed in sunshine," and "it is a luxury to breathe the breath of life." God as little grudges you these as he grudges to the weary traveller his draught of the desert spring; and he who will work but faithfully will assuredly receive of God many a free and happy day spent under the blue sky, in which he may, as it were, draw large draughts of sunshine into his bosom, and rise for happy hours with thoughts fragrant as roses, and pure as the dew upon their leaves. The man . . . who has first thoroughly done his duty, — not with eye-service, as a man-pleaser, but with singleness of heart serving God — may afterwards enjoy to the very utmost his innocent delight; —

> The hour so spent shall live
> Not unapplauded in the book of Heaven.

Only *put duty always before pleasure*. Never invert this order; never let pleasure interfere with the times of duty. . . . To do this is to imitate those ancient Egyptians who worshipped a fly and offered an ox in sacrifice. . . . But if you take work — not amusement, not indolence, not folly — as the noble law of life, it shall save you from a thousand petty annoyances, a thousand sickly day-dreams and morbid discontents. X. 167.

A sower went out to sow his seed: . . . and some fell among thorns. — LUKE viii. 5, 7.

NOT, observe, on full-grown thorns — no sower would be so senseless as to sow seed there — but on thorn-roots lying under the surface, hidden, unnoticed, of which we are afterwards told that they sprang up. Yes, the soil looked good enough, but roots of bitterness were in it, and under it ; . . . and so when the sunbeams fell on it, and it was watered from above with the gracious dews of God, the seed grew indeed, but the thorns grew also, and stronger and more rapidly, and the more they grew the more they robbed the good seed of heat, and light, and moisture, and so absorbed into their own evil nature the whole strength and energy of the soil, that the green blade could never become the ripened ear, and at last, as you looked upon the field, you could hardly tell that there had been corn in it at all ;

"Things rank and gross in nature
Possessed it merely."

Thank God, there are also soils rich, and good, and deep, which bring forth fruit to perfection. VI. 170.

We receive everything ; . . . but the *manner* in which we receive, this is what is still ours. AMIEL.

FEBRUARY 10.

Therefore I say unto you, Take no thought for your life what ye shall eat or what ye shall drink; nor yet for your body what ye shall put on. Is not the life more than meat, and the body than raiment? — MATT. vi. 25.

YOU are doubtless aware that the words, "take no thought," did not, when the Bible was translated, mean as they now mean — "be wholly indifferent to," "never cast a thought upon" — but . . . "be not anxious," "be not over-careful about." To take no thought for the morrow would, in the present sense of the phrase, be at once impracticable and immoral. . . . No man has any right to live on the toil of his neighbors; no man has a right to be a useless burden on others. . . . I need hardly pause to correct this abuse. I trust that all of us, of every rank, of every age, have learnt the dignity of work, the innocence of work, the holiness of work, the happiness of work. . . . The idler and the sluggard have no right either to heaven or to earth. VIII. 1, 2.

Work may be drudgery; it is so only
  When we leave God out of the task He gives,
Or choose our own apart from Him, — a lonely
  Treadmill of selfishness, where no joy lives.

    . . . .

Work is the holiest thing in earth and heaven:
  To lift from souls the sorrow and the curse, —
This dear employment must to us be given,
  While there is want in God's great universe.
                      LUCY LARCOM.

FEBRUARY 11.

Take no thought for the morrow. — MATT. vi. 34.

"TAKE no thought," "Be not anxious:" strange exhortation! How many nominal Christians even pretend to follow it! Go forth into the roaring, surging streets of any of our great cities, and how many are there of these careworn myriads . . . who are not . . . full of a restless and devouring anxiety about the concerns of this life — of this brief day, which, in an hour or two, shall plunge into irrevocable night? . . . Yes, and they will maintain it to you, that so it ought to be; that in this — to them — unintelligible world, they could not possibly get on without dubious dealing; that (as they phrase it) "business is business;" that the Sermon on the Mount is too romantic, too angelical, for the warehouse and the street; and that the heaven, which is so near to us, since we all may enter it, is impossibly far away, because so very few of us do. And thus the voice — the human voice — the still small voice of Jesus on the hill — becomes to us but like the half-remembered echo of music out of some heavenly dream. VIII. 3.

> O Lord, seek us, O Lord, find us
>   In Thy patient care;
> Be Thy love before, behind us,
>   Round us, everywhere;
> Lest the god of this world blind us,
>   Lest he speak us fair,
> Lest he forge a chain to bind us,
>   Lest he bait a snare.
>
> CHRISTINA ROSSETTI.

FEBRUARY 12.

The archangel, Hope,
Looks to the azure cope,
Waits through dark ages for the morn,
Defeated day by day, but unto victory born.

EMERSON.

NOT to despair of good either for ourselves or for the world; not to acquiesce in evil, whether the world's evil or our own, these alone are grand lessons. For the truest men are they in whose bosom there burns an inextinguishable hope. The day may set for them into starless night, but still on the dark horizon,

> "Hope, a soaring eagle, burns
> Above the unrisen morrow."

Is not this a part at least of St. Paul's meaning when he says that "We are saved by hope"? Even at the moment of the lost Paradise, the hope was granted that we should one day crush the serpent's head. We have plucked the bitter fruit of the Tree of the knowledge of evil, yet the Tree of Life still stands in the garden of God, and it was a legend of deep meaning which told that a seed of that tree was brought to Adam, and that from it sprang that other Tree of Life from which the Cross was made.

II. 160.

FEBRUARY 13.

The vision is yet for an appointed time; at the end it shall speak and not lie. — HAB. ii. 3.

THE existence of evil in the world is an insoluble mystery. It is one of the secret things of God. . . . In vain have philosophers brooded over it; saints have wept and prayed over it in vain. It surrounds us like a wall of impenetrable darkness, on which the lifted torch of the poet and the odorous lamp of the sage have shed no gleam. Rage against it has driven some men into atheism; some into pessimism; some into the belief in an evil as well as a good God; some into desperation, or the yet worse wretchedness of unclean living. Had it been possible to lift but one corner of this curtain, opaque as midnight, or to lighten this crushing burden of mystery, the Lord Jesus Christ, who has done *all* for us, would have done this for us. But it could not be. Something in the nature of things, something in the inexorable decrees of eternal destiny, rendered it impossible. "Verily, Thou art a God that hidest Thyself." If we are wise, we shall leave the mystery of the existence of evil in the hands of that inscrutable God. IV. 158.

> Out of labyrinths of thought,
>   Where bewildering gleams confuse,
> From our wanderings we have brought
>   Only broken, tangled clues.
> But this one thing certain is:
>   In Thy world, O God, Thou art!
> Wearied with earth's mysteries,
>   We would rest upon Thy heart.
> LUCY LARCOM.

FEBRUARY 14.

The things which are seen are temporal; but the things which are not seen are eternal.
                               II. COR. iv. 18.

ST. Paul does not say "the things which are *future* are eternal," but "the things which are *not seen* are eternal." Unseen they may be to us, yet they are neither distant nor future; they are here; they are now. . . . No man can pass into eternity, for he is already in it. The dead are no more in eternity now than they always were, or than every one of us is at this moment. We may ignore the things eternal; shut our eyes hard to them; live as though they had no existence; nevertheless Eternity is around us here, now, at this moment, at all moments; and it will have been around us every day of our ignorant, sinful, selfish lives. Its stars are ever over our head, while we are so diligent in the dust of our worldliness, or in the tainted stream of our desires. The dull brute globe moves through its blue ether, and knows it not; even so our souls are bathed in eternity, and are never conscious of it. As little can we get rid of the ethereal air of Eternity as the world can get rid of the blue spaces of ether through which it moves.

Let us then strive — ere it be too late for this life — to see Him who is invisible, and the things which are unseen.   VII. 79.

FEBRUARY 15.

Beloved, if God so loved us, we ought also to love one another. — I. JOHN iv. 11.

GOD is love, His purpose is love; if many of us are lost, He sent His Son to seek and save His lost; if His sheep wander into the wilderness, the Good Shepherd in the parable searches for His sheep, until He find them. Why? Because He grieves over human sin, and pities human misery. And therefore to remedy evil, to strive for good, — not to neglect the little daily duties and beneficences of life, the gracious acts, the tender courtesies, the tolerant appreciations, the public magnanimities, the social efforts, the national aims of nobler manhood, either in selfish absorption in the effort to save our own souls, or in fury against others because they will not save their souls in our way, — in one word to love God and our neighbor, and to believe on the name of Jesus Christ, and to love one another as He gave us commandment, — this is to live as Christ lived on earth.
II. 184.

> As we meet and touch each day
> The many travellers on our way,
> Let every such brief contact be
> A glorious, helpful ministry, —
> The contact of the soil and seed,
> Each giving to the other's need,
> Each helping on the other's best,
> And blessing each, as well as blest.
>
> SUSAN COOLIDGE.

FEBRUARY 16.

Love out of a pure heart, and of a good conscience, and of faith unfeigned. — I. Tim. iii. 12.

AS we have the creed of our faith, ought we not also to have the vow of our practice? and ought it not to run somewhat as follows? — Seeing that God loves us, that He sent His Son to die for us and to save us; — seeing that this world might be made a far happier place . . . than it is if men were wise, and pure, and true to each other, or even if they were not to each other the sorest, surest ill, — therefore, for His sake who died for me and pitied me, I too will be compassionate and active for my brother man. I will pray for him as my Saviour prayed, and work for him as my Saviour worked. If he hates me, I will still try to love him. I will keep my tongue from every species and variety of evil speaking, lying, and slandering. . . . I will put a bad construction on nothing while a good one is possible. I will be kind to many, will wish to be kind to all, will do harm consciously to none. I will think and let think. I will bear and forbear. . . . I will be ashamed of nothing but sin. I will love, I will honor, I will labor for man my brother, because God loves us who is our Father, and Christ died for us, who is the first-born in this great family of man.

II. 245.

FEBRUARY 17.

IN Christ Jesus the end of the commandment is love out of a pure heart, and a good conscience, and faith unfeigned. Nothing can exceed the absolute plainness, the reiterated simplicity of Christ's teaching. A child, a wayfaring man, a fool can understand it. "If ye love me," He says — what? go into the desert? shut yourself up in a monastery? spend your days in the vain repetition of formal prayers? No! but — "If ye love me, keep my commandments." "How commonplace!" you will say; "how elementary! how extremely ordinary! why I learnt all that years ago by my mother's knee; I have got quite beyond all that." Ah! but have you? Like the Pharisee, you may not be an extortioner, unjust, an adulterer; but have you, even in man's judgment, kept, in all their divine breadth, the law of kindness; the law of purity; the law of honesty; the law of truth; the law of contentment? Have you loved God with all the heart? Have you loved your neighbor as yourself? V. 114.

> Father! with contrite grief
> And bitterness of heart we must confess
> How much our good is mingled,
> Its best and greatest, with sin's littleness,—
> Our eye how little singled!
>
> A. E. HAMILTON.

FEBRUARY 18.

If we say that we have no sin, we deceive ourselves, and the truth is not in us. — I. John i. 8.

WE say "I cannot help it; it is fate; it is heredity; it is not volition; it is only with my body, not with my heart, that I serve the law of sin. Even though it is wrong, though I have committed it, it is no part of my real nature; it is, so to speak, a mere accident." With this opiate men lull themselves into fatal sleep. They think that they can be pardoned and yet retain the offence. They think that they can eat the forbidden fruit, yet find in their mouth no gravel and bitterness. They think that they may defile with ten thousand stains the white robes of their baptism, and yet go in to the bridegroom's feast. . . .

Thou hast done with them? Alas! alas! they have not done with thee. Confess them, get rid of them, or they shall be to thee as the garment which is upon thee, as the girdle which thou art girded withal. For, if we say that we have no sin, then actively we are leading ourselves astray; passively the truth is not in us — *i.e.*, our lives are not being spent in the sphere of reality, but in a mirage of self-deceit, of semblance, and of death.

V. 55, 57.

Dare to be true. Nothing can need a lie;
A fault, which needs it most, grows two thereby.
GEORGE HERBERT.

FEBRUARY 19.

I wove the crown for the Brow divine,
  I pierced the Hand that was stretched to save;
I dare not pray that the moon may shine
  To show me the prints of the nails I drave, —
I beat this night on my sinful breast,
  I dare not pray Him to succor me.
. . . .
But the Watchman opened the Gate of Rest, —
  "I am willing with all My heart," said He.
B. M.

THE frank, humble, penitent acknowledgment of sin must precede the possibility of grace. To no human being, until with conscience-stricken David he has sobbed forth, "I have sinned," can the gracious message possibly come, "The Lord also hath put away thy sin." We can have no faith, no fellowship, no joy, nothing of that eternal life which St. John proclaims, until we have recognized, in something more than words, that God is infinitely holy, and that we are infinitely guilty. Let this great lesson suffice for our present meditation, and so shall we begin by God's grace to realize the counter-condition which St. John here lays down: v. 60.

"If we confess our sins, He is faithful and righteous to forgive us our sins, and to cleanse us from all unrighteousness."

FEBRUARY 20.

WHAT he who would be rescued from evil must say is — This one thing I do. When — whether from new passion for the good, or new pain at the evil — the soul collects itself for a supreme effort, it must attend to nothing else. For the mountain of penitence is steep. The entrance to it, indeed, by a good resolution, is so easy that it is like a mere gap in the hedge filled up by a forkful of thorns; but, once entered, the soul must climb, and climb, and climb, however weary, with only this consolation, that the more resolutely we climb the more easy will the climb become. . . . But to the soul that perseveres there are on the road sweet resting-places of hope, wherein it seems carried up as on the wings of eagles; and the more one mounts the less it pains; and so, the first thought followed by a resolve, the first divine resolve followed by an action, leads to the portal of conscious deliverance. . . . And the soul that is in earnest, the soul which is aroused sufficiently not to grow weary in the effort after salvation, does not shrink from the toil, does not murmur at the penalties. For

> "Hearts that verily repent
> Are burdened with impunity,
> And comforted by chastisement:
> That punishment's the best to bear
> Which follows soonest on the sin,
> And guilt's a game where losers fare
> Better than those who seem to win."
>
> IV. 194, 197.

FEBRUARY 21.

GOD does not promise you a noble life without faith; for in faith lies the mainspring of all true nobleness. And still less can He promise you a happy life. . . . For Christ's voice is a still small voice; . . . and when man deafens his ear thereto, the voices of the passions are sweet as the songs of sirens; and the peal of ambition stirring as a clarion's note; and the glitter of dull gold gleams more brightly than the stars of heaven to the downward eye; and if you have no faith, nor seek it, you will therefore live the life of sin, and the life of sin is the life of baseness and of misery. But oh, thou — be thou servant, or clerk, or artisan, or statesman, or poor woman, or professional man, or who thou wilt — climb thou, and fear not to climb, this ladder Godwards, Christwards, Heavenwards — from faith unto faith. And then I tell thee, in the name of the Lord, that both happy and noble shall be thy life. Noble it shall be — however obscure, however poor — for every life is noble which attains the end of the commandment, which is love out of a pure heart, and a good conscience and faith unfeigned; and every life is happy, which, it may be after fierce struggles, has attained to peace in victory. v. 348.

Thanks be to God, which giveth us the victory through our Lord Jesus Christ. — I. Cor. xv. 57.

FEBRUARY 22.

> Straight-fibred Soul of mighty grain,
> Deep-rooted Washington, afire, serene.
> SIDNEY LANIER.

> His honor and the greatness of his name
> Shall make new nations.
> SHAKESPEARE.

WHEN the sword of Cornwallis was surrendered to Washington at Yorktown, some of the Americans . . . began to cheer. But, turning to them, the noble Virginian said, with a fine rebuke, "Let posterity cheer for us." You, as the youngest of the nations, may put your sickle into the ripened harvest of the world's experience, and if you learn the lessons which that revelation has to teach, Posterity will raise such a cheer for you as shall ring through all the ages.

When statesmen and nations have learned these lessons they . . . will aim at only such conditions of life and government as shall make it easy to do right and difficult to do wrong. They will see that politics, no less than individual conduct, have no other rule than the law of God. . . . Like Washington and Lincoln, they will be just and fear not, putting their trust in God. . . . Happy are the people that are in such a cause. Blessed are the people that have the Lord for their God.
VIII. 337, 235.

Keep, therefore, and do them; for this is your wisdom . . . in the sight of the nations, which shall hear all these statutes, and say, Surely this great nation is a wise and understanding people.
DEUT. iv. 6.

FEBRUARY 23.

We may win by toil
Endurance; saintly fortitude by pain;
By sickness, patience; faith and trust by fear;
But the great stimulus that spurs to life
And crowds to generous development
Each chastened power and passion of the soul,
Is the temptation of the soul to sin,
Resisted, and reconquered, evermore.
J. G. HOLLAND.

CHRIST overcame for us the threefold sources of temptation in their subtlest and most virulent form, to show us what we can, and how we can, conquer. He conquered the devil, because never, even in thought, had He suffered the spirit of evil to enter the precincts of His soul; He could say, "The prince of this world cometh, and hath nothing in Me." He conquered the appetites of the body by feeding on the bread of heaven, which is to do the will of God. He conquered the allurements of the world by the constant sense of the divine, the eternal life, which prevents a soul from imbruting itself in the unlawful impulses of that lower life which we share with the beasts that perish. He looked to His Father in heaven. . . . My friends, we are in danger; always in danger. Yet we . . . may feel a high, unflinching courage, if we say with Jehoshaphat, "We have no might against this great company that cometh against us, neither know we what to do; but our eyes are upon Thee." IV. 153, 154.

FEBRUARY 24.

NO good man, no saint of God, has ever lived or died in vain. They have died, almost always, in loneliness, or disappointment, or at the stake, or in the prison, or with hearts broken by man's ingratitude — so often that something seems wanting to the holiest careers which have not ended, even as Christ's did, each in its own Calvary; but they have never ended in vain. No! for the seed is not quickened except it dies. Even in its death, but only by its death, comes the promise of the golden grain.

And even when the effort against drunkenness, and vice, and Pharisaism, and wrong has failed, there has still been the effort, and the world is better for it. The very best of us leaves his tale half untold, his message imperfect; but if we have but been faithful, then, because of us, some one who follows us, with a happier heart and in happier times, shall utter our message better and tell our tale more perfectly. Some one shall run and not be faint; some one shall fly with wings where we have walked with weary feet!

VIII. 212, 213.

For, soon or late, to all that sow,
The time of harvest shall be given;
The flower shall bloom, the fruit shall grow,
If not on earth, at last in heaven.

WHITTIER.

FEBRUARY 25.

I shall restore to you the years that the locust hath eaten, . . . ye shall eat in plenty and be satisfied. — JOEL ii. 25, 26.

CHRIST came to reconcile us unto the Father, to find His lost sheep, to bring His wanderers home. He can give us — if we seek Him, He *will* give us — not only forgiveness, but strength to resist in future ; not only deliverance, but perfect liberty ; not only reconciliation, but assurance ; . . . but can He also restore the years which the locust hath eaten ? Can He undo that which has been done ? Can He disemburden us from the accumulations of guilty years, and make them as though they had never been ? Is not this beyond even the power of Omnipotence ? No, my friends ; and we confess that it is not, every time we say "I believe in the forgiveness of sins." This is the repeated promise of all Scripture. It is expressed by Isaiah: "Though your sins be as scarlet, they shall be as white as snow ; though they be red like crimson, they shall be as wool."

For you there is a blood of sprinkling, which is life, and which

Has this might,
That being red, it maketh red souls white.
V. 72, 78, 91.

FEBRUARY 26.

That henceforth we should not serve sin.
ROM. vi. 6.

IF a man will serve his sin, let him at least reckon upon this, that in one way or other it will be ill with him; his sin will find him out; his path will be hard; there will be to him no peace. It is marvellous in how many ways the retribution works, sometimes by divers diseases and sundry kinds of death; sometimes by utter unspeakable weariness of life; sometimes by a bitter series of unbroken disappointments; sometimes by the interferences of human law and the humiliation of open shame; sometimes by terrible surprises of strong temptation which shock the soul into despair. And sometimes on the other hand by none of these things, so that on the contrary the sinners have been wealthy and prosperous and to all appearance preëminently blessed, and yet at the very summit of their hopes have been tortured by the sense of an aimless existence, and the thirst and hunger of an unsatisfied soul. . . . God does not avenge himself by thunderbolts, He but leaves the sinner to the necessary outcome of his sin; aye, even the repentant sinner. XI. 29, 31.

What we have to recognize is that each of us carries within himself his own executioner, his demon, his hell, in his sin; that his sin is his idol, and that this idol, which seduces the desire of his heart, is his curse.
AMIEL.

FEBRUARY 27.

ALL revolt against God, all rebellion against His law, is simply the assertion of self; the determination to do what we like, not what we ought; the burning, fatal, and ill-regulated curiosity to pluck the fruit of the tree of the knowledge of evil as well as good. Read the story of the Fall in the Book of Genesis, a story of unequalled depth and truth, and you will see that sin came from listening to the deadly whisper, "Ye shall be as gods, knowing good and evil." So, then, all sin is, in its ultimate analysis, the sin of self. Self-assertion, hatred of reproof, the effeminate scream of wounded vanity, spurious independence, these are the root of sin, the principle of wrong-doing; and they tend to those special acts of transgression against the moral law which are separate sins. And these special acts of wrong-doing react upon, and at last constitute, the character. Acts pass into habits. We become what we do. The terrible consequences recall the dreadful parentage. V. 64, 67.

> Hope not the cure of sin till Self is dead:
> Forget it in love's service, and the debt
> Thou canst not pay the angels will forget.
> Heaven's gate is shut to him who comes alone;
> Save thou a soul, and it shall save thine own.
> WHITTIER.

FEBRUARY 28.

Put ye on the Lord Jesus Christ, and make not provision for the flesh, to fulfil the lusts thereof.
ROM. xiii. 14.

IT is a touching story of the late Archbishop Whately, that, when he lay in agony on his deathbed, his chaplain tried to comfort him with the words, "Who shall change our vile body," . . . from our English Bible. "Read it," said the dying Archbishop, "in his own words." The chaplain read it in the Greek, and there the words literally are, "Who shall change the body of our humiliation." "Ah!" said Dr. Whately, "that is it; nothing that God has made is *vile.*" No, our bodies are not vile; but they are, alas, too often bodies of humiliation — of humiliation deepened into abjectness by the sins of others or our own. . . . If we would but strive to live by "putting on the Lord Jesus Christ, and making no provision for the flesh to fulfil the lusts thereof," — how vast a change would even one single generation see in the health, the happiness, the ennoblement of mankind! . . . how soon would these mortal bodies of ours, these harps of a thousand strings, not only keep in tune, but ring with the very melodies of heaven! II. 211.

> They whose hearts are whole and strong,
>   Loving holiness,
> Living clean from soil of wrong,
>   Wearing truth's white dress, —
> They unto no far-off height
>   Wearily need climb;
> Heaven to them is close in sight
>   From these shores of time.
>   LUCY LARCOM.

FEBRUARY 29.

The fathers have eaten sour grapes, and the children's teeth are set on edge. — EZEK. xviii. 2.

WE talk with deep self-pity of the ravages of gout, and cancer, and consumption, and mental alienation. Alas! how many of these might in one or two generations cease to be, if we all lived the wise and temperate and happy lives which nature meant us to lead! And the voice of nature rightly interpreted is ever the voice of God. . . . By unwholesome narcotics, by burning and adulterated stimulants, by many and highly-seasoned meats, . . . the vast majority of men . . . clog and carnalize the aspirations which they should cherish, and feed into uncontrollable force the many-headed monster of the passions which they should control. Hence it is that millions of lives are like sweet bells jangled out of tune.

But in spite of these trials God does not mean us to be disheartened. Those laws of His to which we give the name of nature, have in them a strong recuperative force; they tend back from the degeneracy to the original perfection.

II. 207. 209.

Whiteness most white! Ah, to be clean again
  In mine own sight and God's most holy sight!
To reach through any flood of fire or pain
        Whiteness most white!
   . . . Bliss for bane
 Give me; for mortal frailty give me might;
Give innocence for guilt, and for my stain
        Whiteness most white.

CHRISTINA ROSSETTI.

MARCH 1.

Know ye not that ye are the temple of God? — I. Cor. iii. 16.

Reverence my sanctuary. — Lev. xix. 30.

WE reverence God's holiest sanctuary when we reverence ourselves. . . . A poet has said —

> Self-reverence, self-knowledge, self-control,
> These three alone lead life to sovran power.

It is most true. Self-reverence depends upon self-knowledge, and leads to self-control, and these are the elements of true greatness. Let us sweep aside the world's estimate of greatness. The puppetries of wealth and rank, the pretentious dignities of a little brief authority have no place here. Our smart apparel, our small pomposities, our little lordships — at one touch of Death's finger how do they shrivel and vanish into a nothing less than nothing; only the inherent grandeur of the bare soul remains, and a pauper's may be far grander than a king's. . . . Measure life by the measure of a man, that is of an angel, and you will find that the divinest souls have been swayed, more than all, by the inner reverence for their own personality; by the awful sanctity of their own being; by the honor they have felt, not for their own poor gifts or acquisitions, but for themselves as in Christ, as being partakers of the Divine in the essential nature which God gave them; as being a little lower than the angels, and as souls for which Christ died. VII. 223.

MARCH 2.

LIFE would be utterly different if men would make it different; unutterably more blessed if men sought or cared for the elements of blessedness. Oh! that men would but be true men, and that women would be the holy and gracious things which God meant women to be. . . . Expel from the human heart the ape's vileness, the serpent's hiss, the tiger's fury, the vulture wings which hasten to carrion; and then indeed man will become but little lower than the angels, crowned with glory and honor! Man may be like the brutes or like the angels, as he will. A society of men as God meant them to be, a true Church of Christ — ah! it would be a place which angels themselves might love. And we might help, each one of us, to make earth so. And the more heartily we do this, each for ourselves, the more surely will others do it, for "it is astonishing how much good goodness makes."

VII. 41.

Every man is a centre of radiation like a luminous body; he is, as it were, a beacon which entices a ship upon the rocks if it does not guide it into port. Every man is a priest, even involuntarily; his conduct is an unspoken sermon, which is forever preaching to others; — but there are priests of Baal, . . . and of all the false gods.

AMIEL.

MARCH 3.

Walk in the ways of thine heart and in the sight of thine eyes: but know thou that for all these things God will bring thee into judgment.

ECCLES. xi. 9.

GOD is the Amen, the Eternal Reality. He has set His canons against fraud, and lies, and hate, and lust. Obey Him or disobey Him, "at your pleasure and at your peril." Believe in Him or disbelieve in Him, at your pleasure and at your peril. But He is, and His law is, the sole truth of your life.

Sow a pleasant vice, and reap its poisonous harvest; sow a crime, and reap a retribution; sow a lust, and reap a ruin and a degradation; sow to the flesh, and reap corruption. These things are unreal, as a dream when one awaketh; their fashion passeth away like a vapor. The mere shams of earth, the vain and vile delights of the vicious life, are as the poison of asps. They involve a multiplicity of horrible miseries, as if a man did flee from a lion and a bear met him, or went into a house and leaned his hand on the wall, and a serpent bit him. But God is the Amen, the Eternal Truth, of reality and of righteousness.

IV. 264.

Healed at this fount our inmost ail would be,
Did we but health before disease prefer.

LUCY LARCOM.

MARCH 4.

IT is an age not of great crime, but of little meannesses ; . . . little blasphemy, but universal cynicism ; rare open thefts, but widespread secret dishonesty. And the worst sign is that the Church has well-nigh ceased to be fruitful of preëminent saintliness ; few lights shine out distinctly from the general darkness. Good and evil seem to be at truce, "lying together flat upon the world's surface." Our very conception of goodness seems to be dwarfed and impoverished ; and so little do we attain the high and heroic ideal of the Gospel, that men have begun to argue openly that it is an ideal which is in these days obsolete and impossible. . . . Oh, better by far that God should break us with His indignation, and vex us with all His storms, — better that He should make us suffer in every fibre of our being the ignoble martyrdom of sin, — better that His lightnings should shatter the lowest bases of our earth-born happiness, and let the nether fires glare in our very faces, than that He should thus suffer our souls, under this terrible danger of His wrath, to slumber on, in this trance of despairing insensibility, in this unconsciousness of commencing death.

X. 195, 201.

    And all is well, tho' faith and form
      Be sundered in the night of fear ;
      Well roars the storm to those who hear
    A deeper voice across the storm.

TENNYSON.

MARCH 5.

FOR the Christian life no means of grace is so absolutely indispensable as prayer. The soul of man is like a kindled brand; so long as the air breathes on it, it will retain till the last its genial warmth and crimson glow; but let the air stagnate around it, and, flake on flake, the white ashes will gather over it, and the fire will die away within it, and under those ashes it will be left black and charred, a cold and useless log. What the breath of wind is on the glowing brand, that prayer is to the soul. Let a man or a woman live a prayerless life, and all the light and the fire and the glow, all the wisdom and generosity and love will die away, because these are the result of spiritual grace alone; and covered with the dead, white embers of its own selfishness and pride, the soul will soon become cold and dead and hard — a useless thing, half consumed with impenitence and sin.

VII. 93.

"I know not by what methods rare;
But this I know, God answers prayer.

I know that He has given His word,
Which tells me prayer is always heard,

And will be answered, soon or late,
And so I pray, and calmly wait;
. . . .
Assured that He will grant my quest,
Or send some answer far more blest."

When thou prayest, enter into thy closet, and when thou hast shut thy door, pray to thy Father.
                              MATT. vi. 6.

"WHAT should we pray for?" . . . Everything which you need, . . . both for yourselves and for those whom you love. . . . Remember only two things — one, that to ask only or mainly for earthly blessings is a dreadful dwarfing and vulgarization of the grandeur and holiness of prayer, as though you asked for a handful of grass when you might ask for a handful of emeralds; the other, that you must always ask for earthly desires with absolute submission of your own will to God's, lest God should grant you your own bane, and ruin you at your own desire.
                                    VII. 101.

How oft has bitter tear been shed,
  And heaved how many a groan,
Because Thou wouldst not give for bread
  The thing that was a stone!

How oft the child Thou wouldst have fed
  Thy gift away has thrown!
He prayed; Thou heardst and gav'st the bread;
  He cried: It is a stone!
                    GEORGE MACDONALD.

Let, then, our prayers be "the key that opens the day, and the lock that shuts the night," and also from morning to night our staff and stay in all our labors, enabling us to go cheerfully up to the mount of God.
                                    VII. 106.

Hear ye the word which the Lord speaketh unto you. — JER. x. 1.

ALAS! the very best among us all fails too often to realize, as a guiding thought in life, that God *does* speak, and speaks *to us*, and speaks distinct messages in voices awfully articulate. . . . The Jews, in a legend that is not meaningless, tell us how, on the Mount, the great law-giver needed no human sustenance, because the subtle harmonies of the universe so filled his soul as to satisfy and sustain his whole being with their heavenly diapason; but when he came down out of the rolling clouds, the vesture of decay closed his ears and he heard no longer, and hungered for earthly food. Is it not so with us? Times there are when we hear the voice of God walking in the garden in the cool of the day, yea, when we hear it all the day long; and there are other times when we too listen with fainting hearts to those who tell us that we have but mistaken the pulse of our own beings for a sound above us. X. 24.

>   And so we yearn, and so we sigh,
>   And reach for more than we can see;
>   And witless of our folded wings,
>   Walk Paradise unconsciously;
>
>   And dimly feel the day divine,
>   With vision half redeemed from night,
>   Till death shall fuse the double life,
>   And God himself shall give us light.
>   ADELINE D. T. WHITNEY.

He that doeth truth cometh to the light.
JOHN iii. 21.

LIGHT is the analogue to Life, Truth, Holiness. If we would have fellowship with God we must walk in the light, as He is in the light. If we love the charnel-house of death and darkness then the light shineth in vain in the darkness, and the darkness comprehendeth it not. The condition then of fellowship with God is that there should be no darkness in us — no subterfuges; no duplicity; no dishonest and guilty concealments; no hidden chambers of the Temple full of shame and sin; not two lives in one; no self-deceit, or even self-delusion; no mask of hypocrisy; no base secondary motives; nothing jesuitical; no manipulations of truth or of doctrine; no telling of lies or blackening of names to serve a party or promote a cause; no suppression of truth or suggestion of falsehood; no vile pretence of doing evil that good may come. . . . The earthly correlative to "God is Light" is "Walk in the Light," "Be children of the Light," "Bring forth the fruits of Light." v. 44.

Come nearer, Sun of Righteousness! that we
  Whose swift short hours of day so swiftly run,
So overflowed with love and light may be,
  So lost in glory of the nearing Sun,
That not our light, but Thine, the world may see,
  New praise to Thee through our poor lives be won.

FRANCES R. HAVERGAL.

MARCH 9.

If we say that we have fellowship with Him, and walk in the darkness, we lie, and do not the truth. — I. JOHN i. 6.

STRANGE to say, it is possible to "walk in the darkness," and yet, all the while, to assume that we have fellowship with God, who is Light. Such a thing could not be believed if we did not continually see it. It is the utter indifference to, and unconsciousness of, sin which is the obduracy of callous hearts. . . . How many practically say, each of his own special temptation, "There is no harm in it." This may happen before the conscience has been awakened, or after it has been seared. In either case it may be said, Ephraim is turned to idols, let him alone; Ephraim hath gray hairs upon him here and there, and knoweth it not. . . .

Are not all who act thus, in one sphere of their lives, walking in the darkness, while yet they say that they have fellowship with the Light? My friends, let us search ourselves with candles to see that we be not renegades to our own knowledge. V. 50, 53.

Go to your bosom,
Knock there, and ask what it doth know.
SHAKESPEARE.

For if our heart condemn us, God is greater than our heart, and knoweth all things.
I. JOHN iii. 20.

MARCH 10.

For as many of you as were baptized into Christ, did put on Christ. — GAL. iii. 27.

THIS mystic union with Christ, this putting on Christ, this justification by faith, . . . is not a mere fantastic phraseology, which has nothing to do with daily interests, but is, to a Christian, as his inmost life. It is the very central thought of Scripture, the brightest gem of that oracular Urim and Thummim which gleams on the breast of the great High Priest. If the Old Testament be as a ring of gold which forms a precious setting for the jewels of the New, then the central diamond of all those jewels — the one for the sake of which the whole ring was designed — . . . is this thought of the life of Christ. Do not throw it away as valueless, or valueless to you: if you do, you will be poor indeed. Nay, rather test it. Smite it, if you will, to test its genuineness, with the strongest hammer of inquiry; fling it into the fiercest flame of criticism; pour on it the most corrosive acid of doubt. It has stood all these tests for eighteen hundred years, and is still the same priceless, flawless, eternal gem; the one jewel of the saints of God, which the world can neither give nor take away.

V. 313.

MARCH 11.

According to the measure of a man, that is of an angel. — REV. xxi. 17.

HE who would make life what God meant it to be, he who would make the angel's measure a man's measure, must . . . remember that true human nature is not only angelic but divine; that Jesus Christ our Lord became man, and so took up the manhood into God. In our faith in the Incarnation lies the very heart and essence of our Christianity. The most awful sanctions of purity, the most living impulses to nobleness, the most powerful stimulus to active service, lie in that. To purity — for know ye not that your bodies are temples of Christ? To nobleness — for He taught us to follow His example and walk in His footsteps; to loving service — for can there be work more nobly blessed than to live for the good of those souls for which Christ died? . . . He who measures his life by the measuring reed of these high purposes, measures it as angels measure it, and so measures it indeed with the measure of a man, that is of an angel — nay, rather of the King of the Angels.

VII. 91.

Bring forth the measure, and measure us all:
Alas, how short does our stature fall!

Then measure our Saviour, our King and Friend, —
Ah, how does His stature the measure transcend!

We, lower than angels; He, far, far higher:
But His is our nature, to Him our desire.

J. L. M. W.

MARCH 12.

"He that hath light within his own clean breast,
May sit i' the centre and enjoy clear day."

WHY do even we who profess and call ourselves Christians make our minds miserable by care and envy as we make our bodies miserable by sin? God gives us bread, and we turn it into a stone. We drive away from us our best friends and arm our enemies with scorpions. And yet surely every one of us who has at all realized the central thoughts of Christianity, and the inner meaning of the Saviour's life, must feel that if not all forms of care, yet all those forms of earthly care which are most potent to make man wretched, *ought* to have been dispelled from the heart of him who has listened to the calm and loving invitation, "Come unto Me all ye that labor and are heavy laden, and I will give you rest."

II. 220.

> Onward, onward through the night!
>   Matters it I cannot see?
> I am moving in a Might
>   Dwelling in the dark and me.
> End or way I cannot lose —
>   Grudge to rest, or fear to roam;
> All is well with wanderer whose
>   Heart is travelling hourly home.
>
> GEORGE MACDONALD.

MARCH 13.

> "Not to ourselves are we living,
> Not to ourselves do we die."

NO true work since the world began was ever wasted; no true life since the world began has ever failed. Oh, understand, my brethren, those two perverted words, *failure* and *success*, and measure them by the eternal not by the earthly standard. What the world has regarded as the bitterest failure has often been in the sight of Heaven the most magnificent success. When the cap, painted with devils, was placed on the brows of John Huss, and he sank dying amid the embers of the flame, — was that a failure? . . . When the frail worn body of the Apostle of the Gentiles was dragged by a hook from the arena, and the white sand scattered over the crimson life-blood of the victim whom the dense amphitheatre despised as some obscure and nameless Jew, — was that a failure? And when, after thirty obscure, toilsome, unrecorded years in the shop of the village carpenter, One came forth to be preeminently the Man of Sorrows, to wander from city to city in homeless labors, and to expire in lonely agony upon the shameful cross, — was that a failure? Nay, my brethren, it was the life, it was the death, of Him who lived that we might follow in His steps.

X. 178.

MARCH 14.

He that saith he abideth in Him ought himself also to walk even as He walked. — I. JOHN ii. 6.

"TO walk as Christ walked"! . . . We teach a child to write not only by showing him the shape of the letters, but by giving him letters over which he forms his own. Such a copy was Christ to us. St. Peter used the very word. That which we render "example" is ὑπογραμμὸς, the letters of that Divine word over which must be written the epistle of our lives. And with this St. Peter mingles the other metaphor of walking in Christ's steps. We know the old legend of the saintly king who went before his fainting page on the wintry night:

> In his master's steps he trod
>   Where the snow lay dinted;
> Heat was in the very sod
>   Which the saint had printed.

If we are to be with Christ, or in Christ — if we are to be Christians in more than name — we must imitate Christ, we must follow Him.

V. 128.

> But lead me, Man divine,
> Where'er Thou will'st, only that I may find
> At the long journey's end Thy image there,
> And grow more like to it. For art not Thou
> The human shadow of the infinite Love
> That made and fills the endless universe?
> The very Word of Him, the unseen, unknown
> Eternal Good!   R. W. GILDER.

One of His disciples . . . saith unto Him, There is a lad here, who hath five barley loaves and two small fishes; but what are they among so many? — JOHN vi. 8.

BARLEY loaves and only two small fishes! — but it was enough for the Lord of all; and with that scant, poor food, blessed and multiplied, He fed the hungry, and refreshed the weary, and spread a table in the wilderness, and made them sit on the green grass in the sunset, and gave them that which, to their hunger, was sweet as manna, and sent them rejoicing on their way.

We are in the wilderness, the day is far spent, the night is at hand, on every side of us are the hungry, and the thirsty, and the weary; we feel ourselves utterly helpless to help these helpless; we have not two hundred pennyworth of bread for them, and even that, if we had it, would be insufficient that every one of them might take a little. Yes! but have we tried to use the poor and scant store which we have? Have we, like that lad, offered our barley loaves for Christ to bless? If not, can we expect that they should be used? Still less can we expect that they should be multiplied!

VII. 265.

    Too great Thy heart is to despise;
    Thy day girds centuries about;
  From things we "little" call, Thine eyes
    See great things looking out.

GEORGE MACDONALD.

MARCH 16.

God also, bearing them witness, both with signs and wonders. — HEB. ii. 4.

IT seems as though against the doctrines, and above all against the miracles of Christianity, there were, so to speak, "a conspiracy of silence," an agreement of contemptuous indifference; as though forsooth it were too late in the day to argue or to refute, and it were at once more effectual and more courteous to ignore. . . . And are we timidly to admit these haughty assertions, . . . are we, the successors of those who overcame the world, to accept the patronizing condescension which is willing to spare our venerable prejudices? Nay, unshaken amid the storm of contemptuous assertion, we reply that it requires a loftier height of intelligence to believe in miracles than to reject them, because it involves the realization of loftier than mere material verities, and the recognition of wider than purely physical laws. . . . Nay, but beside the graves of a Whewell and a Faraday let all at least that is noisy and shallow in modern atheism, learn the humility of science, and the calm dignity of unshaken Christian faith! XII. 14.

> I grant to the wise his meed,
> But his yoke I will not brook,
> For God taught *me* to read, —
> He lent me the world for a book.
> JEAN INGELOW.

MARCH 17.

A holy life is Heaven's unquestioned text;
That shining radiance doubt can never mar, —
The pillar's flame, the light of Bethlehem's star!
OLIVER WENDELL HOLMES.

IT may not be ours to utter convincing arguments, but it may be ours to live holy lives. It may not be ours to be subtle and learned and logical, but it may be ours to be noble and sweet and pure. Oh! believe me, not to the diadem of Constantine, not to the tiara of Gregory, not to the gorgeousness of Leo, not to the fagots of Torquemada, not to the sword of the Crusaders, not to the logic of the schoolmen, does Christianity owe one half-hour of her dominion over any human heart; but to the majesty of her self-denials, to the beauty of her holiness, to the meekness of her saints, to the truth, the zeal, the faithfulness of those who asked for nothing better than to follow His example who died as a malefactor to save the world. And these lessons are open to us no less than to them. "They ask me for *secrets* for attaining to perfection," said St. Francis de Sales; "for my part I know no other secret than this: to love God with all one's heart, and one's neighbor as one's self." This was the great lesson of Christianity, but Christianity was not only a doctrine but a Life. Oh, let us strive to imitate that Life! XII. 124.

MARCH 18.

WHO are the real enemies and underminers of Christianity? Far less the publicans than the Pharisees. Far less the avowed sceptics than the insincere formalists. Far less the open worldlings than those who with the most tremendous professions on their lips, and the most ostentatious religiosity in their actions, go away to defraud their neighbors, or to dawdle away their own useless and self-indulgent lives, or to be absorbed in their own callous egotism, or to tell lies of their brethren, or to be lovers of pleasure more than lovers of God.

> " They passed before my threshold,
>   The lost souls one by one;
> I watched them from the daybreak
>   Unto the set of sun.
>
> " I said, ' My soul's unshaken,
>   Because I have not sinned,
> Surely they reap the whirlwind,
>   They who have sown the wind.'
>
> " The burden of their failure,
>   It was no more my own
> Than a far-distant struggle
>   Lost in a land unknown.
>
> . . . . . .
>
> " Till, it seemed, a sudden shadow
>   Over my threshold crossed;
> And I knew the play was ended,
>   And my own soul was lost."

Alas! if our sins were written on our foreheads in the too legible autograph of the Recording Angel, how many a man would be horribly startled to read the plain indictment!

V. 54, 56.

IN one form or another, . . . having long ago repented, or having not repented but only suffered from remorse and fear — we have . . . all disobeyed the will of God. . . . The sentence of death has passed upon us; and, unless we have repented long ago in dust and ashes, the flaming sword of the cherubim waves every way between us and the Tree of Life. Which of us all shall cast the stone at our fallen father Adam, at our frail miserable mother Eve? Have we made any wiser choice? If they did so badly, did not God put it afresh in our power to have done better? After millenniums of experience have proved that the crude apple which perverted Eve was so ruinous and so bitter, have we not plucked it? Have not we too been driven from the Eden of innocence? Was it only in that garden by the Euphrates, or is it also in the ruined garden of every human soul, that by the Tree of Life there grows also the Tree of the Knowledge of good and evil? VII. 163.

If we can forget the Tree of Life, can we forget that Tree of Death whereon Christ hung so that He might be indeed our Life?

CHRISTINA ROSSETTI.

MARCH 20.

HOW many of us can say with the Apostles, "Lo! we have forsaken all and followed Thee"? Ought the Christian life to be so easily harmonized as we harmonize it with luxury, with eager worldliness, with murmuring ambition, with greed, with malice, with lack of charity, with love of self? Ought the Christian warfare to be, as it so often is, little more than a comfortable profession of languid virtues; a thin veneer of conventional respectabilities; a hypocritical semblance of dead, or at least of inoperative, of ineffectual, of passively received beliefs? Death, judgment, eternity — how many of us live with these habitually in view? To eat, and drink, and sleep, to accumulate, to laugh, to die, with no thought of a besetting God, with no shame for our unworthiness, no bitter penitence for sin, no serious effort for amendment, no thrill of gratitude to Christ, no solemn looking forth to heaven: — does this describe the life of any of us? and if it does — oh, is this the life on which has fallen the shadow of the cross?
VII. 289.

> Go up, go up, my heart!
>   Be not a trifler here;
> Ascend above these clouds,
>   Dwell in a higher sphere.
>
> Waste not the precious stores
>   On creature-love below;
> To God that wealth belongs,
>   On Him that wealth bestow.

Horatius Bonar.

MARCH 21.

OF worldliness I accept no such cheap and vulgar definition as that which makes it consist in going to races, and theatres and balls. No, I mean something infinitely deeper than this. I mean living for what is temporal, and not for what is eternal. . . . And oh, what a great blank of the soul comes upon the man who accepts this life; how all the ardors of his early enthusiasm die away; how all that was free, and delicate, and noble, and attractive about him, . . . all the poetry of his existence gets congealed and hardened into conceit and commonplace, . . . how in his easy life evils come upon him which " vex less, but mortify more, which suck the blood though they do not shed it, and ossify the heart though they do not torture it." . . . The scurf of a heartless conventionality lies thick all over the daily life.
XI. 96.

Upon his life Sanjarim looked in pain,
And saw its incompleteness and its stain.

From these he sought with tears to wash him free,
Nor knew how blest a thing it is to see.

Again Sanjarim looked upon his life,
And noted not that sin and self were rife;

Then, smiling, went his way among mankind,
Nor ever dreamed, alas, that he was blind.
ROBERT GILBERT WELSH.

MARCH 22.

Which of you convinceth me of sin?

JOHN viii. 46.

THE fierce light of envy and anger has beaten on the minutest incidents in the life of Christ, yet none in these two thousand years can lay any sin to His charge. The microscope of historical criticism, the spectral analysis of philosophic inquiry, have failed to discover one speck in that Sunbeam from the Father of Lights. The fierce hatred of the Jews, the bitter controversies of the atheists, alike acquit Him. . . . The most outspoken of modern rationalists, as they gaze on Him with dubious wonder, seem one after another to fall on their knees. . . . His life was confessedly a copy over which has been fondly traced the biography of all His truest saints.

Let us remember that He died to take away our sins. This sinless and stainless Saviour, the Son of God, has a heart of tender compassion and infinite forgiveness.

IX. 69, 72, 76.

But Thee, O man's best Man, O love's best Love,
O perfect life in perfect labor writ,
O all men's Comrade, Servant, King, or Priest, —
What *if* or *yet*, what mole, what flaw, what lapse,
What least defect or shadow of defect,
What rumor, tattled by an enemy,
Of inference loose, what lack of grace
Even in torture's grasp, or sleep's, or death's, —
O what amiss may I forgive in Thee,
Jesus, good Paragon, thou Crystal Christ?

SIDNEY LANIER.

For God . . . hath shined in our hearts.

II. COR. iv. 6.

YOU have seen the heavens gray with dull and leaden-colored clouds, you have seen the earth chilly and comfortless under its drifts of unmelting snow: but let the sun shine, and then how rapidly does the sky resume its radiant blue, and the fields laugh with green grass and vernal flower! So will it be with even a withered and a wasted life when we return to God and suffer Him to send His bright beams of light upon our heart. I do not mean that the pain or misery under which we are suffering will necessarily be removed, — even for Christ it was not so; but peace will come and strength will come and resignation will come and hope will come, — and we shall feel able to bear anything which God shall send, and though He slay us we still shall seek Him, and even if the blackest cloud of anguish seem to shroud His face from us, even on that cloud shall the rainbow shine.　　　　X. 233.

   Shine, shine; make me Thy shadow still —
   The brighter still the more Thy shade;
   My motion be Thy lovely, moveless will!
   My darkness, light delayed!

GEORGE MACDONALD.

MARCH 24.

Thine eyes shall see Jerusalem, a quiet habitation, a tabernacle that shall not be taken down.
                                    ISA. xxxiii. 20.

OUR path in life is like that of the traveller who lands at the famous port of the Holy Land. He rides at first under the shade of palms, under the golden orange-groves, beside the crowded fountains, with almonds and pomegranates breaking around him into blossom: soon he leaves behind him these lovely groves; he enters on the bare and open plain; the sun burns over him, the dust-clouds whirl around him; but even there the path is broidered by the quiet wayside flowers, and when at last the bleak bare hills succeed, his heart bounds within him, for he knows that he shall catch his first glimpse of the Holy City, as he stands weary on their brow.   X. 138.

O happy harbor of God's saints!
  O sweet and pleasant soil!
In thee no sorrow can be found,
  Nor grief, nor care, nor toil.

No murky cloud o'ershadows thee,
  Nor gloom, nor darksome night;
But every soul shines as the sun,
  For God Himself gives light.
                                    UNKNOWN.

MARCH 25.

Are they not all ministering spirits? — HEB. i. 14.

WHAT is told us respecting [the angels] is not for the luxury of the imagination; it is for the example of our lives. . . . These are they by whom God's will is done in heaven. How is it done? As differently as possible from the slack and unwilling way in which it is done on earth. God's angels, we know, do it contentedly and unquestioningly, whatever it is. . . . And they do it cheerfully.

Man has his insect ambition, his ephemeral distinctions. To the angels, if it be God's will, it is just as dignified to sweep a room as to rule a kingdom. When Raphael conducted to Babylonia the boy Tobias and his dog,

"He did God's will, to him all one,
Or on the earth, or in the sun." . . .

To those myriads of waiting ministrants

"Naught is too high or low,
Too mean or mighty, if God wills it so;
Neither is any creature, great or small,
Beyond His pity, which embraceth all;
Nor any ocean rolls so vast that He
Forgets one wave of all that restless sea." . . .

The quintessence of the way in which angels do, and men should do, God's work is *love*.

IV. 78, 79, 80.

MARCH 26.

. . . THERE is the world of sorrow; and though it must continue while time lasts, there is not one of us who cannot help to make it *less* sorrowful. We can do so passively by abstaining from all churlish deeds and all false and cruel words. We can do so actively by the constant endeavor to cultivate every gentle and kindly feeling, to rejoice with them that do rejoice, and weep with them that weep.

We can do so both actively and passively by the strenuous determination to be kind to many, to wish to be kind to all, willingly to do injury to none. "Be ye kind one to another, tender-hearted, forgiving one another, even as God in Christ forgave you." . . . This we can all do. All this let us do, and, if often in doing it, we shall have to sigh as Jesus sighed, we shall find that, however the world may treat us, He will also grant to us to become "partakers of His vision and His Sabbath," to share in the infinitude of His peacefulness, to enter into His boundless joy.   II. 39.

> And some day God shall bid me dwell
> Where the great visions shine;
> The sight of the Lord and all He is
> Shall be the world's and mine.
>
> DENIS WORTMAN.

MARCH 27.

RELIGION is neither a diseased self-retrospection, nor an obtrusive impertinence, nor an agonizing inquiry. What is it? It is the way of the supreme good, plain and indisputable, and ourselves travelling upon it. It should be "an all-embracing heavenly canopy, an atmosphere, a life-element;" not always spoken of, but always presupposed. It should be like the bottom of the ocean, always there, always necessary, though not always seen. . . . Let us do our duty, and pray that we may do our duty here; now; to-day; not in dreamy sweetness, but in active energy; not in the green oasis of the future, but in the dusty desert of the present; not in the imaginations of otherwhere, but in the realities of *now*.

I. 204.

> Balance not in scales of time
> Deathless destinies sublime!
> What vague future can weigh down
> This great Now that is thine own?
>
> . . . .
>
> This a star is - - this, thine earth;
> Here the germ awakes to birth
> Of God's sacred life in thee —
> Heir of immortality!
>
> LUCY LARCOM.

MARCH 28.

O CHRISTIAN men and women, do not deceive yourselves! Remember that God sees through shams, remember that God does not care for anything except the heart. He will not in the least value you for your professions, or for your observances: but, "as He Who hath called you is holy, so be ye holy in all manner of conversation." If you want to make religion lovable, you must make it lovely; if you want men to accept your opinions, enable them, if you can, to respect your character; let men see in you a purer standard than their own, a loftier stature, a kindlier sympathy. The centuries do homage to real goodness; it is fairer than the morning or the evening star; it is the reflection of the life of Christ; it is as "a city set on a hill;" it is as a pillar of fire moving over a wilderness of graves.

IX. 118.

God gives each man one life, like a lamp, then gives
That lamp due measure of oil: Lamp lighted — hold
    high, wave wide,
Its comfort for others to share.

BROWNING.

He that believeth on the Son hath everlasting life. — JOHN iii. 36.

HERE is the mystery of all mysteries — the unsearchable depth of the riches of the love of God — in that, while we were yet sinners, He sent His Son to die for us. He who has apprehended this secret of the ages needs no other wisdom. God became man, that man might be as God. Even so did God cast a bridge over the seemingly immeasurable abyss, which separates His infinitude from man's insignificance. He did so when He, who was in the form of God, made himself of no reputation, and took upon Him the form of a servant. . . . Where shall we find help in time of need if we reject a Saviour who is all love; who is ever near; who lived, and died, and rose again for us; in whom alone we can obtain forgiveness for the sins of the past, or any strength in the present, or any hope and peace in the long days that are to come?

V. 10.

In Thee God's promise is Amen and Yea:
  What art Thou to us? Prize of every lot,
Shepherd and Door, our Life and Truth and Way: —
  Nay, Lord, what art Thou not!

CHRISTINA ROSSETTI.

MARCH 30.

The redeemed of the Lord . . . shall obtain gladness and joy; and sorrow and mourning shall flee away.

I, even I, am He that comforteth you.

ISA. li. 11, 12.

WE all, in turn, must face our forlorn hours of bereavement. For us, sooner or later, our house must be left unto us desolate. But . . . these natural sorrows are, and are meant to be, full of blessedness; the light of God shining upon them transmutes them into heavenly gold. The wounds which God makes, God heals. The fire which kindles the grains of frankincense upon His altar, at the same time brings out their fragrancy. All that He sends, if borne submissively, becomes rich in mercy. Upon the troubled soul which seeks Him His consolations increase "with the gentleness of a sea which caresses the shore it covers."

VII. 26.

Patience must dwell with Love, for Love and Sorrow
  Have pitched their tent together here:
Love all alone will build a house to-morrow,
    And Sorrow not be near.

To-day, for Love's sake, hope; still hope in Sorrow,
  Rest in her shade, and hold her dear;
To-day she nurses thee; and lo! to-morrow,
    Love only will be near.

CHRISTINA ROSSETTI.

MARCH 31.

And being in agony, He prayed.
LUKE xxii. 44.

HOWEVER bright the brightest of your lives may hitherto have been, . . . yet for every one of you, I suppose, sooner or later the Gethsemane of life must come. It may be the Gethsemane of struggle, and poverty, and care;—it may be the Gethsemane of long and weary sickness;—it may be the Gethsemane of farewells that wring the heart by the deathbeds of those we love;—it may be the Gethsemane of remorse, and of well-nigh despair, for sins that we will not, but which we say we cannot, overcome. Well, my brethren, in that Gethsemane—aye, even in that Gethsemane of sin—no angel merely, but Christ Himself, who bore the burden of our sins, will, if we seek Him, come to comfort us. He will, if, being in agony, we pray. He can be touched, He is touched, with the feeling of our infirmities. He, too, has trodden the winepress of agony alone; He, too, has lain face downwards in the night upon the ground; and the comfort which then came to Him He has bequeathed to us—even the comfort, . . . the light, the hope, the faith, the sustaining arm, the healing anodyne of prayer. . . . Yes, being in an agony, we pray; and the talisman against every agony is there. X. 231.

For thou shalt have thy delight in the Almighty, and shalt lift up thy face unto God.

JOB xxii. 26.

"THOU hast written well of me," said the Vision to the great teacher of Aquinum; "what reward dost thou desire?" — "*Non aliam, nisi te Domine*" — "No other than Thyself, O Lord," was the meek and rapt reply. And when all our restless, fretful, discontented longings are reduced to this alone, the desire to see God's face; — when we have none in Heaven but Him, and none upon earth whom we desire in comparison of Him; — then we are indeed happy beyond the reach of any evil thing, for then we have but one absorbing wish, and that wish cannot be refused. Least of all can it be refused when it has pleased God to afflict us. "Ye now have sorrow," said Christ, "but I will see you again, and your heart shall rejoice, and your joy no man taketh from you." Yes, when God's children pass under the shadow of the Cross of Calvary, they know that through that shadow lies their passage to the Great White Throne. For them Gethsemane is as Paradise. God fills it with sacred presences; its solemn silence is broken by the music of tender promises; its awful darkness softened and brightened by the sunlight of heavenly faces and the music of angel wings.

X. 237.

APRIL 2.

Never man spake like this man. — JOHN vii. 46.

IN the dim hours of sorrow and bereavement; in the hours of painful lassitude, when we hear

"Time flowing through the middle of the night;"

in the hour when, like an uncertain echo in the lonely corridors of some haunted house, we hear far off the monotonous footfall of approaching death; what is it that calms, and comforts, and soothes us then? Is it any discovery of science? is it any scheme of philosophy? is it even the sublime vision of Dante, or the lordly eloquence of Milton? is it anything that orator has uttered and poet sung? Nay, when the melody of lyric songs has lost its charm, and the music of memory and her siren daughters has been brought low, we still listen — when we can listen to nothing else — to the beatitudes which Christ spake to the multitudes as they sat listening among the mountain lilies, or to those last words, more precious than archangel's utterance, which on the same night that He was betrayed He spake to His beloved ones, when the traitor had gone out and it was night.   XII. 75.

Thou, O Friend,
From Heaven, that madest this our heart Thine own,
Dost pierce the broken language of its moan;
Thou dost not scorn its needs, but satisfy.
DORA GREENWELL.

APRIL 3.

This man, after He had offered one sacrifice for sins, forever sat down on the right hand of God.
HEB. X. 12.

NO priest was He, robed only in symbolic innocence; no offerer of a blood which could not purge the conscience from dead works; no, but in His perfect sinlessness, with His own blood, that is, with the perfect sacrifice of His vivifying life, He passes into the Eternal Presence, so that in His Person our glorified human nature might sit forever upon the sapphire throne. Henceforth for every one of us the way is open, the parting veil has been forever rent in twain.

And when the last hour hath come, when the still shadow hath reached its appointed line on the dial-plate of Eternity, He shall come once more to judge the world, and to give unto every man according as his work shall be. Oh, may we then be found cleansed by His propitiation, forgiven by His intercession, safe in His advocacy; washed, justified, sanctified, accepted in the Beloved. V. 105, 107.

Apart from Thee all gain is loss,
All labor vainly done;
The solemn shadow of Thy Cross
Is better than the sun.
WHITTIER.

APRIL 4.

Wherefore if any man be in Christ he is a new creature. — II. COR. V. 17.

IN Christ. Those two words contain the very secret, the sole secret, of the Christian life. To have died with Christ unto sin; to have risen with Christ to righteousness; to grow in Christ by holiness — that is to be a Christian. The righteousness of God; the non-fulfilment of it by man; the fulfilment of it by Christ; the forgiveness of past sins through Him; the strength in Him amid the temptations of the present; the identification with Christ by faith — there you have the Gospel of salvation. Are you troubled by any or all of the forms of evil passion? Die to them — Christ did. So shall you rise with Him, become a new creature, and be transformed by the renewing of your minds.

V. 299.

> By Thine anguish cleanse my soul,
> By Thy Passion make me whole;
> Weak and helpless on the Tree,
> Thou didst gain the victory, —
> Weak and helpless as I lie,
> Thou canst triumph, sin can die.
>
> CAROLINE M. NOEL.

APRIL 5.

As in Adam all die, even so in Christ shall all be made alive. — I. COR. XV. 22.

DEATH smote for ages God's fair creation, he lifted up his hand against the Lord's anointed, he seemed as irresistible as terrible; and yet not kings only and mighty men, but the soul of the meanest beggar that ever died of want in the crowded city street, and the soul of the tenderest newborn infant that passed away like a thin breath of air a thousand years ago, shall be delivered safe and uninjured, yea, glorified and immortal, out of his armed and icy hand! What a hope, . . . what a change in the thought of life! Bravely and happily let us walk through this Dark Valley; for though the rocks overshadow, and the Phantom haunts it, at the end of it is a door of hope — a door of Immortality that opens on the gardens of Heaven and the trees and streams of life. . . . This is the Christian's hope, and truly herein Christ maketh us "more than conquerors," for we not only triumph over the enemy, but profit by him, wringing out of his curse a blessing, out of his prison a coronation and a home.

XI. 71.

> Shine, then, Thou Resurrection Light!
>   Upon our sorrows shine!
> The fulness of Thy joy be ours,
>   As all our griefs were Thine.
> Now, in this changing, dying life,
>   Our faded hopes restore,
> Till, in Thy triumph perfected,
>   We taste of death no more.
>
> A. L. WARING.

APRIL 6.

We have not only to look back at a dying Saviour, but to look up at a living one.   F. R. HAVERGAL.

IF you will faithfully set to work; humbly do your duty; sincerely try to benefit your neighbor; earnestly strive to mortify the flesh; . . . you will find that Christ is not dead. Even though He died, He also rose, He ascended. It is not only that He once walked this earth, but that His life is in it; it is not only that He is in His unseen heaven, far away; nay, but He is very nigh thee, even in thy mouth, and in thy heart. . . . He will not cast thee out, however poor and stained thou art; however vulgar and wretched and bad a Christian thou mayst be. . . . Begin at the beginning. Pray to Him. Try to do His will. Then His Father will come, and He will come. Do not trouble yourself about finding them, for then you shall be found. Have you not often heard in lovely melody, "If with all your hearts ye truly seek me, ye shall ever surely find me"? and if those be not exactly the words of Scripture, these are: If from thence thou shalt seek the Lord thy God, thou shalt find Him if thou seek Him with all thy heart.
    V. 319.

   Who shall cry, and He not hear?
   When the night comes down in dread,
Lo! He standeth very near:
   "Child of Mine, be not afraid;
In Mine arms you need not fear,
   In My hands your hands are laid."
          KATHERINE TYNAN HINKSON.

APRIL 7.

The blood of Jesus His Son cleanseth us from all sin. — I. John i. 7.

TO use the language of the Mystics, "the white rose of purity grows on the same stem, and springs from the same root, as the red rose of pardon." And do not let the expression, the "blood of Jesus," lead you into all kinds of repellant language, and notions of Pagan expiation. By "the blood of Jesus" is meant the spirit, the essential life of Jesus; the phrase, in this context, scarcely ever alludes to the *physical* blood shed from the veins. The expression is explained by the constant clause in the Pentateuch, "the blood thereof, which is the life thereof." . . . The blood — that is, the essential life of Jesus — is at once the price by which we were purchased, and the power by which we are kept pure. By His death He completed our redemption; by His blood — *i.e.*, by the continuous efficacy of His life thus given for us — He cleanses us. "To drink of His blood is to partake of His immortality." V. 83, 85.

>Now the Holiest with boldness
>   We may enter in,
>For the open fountain cleanseth
>   From all sin.
>
>Precious, precious blood of Jesus,
>   Ever flowing free!
>O believe it, O receive it,
>   'Tis for thee!
>
>   Frances R. Havergal.

APRIL 8.

The creature itself also shall be delivered from the bondage of corruption. — ROM. viii. 21.

YES, Christ is risen. . . . The sunlight that gleams forth after the world has been drenched, and dashed, and terrified with the black thunder-drops, re-awakening the song of birds and re-illuminating the bloom of the folded flowers, does not more gloriously transfigure the landscape than those words transfigure the life of man. Nothing short of this could be our pledge and proof that we also shall arise. We are not left to . . . vague hopes of it in exalted moments; splendid guesses of it in ancient pages; faint analogies of it from the dawn of day, and the quickened grain, and the butterfly shaking itself free of the inclosing chrysalis to wave its wings in the glories of summer light: all this might create a longing, the sense of some far-off possibility in a few chosen souls, but not for all the weary and suffering sons of humanity a permanent and ennobling conviction, a sure and certain hope. But Christ is risen, and we have it now; a thought to comfort us in the gloom of adversity, a belief to raise us into the high privilege of sons of God.

XI. 70.

"Forever with the Lord!
Amen, so let it be.
Life from the dead is in that word,
And immortality."

APRIL 9.

The King of kings, and Lord of lords, Who only hath immortality. — I. TIM. vi. 15.

WHEN, three centuries ago, in 1557, the Spaniards, under Philip II., were besieging Coligny in the little town of St. Quentin, they shot over the city walls a shower of arrows to which were attached little strips of parchment with promises meant to seduce from their allegiance the starving and fever-stricken inhabitants. Coligny thought it sufficient to take a piece of parchment, to write on it two words, *Regem habemus*, to tie it on a javelin, and hurl it into the Spanish camp. . . . Have we then no king? Is not Christ our King — the King of verity and judgment, the King of mercy and tenderness, the King who loved us and died for us, the King who sits at the right hand of the Majesty on high? . . . Oh! that we, too, would seize our lives as a javelin, and writing on them the two words *Regem habemus*, would hurl it with all our force into the serried ranks of the enemies of God.

IV. 225.

Stainless soldier on the walls,
  Knowing this, — and knows no more,
Whoever fights, whoever falls,
  Justice conquers evermore,
  Justice after as before, —
And he who battles on her side,
God, though he were ten times slain,
  Crowns him victor glorified,
Victor over death and pain.

EMERSON.

APRIL 10.

THOUGH we have no power of ourselves to help ourselves; though we are not sufficient of ourselves to think anything as of ourselves; yet our sufficiency is of God. The doctrine may not be palatable to human pride, which likes to stand on its own manhood, and with its own thews and sinews to wrestle with the principalities and powers of evil. But when human pride has been humiliated to the dust by utter failure; when, with infinite sadness, our own efforts, though aided by a Father's unseen grace, have only succeeded in establishing the unstable equilibrium of a most weak and imperfect goodness, then we are driven to find strength and refuge in the thought that without God we can do nothing. It is God who worketh in us both to will and to do of His good pleasure. If we have advanced but a very small way in the godly life, it is solely by the grace of God that we are what we are. The point is this: that the true life of a Christian is not a natural but a supernatural life. v. 293.

> What man is he, that boasts of fleshly might
> And vain assurance of mortality,
> Which, all so soon as it doth come to fight,
> 'Gainst spirituall foes, yields by and by,
> Or from the fielde most cowardly doth fly!
> Ne let the man ascribe it to his skill,
> That thorough grace hath gainèd victory:
> If any strength we have, it is to ill,
> But all the good is God's, both power and eke will.
> **SPENSER.**

APRIL 11.

Serve the Lord with gladness. — Ps. c. 2.

THE full, rich, innocent use of gifts and opportunities — how little do we understand it! For every purpose of noble gladness, how much more might almost every one of us make of our life than we do! How do we throw away the substance for the shadow, and the healthy reality for the feverish dream! How do we crowd out the natural effects, and make all life artificial. We spend our life, as it were, on the stage and under the gaslight, when we might be walking in the sunlight under heaven. We talk of poverty and limitation, while we make life "a haggard, malignant running for luck," and are daily neglecting the elements of purest and loftiest pleasure. "Give me," says an American writer, "health and a day, and I will make the pomp of emperors ridiculous." But to enable us thus to enjoy the gifts of nature we all need more open eyes, more grateful hearts. II. 197.

Soul, perceive thy perfect hour!
Let thy life burst into flower;
Heaven is opening to bestow
More than thou canst think or know:
Now to thy true height arise,
Enter now thy paradise.
In to-day to-morrow see, —
Now is immortality! LUCY LARCOM.

APRIL 12.

NEARLY nineteen centuries have sped away since the great Sacrifice was offered on Calvary, and we are living still in a world of error and ignorance, of misery and sin. And yet we do not despair. When the deep gloom settled down on Calvary, when the disciples had forsaken Him and fled, when priests and rulers, Jews and Gentiles, the soldiers and the mob, nay, even the crucified robbers at His side, had all been joining in insult and execration, when for one awful moment it seemed as if even His Father had forsaken Him, He, the Son of man and the Son of God, was still the Lord, the Victor, the Deliverer, and His "It is finished!" was the cry of triumph. That triumph, though still but partial, shall hereafter be universal. From the gloomy background of history, from the clouds and darkness which so often seem to settle down on our human lives, the eye of faith not only sees that cross stand out in holy light, but over it and around it we still read the name of Him who died thereon, and the promise of the vision which the first Christian emperor wove in letters of gold upon his labarum, "*By this thou shalt conquer!*"

II. 234.

"All is of God that is, and is to be,
And God is good!" Let that suffice us still,
Resting in child-like love upon His will,
Who moveth His great ends unthwarted by the ill.

WHITTIER.

Hereby we do know that we know Him, if we keep His commandments. — I. JOHN ii. 3.

WHAT is the test? To be a nominal Christian, to have been baptized, to be a member of the Church? By no means. It was to the baptized, it was to nominal Christians, that St. Paul said, "Some have not the knowledge of God; I speak this to move you to shame." Is it so with us? How may every soul find out what must be the individual answer to that which is the most solemn question of all life, "Do I know God?" . . . The test is nothing superfine; nothing transcendental; nothing disputable; but just simple, plain obedience. The love of a true child for its parents is not shown by fondling and talking; the truest, deepest love is not demonstrative, not sentimental, not emotional. It is shown by meeting the parents' wishes, and trying to fulfil their hopes; and so Cordelia loves King Lear better than Regan and Goneril.

We know God if we keep His commandments, not merely as a dead deposit, but with a watchful heed; with a living observance.

V. III.

Master, speak! and make me ready,
When Thy voice is truly heard,
With obedience glad and steady,
Still to follow every word.

FRANCES R. HAVERGAL.

APRIL 14.

The man, Christ Jesus. — 1. TIM. ii. 5.

JESUS, who is Christ the Lord, was the perfect man, the representative man, man in the image of God, God as a man with men; God not merely revealing Himself to man, not merely uniting Himself to man, but God *becoming* man. We do not judge of the tree from the blighted trunk, the cankered leaves, the bitter roots — but from its glory of foliage, of blossom, and of fruit. We do not estimate the ship from the miserable wreck which the rocks have gored, and the waves shattered, and the winds flung in scorn upon the shore — but from the gallant barque, when, with streaming flag and bellying sails, "she walks the waters like a thing of life." Even so we must take our estimate of man, not from the churl and the villain, not from the liar and the scoundrel, not from the selfish miser and the staggering drunkard, not from the indolence of the slothful and the wretchedness of the depraved; not from the harlot and the felon, and those yet more guilty, who made them what they are — but from the pure, the good, the spiritually minded. These alone are true men and true women. . . .

And in the light of this truth we escape from that snare of the devil which would lead us to despise our human nature. We say, "I trust in the nobleness of human nature, in the majesty of its faculties, in the fulness of its mercy, in the joy of its love."

IF Abraham Lincoln was not great by genius he was something more; he was great by exalted goodness. Never, perhaps, did a simpler, a sweeter, a homelier nature, shape the decrees of a great people; never certainly did a leading ruler depend with so steady and entire a humility on God, or feel with deeper piety, and avow with manlier courage, that he was but a weak instrument for the purposes of the Almighty. He was a truly good man; — a man who, encircled with temptations, yet lived without avarice and without ambition; — a man who, while others blustered, never uttered one boastful sentence, and while others raved, never penned one vindictive word; — a man whose very face, they say, in his last days was illuminated with the hopes of peace and the power of mercy; — a man whom misfortune did not depress, nor success unduly elate —

"A good man, struggling with the storm of fate,"

through good report and through ill report calmly, humbly, hopefully bearing up, and doing his manful duty to the bitter end.

XI. 222.

Yes, this is he who ruled a world of men
  As might some prophet of the elder day —
  Brooding above the tempest and the fray
With deep-eyed thought and more than mortal ken.
  A power was his beyond the touch of art
  Or arméd strength — his pure and mighty heart.
               RICHARD WATSON GILDER.

APRIL 16.

IT is one of the very finest and deepest sayings of the great sage of China that "Heaven means Principle." With him, with all good men who have ever lived, this was the solid result and outcome of experience. Other sources of happiness are but as transient gleams of sunlight, but this is life eternal; other blessings fade as the flowers fade, but this is an everlasting foundation. How full is all Scripture of this one lesson! With what a glow of belief, with what a force of conviction, do those divine utterances crowd upon us, "Blessed is every one that feareth the Lord, oh, well is he, and happy shall he be." "The Lord ordereth a good man's going, and maketh his way acceptable to Himself." "Thou wilt shew me the path of life; in Thy presence is the fulness of joy; at Thy right hand there are pleasures for evermore." X. 50.

"Take thou no thought for aught but truth and right,
  Content, if such thy fate, to die obscure;
  Youth fails, and honors; fame may not endure;
  And loftier souls seem weary of delight.
  Keep innocence; be all a true man ought,
  Let neither pleasure tempt nor pain appal:
  Who hath this, he hath all things having naught;
  Who hath it not, hath nothing having all."

APRIL 17.

THE assertion, "Thine is the kingdom," is not only a conclusion of the reason, it is the sole explanation of the life of man. Men who have tried to get rid of it have only proved it with more overwhelming force, as if one should fling up a stone to disprove the law of gravitation, and it fell back and crushed him. Over and over again colossal human tyrannies have been dashed to pieces by the stone cut without hands, and have proved that no kingdom which is not based on God's righteousness can ever stand. . . .

And when we say, "For Thine is the kingdom," we acknowledge this. We mean, if we mean anything, that in the long run righteousness will justify itself; that goodness only is divine and eternal; that injustice and wickedness may be long-lived, but doomsday comes to them at last. IV. 220.

> It looked so grim, it looked so strong!
> So high it reared its haughty head!
> "'Tis vain to cry, 'O Lord, how long!'"
> The hopeless captives sadly said.
> Yet no one liveth now to tell
> What day that tower of evil fell.
> We only know that where it stood
> Upsoars the anthem, "God is good."
>
> J. L. M. W.

APRIL 18.

God hath chosen the weak things of the world to confound the things which are mighty.

I. Cor. i. 27.

THE intellect of Greece was keen, her poetry splendid, her art unrivalled; and yet, when the poor worn Jew of Tarsus trod the streets of Athens, a hunted, persecuted man, . . . who could have believed that the might and glory of the future was with the poor Jew, not with those philosophic and gifted Athenians? Who would have guessed that . . . the awful Pallas of the Acropolis should be forced to resign her Parthenon to the humble virgin of Nazareth? Not many years afterwards that same suffering missionary . . . was dragged a prisoner to Rome. At that time her Cæsar seemed omnipotent, her iron arms unconquerable. And Rome did not yield without a desperate struggle. Yet it was all in vain. The worshippers of the Capitol succumbed before the worshippers in the Catacombs, . . . and the greatest of earthly empires . . . embraced the gospel preached by the unlettered peasants. Why was it? It was because "every tree that bringeth not forth good fruit is hewn down and cast into the fire." The fruits of heathendom had been selfishness, and cruelty, and corruption; the fruits of Christianity were love, joy, peace, faith, meekness, charity, and the leaves of that tree were for the healing of the nations.

VII. 191, 193.

APRIL 19.

O come, let us sing unto the Lord. — Ps. xcv. 1.

IF we be Christians at all we are all joining, or trying to join, somehow, in the one great Psalm of life. To one who hears it near at hand many of our notes may seem hideous and most discordant; but a little farther off in time and space, as with a Scotch psalm amid the mountains, "the true notes alone support one another, all following the one true rule; the false notes, each following its own false rule, quickly destroy one another, and the psalm, which was discordant enough near at hand, is a perfect melody when heard from far." Oh, that our lives might add to the dominant melody, might help to subdue and drown those disproportionate and jarring notes.

II. 189.

Tune me, O Lord, into one harmony
  With Thee — one full, responsive, vibrant chord;
Unto Thy praise all love and melody,
    Tune me, O Lord.

Devil and world, gird me with strength to flee;
  To flee the flesh, and arm me with Thy word;
As Thy heart is to my heart, unto Thee
    Tune me, O Lord.

CHRISTINA ROSSETTI.

APRIL 20.

And in every work that he began in the service of the House of God, and in the Law, and in the Commandments, to seek his God, he did it with all his heart, and prospered.
II. CHRON. xxxi. 21.

WORK, Energy, Success — those are the prominent conceptions brought before us by this text. . . . Work — aye, and hard work — is, in some form or other, the law of life. There is nothing whatever stern, or repellant, or wearisome in the thought. On the contrary, if God said, "In the sweat of thy brow shalt thou eat bread," He said it in mercy to a race fallen from innocence; . . . work is the best birthright which man still retains. It is the strongest of moral tonics, the most vigorous of moral medicines. All nature shows us something analogous to this. The standing pool stagnates into pestilence; the running stream is pure. The very earth we tread on, the very air we breathe, would be unwholesome but for the agitating forces of wind and sea. X. 165, 166.

THE MILL.

Winding and grinding,
  Work through the day,
Grief never minding —
  Grind it away!
What though tears dropping
  Rust as they fall?
Have no wheel stopping —
  Work comforts all.
DINAH MULOCK CRAIK.

APRIL 21.

Work: for I am with you, saith the Lord of Hosts. — HAG. ii. 4.

BUT then the work must be approached in a right spirit, must be work in God's vineyard, and work for God. Thousands of men work, nay, toil, nay, grind and slave . . . simply to further their own emmet interests. Such work followed in such a spirit is but a little less baneful than idleness; if it does not corrupt the habits, it ossifies the heart. . . . But, on the other hand, few earthly paths are more rich in intrinsic and immediate blessing than when, with earnest undivided hearts, with lofty unselfish purpose, we devote our lives to God's service. The man who does it . . . will have no time for evil thoughts; every day he will work as if he had to live forever; he will live as if he had to die at once; and when he lies down at night in happy and trustful weariness, the angels of God will breathe over him an evening blessing, and shut to the doors of his heart. Till at last the weary day is over, and it ringeth to evensong: the work is done, the rest is prepared for him in heavenly mansions, and God giveth His beloved sleep. XI. 52, 53.

Work on. One day, beyond all thought of praise,
A sunny joy will crown thee with its rays;
Nor other than thy need, thy recompense.
GEORGE MACDONALD.

APRIL 22.

> All we have willed or hoped or dreamed of good shall exist.
> BROWNING.

THIS, then, is the only thing which every Christian, every good man, has to bear in mind — that he ought to "deal courageously, and then the Lord shall be with the good." God gives thee the high privilege of being a fellow laborer with Him. Do not be troubled if, in spite of all that thou triest to do, the times are out of joint and things go wrong, and thou seemest to do no good. God made the world, not thou. He has patience; shouldest not thou have patience? Even thy poor good deeds cannot die. If they seem at first to yield no fruit, they shall still be as seeds shut up in the darkness of a sepulchre, and when they are taken from the dead hand of time, years afterwards, it may be, they shall rise in golden grain. Be it little, be it much, God will accept thy honest offering. Better than the holocausts of the wicked shall be the fragment of bread given to the world's hunger, or the grain of salt flung into its corruption. For —

> "God doth not need
> Either our work, or His own gifts; who best
> Bear His mild yoke, they serve Him best. His state
> Is kingly; thousands at His bidding speed,
> And post o'er land and ocean without rest;
> They also serve who only stand and wait."
> II. 50.

And Jacob said, Sell me this day thy birthright.
GEN. xxv. 31.

SATAN is a harder bargainer than ever Jacob was. He grants the momentary desire, but he exacts, sooner or later, to the uttermost farthing, the lifelong forfeiture. After the red pottage comes the exceeding bitter cry. After the one hour's disgrace, or the long, pleasureless yielding to temptation, comes the hard entail of suffering. . . . The consequences come as diversely as the sin, but they do come; sometimes creeping, snakelike, through the dry leaves of a wasted life; sometimes bursting out as from a thicket, "terrible and with a tiger's leaps;" sometimes slowly torturing; sometimes waiting to smite once, and smite no more. But whether they come soon or late, they will come, and we cannot avoid them. "The comedy is short, but the tragedy is long. God came not to Adam till the evening; yet He came. The fire fell not on Sodom till the evening; yet it fell." VII. 183.

> We shape ourselves the joy or fear
>   Of which the coming life is made
> And fill our future's atmosphere
>   With sunshine or with shade.
>
> The tissue of the life to be
>   We weave with colors all our own,
> And in the field of destiny
>   We reap as we have sown.
WHITTIER.

APRIL 24.

IS this sin — this contempt for the spiritual, this despising of the birthright — is it so rare? Is it not the very commonest of all sins? Is it not distinctively the sin to which every one of us is tempted; of which, in greater or less degree, in some form or other, nearly all of us are guilty? And why? Because all men have not faith; and this sin is the absence of faith, the opposite of all faith. For faith is the power to recognize the spiritual, and to trample on the carnal. . . . And want of faith often looks like the sin of a moment, but it is the abstract of a tendency, it is the habit of a life. It is that profane self-indulgence to which an ideal blessing is as nothing compared to a momentary pleasure. It is the sin which, selling itself to do evil, sells itself always for naught. It sells the distant for the near, the true for the false, the substance for the shadow, the eternal for the temporal, the peace of life for the follies of boyhood, the hopes of the years of the right hand of the Most High for turbid, evanescent, and envenomed pleasures.

VII. 177, 178.

From building on the sand and not on the rock; from gaining though it were the whole world and losing our own soul ;
Deliver us, Lord Jesus.

CHRISTINA ROSSETTI.

Giving thanks unto the Father, which hath made us meet to be partakers of the inheritance of the saints in light. — COL. i. 12.

CHRIST was the Word of God, and Christ's saints show us the acceptance of His word, the reality of His power. They show us how, through faith in Christ, and by the spirit of Christ, and because of prayer to God through Christ, men weak as we are, tempted as we are, yet did gloriously and conspicuously triumph over sin, the world, the flesh, and the devil, and thereby made manifest to us that we can do the same. They have proved to us that even in such a world as this, and even for hearts so poor and weak as ours, it is possible to be good and pure and true by the help of God, because by the help of God they were so, and that with no greater strength than we may obtain. They refute the excuse of our feebleness; they cut away the lie of our inability.
VIII. 193.

> For Right is Right, since God is God;
> And Right the day must win;
> To doubt would be disloyalty,
> To falter would be sin.
>
> **FABER.**

APRIL 26

Honor all men. — I. Peter ii. 17.

ALL but the brutish understand the duty of giving honor where honor is due. . . . But are we to honor the mean, the base, the despicable, the depraved? Ay! there, my friends, lies the deepest meaning of the rule: their dishonor, their depravity, their baseness we honor not; but we honor the majesty of their nature even in its fall. As Michael Angelo sees in the rough block of marble the winged angel struggling to be free; as Flaxman, walking in the slums, sees the beauties and possibilities of the "human face divine" even under the dirt and squalor of the gutter-child, even so with pity and reverence the true Christian sees even in the lowest the marred work of Him who breathed into man's nostrils the breath of life. In the most fallen of the children of men he still honors the immortality which seemed so priceless to the Lord of Glory, that, for the sake of it, He descended step by step to the lowest round of the infinite abyss, died for it upon the cross, united it with the Godhead forever, and took it up to the right hand of the Majesty on High. .

VII. 235.

King's children are these all. Though want and sin
Have marred their beauty glorious within,
We may not pass them but with reverent eye,
  As when we see some goodly temple, graced
  To be Thy dwelling, ruined and defaced, . . .
  It grieveth us to see this House laid waste,
It pitieth us to see it in the dust!

DORA GREENWELL.

APRIL 27.

Ye know the grace of our Lord Jesus Christ, that, though He was rich, yet for your sakes He became poor, that ye through His poverty might be rich.—II. Cor. viii. 9.

MEN shun poverty; they toil, and moil, and lie, and cheat, and weary themselves in the very fire for money; yet poverty may be a perfect blessing. Christ chose the lot of poverty. There has hardly been a great saint or benefactor of mankind who has not been poor; and often to be a millionaire has proved to be an utter curse, and to die a millionaire has been to die disgraced. There is a poverty, honest and noble, like that of Christ, which is transcendently preferable to riches; a poverty which has "its sweet complete untainted happiness like the intermittent notes of birds before the daybreak, or the first gleams of heaven's amber in the eastern gray."

IV. 180.

"Come ye who find contentment's very core
 In the scant store
 And daisied path
 Of poverty, and know how more
 A small thing that the righteous hath
 Aboundeth than the ungodly's riches great."

FABER.

APRIL 28.

Ye shall be gathered one by one, O ye children of Israel. — ISA. xxvii. 12.

LET no one say, "I am nobody; I know nothing; every one scorns me; what can I do?" Little may be much, my brother. The widow's two farthings were more than the gifts which the rich cast into the treasury. Who knows how much God may increase and multiply our miserable quota towards the stream of human improvement? After all, it is but the dewdrops and the raindrops which go to make the mighty river and the mighty sea.

God cares for the individual. He cares for every one of you. It is the characteristic of an immoral tyranny to deal only with men in masses; but no true child of God can merge the individual in the class. Every soul is precious to Him, because every soul is one for which Christ died. II. 247, 248.

> Not pressing through the portals
>   Of the celestial Town,
> An army of fresh Immortals,
>   By the Lord of Battles won, —
> But one by one we come
> To the gate of the Heavenly Home;
>
> That to each the voice of the Father
>   May thrill in welcome sweet,
> And round each the angels gather
>   With songs, on the shining street,
> As one by one we go
> To the glory none may know.   B. M.

APRIL 29.

FAR better and brighter is the world than we will see, or suffer it to be for us; far more rich in capabilities of power and blessedness than we have made them are the immortal souls which God has given us, the mortal bodies into whose nostrils He has breathed the breath of life.

That is the negative side of the matter,— what we cannot see, what we will not do,— but alas! the positive side is far more humiliating. Man complains of his misery on earth; but "this," it has been said, "we may discover assuredly; this every true light of science, every mercifully granted power, every wisely restricted thought may teach us more clearly day by day, that in the heavens above, and in the earth beneath, there is one continual and omnipotent Presence of life, and of peace, for all who know that they live, and remember that they die." II. 205.

> One adequate support
> For the calamities of mortal life
> Exists—one only; an assured belief
> That the procession of our fate, howe'er
> Sad or disturbed, is ordered by a Being
> Of infinite benevolence and power,
> Whose everlasting purposes embrace
> All accidents, converting them to good.
>
> WORDSWORTH.

APRIL 30.

HOW many of us notice, as loving and gifted observers might help us to notice, the multitudinous beauty and tenderness of the burst of spring, the black ash buds in March, the glistening chestnut buds in April, the blaze of celandines, the golden dust in the catkins of the hazel, the rosy sheath of the larch tree's fresh green leaves. A poet speaks of one to whom

> "A primrose by a river's brim,
> A yellow primrose was to him,
> And it was nothing more."

He means by those lines to express the difference between bare sight and divine insight; between the cold, unfurnished, sensual soul and the soul that sees the Unseen—sees God in all things and sees all things in God. . . .

We all live on far lower levels of vitality and of joy than we need to do. We linger in the misty and oppressive valleys when we might be climbing the sunlit hills. God puts into our hands the book of life, bright on every page with open secrets, and we suffer it to drop out of our hands unread. II. 203.

> O God, O Good beyond compare!
> If thus Thy meaner works are fair,
> If thus Thy bounties gild the span
> Of ruined earth and sinful man,
> How glorious must the mansion be
> Where Thy redeemed shall dwell with Thee!
>
> REGINALD HEBER.

MAY 1.

The saints that are in the earth . . . in whom is all my delight. — Ps. xvi. 3.

ONE morning, among the high Alps, I happened to be on a glacier which lay deep beneath a circle of stupendous hills, when the first beam of sunrise smote the highest summit of Monte Rosa. . . . Until they burned like watchfires of advancing angels, mountain crest after mountain crest caught the risen splendor, and it flowed down their mighty crags in rivers of ever-broadening gold, until not only was the east full of glory and flame, but the west, too, echoed back the dawn in bright reflection, and the peaks which had caught the earliest blaze were lost in blue sky and boundless light, — and it was day. I never think of the saints of God without their recalling to my memory those sunlit hills! *We* may be wandering in the dangerous darkness, but *they* are the proof that the sun has risen — they are the prophecy of the lingering day. . . . And oh, it is good for us thus to lift up our eyes unto the hills! It is good for us, in the midst of lives so inconsistent, so dwarfed, so conventional as ours, to bear in mind how much greater and better others have been — how dauntlessly good, how magnificently victorious over vice and sin. Their high examples teach us how we may rise above our nothingness; how little we are when we live the selfish life of the world; how great we may be if we live as the sons of God.

VI. 337.

MAY 2.

Lord, give me grace
To take the lowest place;
Nor even desire
Unless it be Thy Will, to go up higher.

Except by grace,
I fail of lowest place;
Except desire
Sit low, it aims awry to go up higher.
Christina Rossetti.

WHY should any one of us sorrow for, or be ashamed of, his earthly insignificance, or care how much the world despises him? Ours, as much as any man's, may be the most inconceivable of all blessings — the peace of God here which passeth all understanding, and hereafter a blessedness which eye hath not seen nor ear heard, neither hath it entered into the heart of man to conceive. But be we high or low, rich or poor, clever or stupid, for which God cares nothing, it is equally possible for the humblest of us all to do our duty. It is true that we have but our five coarse barley loaves and two small fishes. In themselves they are useless. Well, then, let us give them to Christ. He can multiply them. He can make them more than enough to feed the five thousand.
VII. 277.

To give ourselves to Thee, to blend
Our weakness with Thy strength, O Lord our Friend,
This is life's truest privilege and end.
Susan Coolidge.

MAY 3.

HE who would follow Christ must not only follow Him on the path of self-denial and of labor, but must follow Him also in the strength of *Enthusiasm,* must be baptized with the Holy Ghost and with fire. And herein too he must let the dead bury their dead. For the dead of this world hate this fiery spirit. "Above all, no zeal," said the witty, crafty, successful statesman; "Fervent in spirit," said St. Paul, or, as it should be rather rendered, "boiling in spirit." It was not the word of a fastidious Atticist, or long-robed Pharisee, but rather one of those words that were thunders, one of the words that have hands and feet. And never was it more needed than now; for never more than now did the world hate enthusiasm, and never was it more certain that by a noble enthusiasm it can alone be saved. For it is an age of unbelief, of hollowness, of cynicism; and these are the inevitable symptoms of decay. And decaying times need no smooth and drowsy voices, no conventional remedies, no flattering words. They need the living zeal that cannot sleep and settle on its lees, but which reels and staggers as with an invincible exaltation.

XI. 57.

> Blow, breath of God, blow keen and strong
>   Across these embers! blow aside
>   These smothering ashes, — self and pride,
> And weak subserviency to wrong, —
> That soon the whole wide world may be
> Ablaze with love of right and Thee!

J. L. M. W.

He drove them all out of the temple. — JOHN ii. 15.

CHRISTIAN art, Christian eloquence, Christian song have long made us familiar with Christ's meekness and lowliness of heart. . . . But there is one side of our Lord's character, which, because it has not sufficiently been dwelt upon, has scarcely exercised its due influence upon our minds. It is His just indignation. The ideal of the Christian life — not the true ideal, but the common one — has been too tame, too timid, too effeminate; strange as it may seem, it has wanted not only that brightness and joyance, that high victorious faith, that royalty of happiness, which of due right belong to it, but it has been lacking also in that fire and force, that iron in the blood, that dauntless courage, that glorious battle-brunt in the heart of man, which are yet necessary to soldiers of the Cross. . . . The old mighty, unswerving heart of Christendom seems dead. We dare not face our thoughts; we dare not act up to our convictions; we are full of conventional phrases, and polite reticence, and soft compromise, under which is smothered that fire which of old burnt in men's hearts till at the last they spake with their tongue. X. 188.

> He's a slave who would not choose
> Hatred, slander, and abuse,
> Rather than in silence shrink
> From the truth he needs must think.
>
> LOWELL.

MAY 5.

ALL common things are lovely so far as man leaves them so; and in their loveliness we read the very autograph of God. Through every gateway of the senses flow pure and delightful impressions to the healthy soul. There are delicious fruits of autumn, there are fragrant odors of spring. For the ear there is the song of birds, and the murmur of the sea, and the warbling of the vernal breeze, and "angelical soft trembling voices," and silver songs and solemn instruments. And for the eye what wealth and worlds of beauty,— . . . the blue distant hills, the yellow wealth of harvest, the trees in their "green plenitude of May," the dewdrop sparkling like a diamond in the bosom of the rose, the gorgeous conflagration of autumn lending beauty even to decay; — the laugh of summer waters, the colorings of the shell upon the shore, the iridescence of the peacock's wing — are not these signs that God is Love? Since the days of Job, mankind has seen that it is only a Father of mercies who could have endowed with all this glory and melody the hearing ear and seeing eye of love.　　　　　　　　　　　　VII. 16.

Art tired?
There is a rest remaining. Hast thou sinned?
There is a Sacrifice. Lift up thy head;
The lovely world, and the over-world alike,
Ring with a song, a happy rede,
"Thy Father loves thee."

　　　　　　　　　　　JEAN INGELOW.

MAY 6.

These things have I spoken unto you, that my joy might remain in you, and that your joy might be full. — JOHN xv. 11.

THERE are two conditions requisite for joy — innocence and fellowship; and both conditions are all too rare. The world, not possessing either, — for its seductions are evil and its fellowships are false, — aims at a guilty substitute for joy. But there is no such thing. Guilty excitement, guilty passion, there is; but one drop of guilt in the sparkling cup of true joy makes it bitter, envenomed, turbid, even in the moment of fruition. It is at the best the sweetness of the fruit whose taste is poison, the glitter of the serpent whose bite is death. Its pleasure is unsatisfying at the moment, and its effects deprave forever. But true joy is a rose of Paradise, which only the hand of innocence can pluck. God only can grant true joy to any human soul. "Thou shalt show me the path of life; in Thy presence is the fulness of joy; and at Thy right hand there are pleasures for evermore." There and nowhere beside.

V. 26.

What will it be, O my soul, what will it be
To touch the long-raced-for goal, to handle and see,
To rest in the joy of joys, in the joy of the blest,
To rest and revive and rejoice, to rejoice and to rest!
CHRISTINA ROSSETTI.

MAY 7.

THE great procession of mankind in its unnumbered millions is ever sweeping across the narrow stage of life, issuing from a darkness in which they are not, passing into a darkness in which they are no more seen. We watch that procession as it winds through the long centuries of history, and we note its most striking figures; . . . but the vast masses of it . . . consist of a nameless throng — the poor, the ordinary, the average, the undistinguished; . . . the meaning, and even the bare fact of their existence as much obliterated from all human memory and from every human record as though it had been a speck of foam on the immeasurable sea. . . . Savage and civilized, in every age, in every region, the immense majority of men — "some with lives that came to nothing, some with deeds as well undone," have vanished like a bubble, have "sunk as lead in the mighty waters." After a year or two they are forgotten in the grave for evermore.

V. 123, 129.

    Yet still
Our change yearns after Thine unchangedness;
Our mortal craves Thine immortality;
Our manifold and multiform and weak
Imperfectness requires the perfect One.
For Thou art ONE, and we are all of Thee —
Dropped from thy bosom, as Thy sky drops down
Its morning dews, which glitter for a space,
Uncertain whence they fell, or whither tend,
Till the great Sun, arising on his fields,
Upcalls them all.
                      DINAH MULOCK CRAIK.

MAY 8.

> O restless spirit! wherefore strain
> Beyond thy sphere?
> Heaven and hell, with their joy and pain,
> Are now and here. — WHITTIER.

CHRIST came not to revolutionize, but to ennoble and to sanctify. He came to reveal that the Eternal was not the Future, but only the Unseen; that Eternity was no ocean whither men were swept by the river of Time, but was around them now, and that their lives were only real in so far as they felt its reality and its presence. He came to teach that God was no dim abstraction, infinitely separated from them in the far-off blue, but that He was the Father in whom they lived and moved and had their being; and that the service which He loved was not ritual and sacrifice, not pompous scrupulosity and censorious orthodoxy, but mercy and justice, humility and love. He came, not to hush the natural music of men's lives, not to fill it with storm and agitation, but to retune every silver chord in that "harp of a thousand strings," and to make it echo with the harmonies of heaven.

XIII. 84.

MAY 9.

JESUS had "received sinners and eaten with them." It was His special characteristic to love those whom none had loved, and to love them as none had ever loved before. Those whom the Priests wholly failed to reach by their officialism, He reached; those whom Scribes failed to move by their learning, or Pharisees by their orthodoxy, He moved to the depths of their sad and guilty souls. The chill wind may play about the Alpine heights, but it only congeals them into a deadlier and more frozen whiteness; but when they thrill to the touch of the sunbeam and the breathing of the western wind, the snow is melted and loosed, till from the burdened bosom of the mountain it slips away in avalanche, and where yesterday the slopes were blank and perilous, to-day there is green grass and purple flower. So is it with the human heart. Coldness and fierceness will not touch it; it will be only hardened by contempt and anathema; it may be broken, not swayed, by authority and domination; but there never yet was human heart so hard as not to be thrilled and melted by sympathy and love. VIII. 93.

Oh, runs not thus the lesson thou hast aught?—
When life's all love, 'tis life: aught else, 'tis naught.
SIDNEY LANIER.

MAY 10.

CEREMONIAL observances are not religion; . . . long prayers are not religion; orthodoxy of creed is not religion. Parts of religion; . . . aids to religious feeling they may be — religion they are not. But to keep ourselves unspotted from the world, that is religion; . . . and to do the things which Christ says, that is religion; and all the charities which bind man to man, and which bless the family, the nation, and the world, these are religion; and this is religion, to love God with all our hearts, and our neighbor as ourselves. . . . If you do not love your brother, however tremendous the truths which you utter with your lips, your Christianity is heathendom, and the kingdom of God is not within you. The throne of Christ can only be set up in the heart of man, not in his actions; in the life of man, not upon his lips. VIII. 41.

For he whom Jesus loved hath truly spoken;
  The holier worship which He deigns to bless
Restores the lost, and binds the spirit broken,
  And feeds the widow and the fatherless.

O brother man, fold to thy heart thy brother;
  Where pity dwells the peace of God is there;
To worship rightly is to love each other,
  Each smile a hymn, each kindly deed a prayer.

Follow with reverent steps the great example
  Of Him whose holy work was " doing good;"
So shall the wide earth seem our Father's temple;
  Each loving life a psalm of gratitude.
                                  WHITTIER.

MAY 11.

And Elisha prayed, and said, Lord, I pray Thee, open his eyes, that he may see. And the Lord opened the eyes of the young man: . . . and behold, the mountain was full of horses and chariots round about Elisha. — II. KINGS vi. 17.

ARE you in sorrow? Prayer can make your affliction sweet and strengthening. Are you in gladness? Prayer can add to your joy a celestial perfume. Are you in extreme danger, whether from outward or inward enemies? Prayer can set at your right hand an angel whose touch "could shatter a millstone into smaller dust than the flour it grinds," and whose glance could lay an army low. When St. Felix of Nola was hotly pursued by murderers, he took refuge in a cave, and instantly, over the rift of it, the spiders wove their webs, and seeing this, the murderers passed by. Then said the saint, "Where God is not, a wall is but a spider's web: where God is, a spider's web is as a wall." What will prayer do for you? I answer, All that God can do for you. When He bids us pray it is as though He said to us, "Ask what I shall give thee."   VII. 99.

> "Lord, if I dip my cup into the sea,
> It rises full! Such cup each soul may be,
> Such ocean is Thy good."

MAY 12.

PRAYERS are to the soul what the dew of God is to the flowers of the field; the burning wind of the day may pass over them, and the stems droop and the colors fade, but when the dew steals down at evening, they will revive. Why should not that gracious dew fall even now and always for all of us upon the fields of life? A life which has been from the first a life of prayer — a life which has thus from its earliest days looked up consciously to its Father and its God — will always be a happy life. . . . For what we desire we ask, and what we ask we aim at, and what we aim at we shall attain. No man ever yet asked to be, as the days pass by, more and more noble, and sweet, and pure, and heavenly-minded, — no man ever yet prayed that the evil spirits of hatred, and pride, and passion, and worldliness might be cast out of his soul, — without his petition being granted and granted to the letter. And with all other gifts God then gives us His own self besides — He makes us know Him, and love Him, and live in Him. X. 235, 236.

> We doubt the word that tells us: Ask,
>   And ye shall have your prayer:
> We turn our thoughts as to a task,
>   With wilts constrained and rare.
>
> And yet we have; these scanty prayers
>   Bring gold without alloy:
> O God! but he who trusts and dares
>   Must have a boundless joy.
>
> GEORGE MACDONALD.

MAY 13.

If we hope for that we see not, then do we with patience wait for it. — ROM. viii. 25.

GOD is patient. "*Patiens quia aeternus.*" His great ones are slandered every day by earth's little, and His wise men judged by fools, and "He makes no ado." His name is blasphemed, His character often hideously misrepresented by those who profess to teach in His name. He bears it all, He has borne with man's falsehood, and littleness, and disobedience, for no one knows how many thousand years. Cannot we too wait? If we do well and suffer for it, can we not take it patiently? "Patient continuance in well doing," there is a grand remedy for idle tears.

II. 146.

Grant us, O Lord, that patience and that faith, —
  Faith's patience imperturbable in Thee,
  Hope's patience till the long-drawn shadows flee,
Love's patience unresentful of all scathe.
. . . .
How gracious and how perfecting a grace
  Must patience be on which those others wait! —
Faith with suspended rapture in her face,
  Hope pale and careful hand in hand with fear,
Love — ah, good love, who would not antedate
  God's will, but saith, Good is it to be here.

CHRISTINA ROSSETTI.

MAY 14.

Lift up your heads, O ye gates; and be ye lift up, ye everlasting doors, and the King of glory shall come in. — Ps. xxiv. 7.

YES, but not He alone. When the triumphs of the chariots of God, even thousands of angels, swept behind Him in their unseen procession, the everlasting portals closed not after them; they are open still, open to us, and to our race, and through them pass, and shall pass till the end of time, the thronging souls of the redeemed. He went to prepare a place for those whom He loved; He went up on high, He led captivity captive, to receive gifts for men, "yea even for His enemies, that the Lord God might dwell among them." He went but as the great forerunner of His people, and we must follow in His course; where the Head is there should the members be; and our treasure, our life, our affection, are meant to be with Him at the right hand of God. XI. 79.

> Thither in mind and heart we go,
>   Where the Saviour went before;
> We climb the steps of the azure steep,
>   We enter the heavenly door.
>
> It is only a moment the vision lasts,
>   But its sweetness haunts us still;
> It smooths the paths for our weary feet,
>   It strengthens our feeble will.
>
> What if the day be dark with woe,
>   The night-watch heavy and dim,
> If that be the way by which we go
>   Forever to dwell with Him!

J. L. M. W.

MAY 15.

And a cloud received Him out of their sight.
                                    ACTS i. 9.

AND that cloud still remains. To *their* eyes doubtless it was luminous as the floor of heaven — soft and beautiful as those that lie cradled near the setting sun, and do but veil its too blinding splendor; but to the eyes of the world, and oftentimes to our own, it has grown thicker, and blacker, and more vast; it has rolled its darkness over the blue sky; it has blotted out the light of day; not even the rainbow circles it; it has become a cloud of wrath and terror, and no gleam save that of the lightning tears a way out of its lurid depths. It is no mere fleeting mist which has hidden Christ the Sun of Righteousness from our eyes, but an earthborn fog, bred in the dismal region of unbelief, reeking upwards from the abysses of human guilt; sin is its very substance, and an unhallowed pride, and a dreary science, and a godless criticism, and an unredeemable despair, have all added fold on fold to that midnight screen.

In the night there is no gracious presence to enlighten; in the storm no gentle voice to utter "It is I, be not afraid." . . . Lord, may it not be so with us; may the dark clouds of sin, and of unbelief, that hide Thee from us be rolled away; may we see Thy face, and see Thee as Thou art, and seeing Thee, be changed into Thy likeness from glory to glory!
                                    XI. 76. 77.

MAY 16.

We all, with open face beholding . . . the glory of the Lord, are changed into the same image from glory to glory. — II. Cor. iii. 18.

WHAT is a jewel in the midnight? It is a cold chip of worthless stone; but let light fall on it, and . . . you may then see the jewel as it is — "see depth opening beyond depth, until it looks as if there were no end to the chambers of splendor that are shut up in that little stone; see flake after flake of luminous color floating up out of the unseen fountain which lies somewhere in the jewel's heart." So is it with the human soul. If your soul is untouched by the transforming light of Christ, it is dull and vile. But when the light of God shines on it, it will be changed from glory to glory. The glory of God is the analogue of holiness in man. IV. 236.

"From glory unto glory" that ever lies before,
Still wondering, adoring, rejoicing more and more,
Still following where He leadeth from shining field
    to field,
Himself the goal of glory, Revealer and Revealed!
F. R. HAVERGAL.

MAY 17.

The grass withereth, the flower fadeth, but the Word of our God shall stand forever. — Is. xl. 8.

THE Word of our God — that, and that alone; and man, only as he listens to that Word, only as he is in harmony with that God. The earth may be shattered, and the heavens pass like a shrivelled scroll; but not the soul of man, which hath become partaker of God's Eternity. The one thing then of real and infinite importance to us, is, not the fruit of our studies, not the success of our efforts, not the things for which men toil and weary themselves and sigh, not anything whereby we are distinguished from other men, but this only, which affects us in common with *all* other men, whether our ears are quick to hear, and our hearts zealous to obey the voice of God. To do this is safety: not to do this is misery and failure; nay, to do this is life, and to do it not is to make life itself an initiation into death.

X. 15.

> Oh, let Thy sacred Will
>   All Thy delight in me fulfil!
> Let me not think an action mine own way,
>   But as Thy love shall sway,
> Resigning up the rudder to Thy skill!

GEORGE HERBERT.

MAY 18.

A MAN may stand, if he will, amid the mirth and music of a breathing summer day, when all the air is vocal with whispering trees, and singing birds, and the quivering of insect wings, and assert to us, contemptuously, that all is silent: what can we answer him save that it *is* silent to the dull deaf ear? A man may close his eyes if he will till they are blind, and then, standing in the burning noonday, may defy us to prove that there is a sun in heaven: what need we care to say to him in answer, but that we see its splendor, but that we feel its warmth? What *can* we say to such, but that which even a heathen said, "God is within thee, and is thy God; thou carriest God about with thee and knowest Him not." And may we not say, my brethren, that as for ourselves we know God; we hear His voice; we see His face; His name is on our foreheads? In joy He increases and purifies our joy; in sorrow He heals and sanctifies our sorrows; in sin He punishes and forgives our sins.

X. 18.

What the soul teaches profits to the soul,
Which then first stands erect with Godward face,
When she lets fall her pack of withered facts —
The gleanings of the outward eye and ear —
And looks and listens with her finer sense:
Nor Truth nor Knowledge cometh from without.
LOWELL.

MAY 19.

> " 'Mid all my store of blessings manifold
> I count this chiefest, that my heart has bled."

HAVE we learned this lesson? . . . Evil, in the form of pain, bereavement, sickness, loss, heartache, care, disappointment, or some other of its Protean varieties, comes without any exception to every one of us. Evils, in their external form, happen alike to the good and to the bad, to the wise and to the foolish. This was a source of immense perplexity to many of the ancient patriarchs and psalmists. But has not Christ taught us the solution of the difficulty? Has He not furnished us with a means of deliverance, and with countless living proofs of its efficacy? To wicked men evils are evils in all their malignity — horrible, hopeless, not to be told. But in the midst of the very same evils, the good are so strengthened by grace, so illuminated with hope, that "our light affliction which is for a moment" is not to be compared with "that far more exceeding and eternal weight of glory, while we look not at the things which are seen, but at the things which are not seen; for the things which are seen are temporal, but the things which are unseen are eternal."

IV. 174.

> There is some soul of goodness in things evil,
> Would men observingly distil it out; . . .
> Besides they are our outward consciences,
> And preachers to us all; admonishing
> That we should dress us fairly to our end.
> Thus may we gather honey from the weed.
> SHAKESPEARE.

MAY 20. 141

In Christ. — II. COR. v. 17.

SINCE our spirits are the breath of God within us; since they can be only renewed by the Spirit of God; since we can only walk in the Spirit when we are in Christ, and so are a new creation; therefore we may say truly that the life of the Christian is a supernatural life. It could not be lived at all but by virtue of that supernatural change, that blessed re-creation, that new life which we draw from union with Christ, even as the vine-branch draws only from the vine its purple fruitfulness. . . . The moralist says that "this time-world flickers on the grand still mirror of eternity, and man's little life has duties which alone are great." The mystic says, "He to whom time is as eternity and eternity as time, he alone is freed from strife." But to the true saints of God the meaning of these sayings is best expressed in those two words, "in Christ."

V. 311.

O soul of mine, I tell thee true,
  If Christ indeed be thine,
Not more made He himself thy kin
  Than makes He thee divine:
As through His heart there frequent beat
  Our human hopes and loves,
So 'midst thy varying joys and fears
  His spirit lives and moves.

DENIS WORTMAN.

MAY 21.

I can do all things through Christ which strengtheneth me. — PHIL. iv. 13.

WHY did the torch which had failed to illuminate the world when it had been upheld by such strong hands as those of the great men in Greece and Rome, shed so sunlike a splendor over a world of sin when carried in the weak grasp of the early Christians? . . . It was because behind the truths, behind the preachers of Christianity, lived and moved, unseen yet ever present, the mighty force of Christ. . . . Why does the march of tidal waters flush the rivers, and flood the great bays with its lustral wave? Because the swing of the living ocean is behind the harbor bar!

Yes! the force of Christianity was Christ; Christ, not preached in eloquent words of man's wisdom, but in demonstration of the spirit and power; Christ not inurned in orthodox dogma, but felt in the inmost heart. The reason why these poor early Christians subdued the world is because they were not good merely, but holy; not moral merely, but full of the indwelling Spirit of God. It wrought in them a mighty and inexplicable change. It presented to the world the hitherto undreamed of spectacle of men who had shifted the moral centre of gravity from self to God.

VII. 197.

MAY 22.

He that soweth to the Spirit shall of the Spirit reap life everlasting. — GAL. vi. 8.

LIFE is not the mere living. It is worship — it is the surrender of the soul to God, and the power to see the face of God; and it is service — it is to feel that when we die, whether praised or blamed, whether appreciated or misinterpreted, whether honored or ignored, whether wealthy or destitute — we have done something to make the world we came to better and happier — we have tried to cast upon the waters some seeds which, long after we are dead, may still bring forth their flowers of Paradise. The seed dies, but the harvest lives. Sacrifice is always fruitful, and there is nothing fruitful else. . . . Out of the suffering comes the serious mind; out of the salvation, the grateful heart; out of the endurance, the fortitude; out of the deliverance, the faith.

VI. 238, 240.

So should we live that every hour
May die as dies the natural flower —
A self-reviving thing of power;

That every thought and every deed
May hold within itself the seed
Of future good and future meed.

R. MONCKTON MILNES.

MAY 23.

THE sun shines, my brethren, and we see the things that are near us, — all the little things that flit in the air, or creep beside our feet. The sun sets, and then first we see the unnumbered stars of heaven, repaying to the sun its sunlight, or burning with independent glory through all the unfathomable space. May it not be so with life and death? Life sets; its insect greatnesses cease to buzz about us; its insect littlenesses cease to sting. We lose sight even of this vault of light and blue which is above our heads; but lo! from under the shadow of death the heavens above us seem to burst open to their depths, and we see not one sun, but systems, and constellations, and galaxies, white with the confluent lustre of suns numberless in multitude and indistinguishable from their distance. May not *death* first reveal to us, as night first reveals to us, the undreamt-of glories, the possibilities hitherto inconceivable, which crowd the universe of God? And through all that universe our Father reigns, — God, who is in Christ reconciling the world unto Himself. II. 255.

> Teach me how to guess aright
> Of the wonders out of sight;
> Let my spirit grow more clear,
> Heavenly whispers let me hear;
> Let the veil become more thin,
> And the glory pierce within.
>
> CAROLINE M. NOEL.

MAY 24.   145

I will pour out of my Spirit upon all flesh.

ACTS ii. 17.

INSPIRATION is a continuous energy of the present, not a mere exhausted and isolated spasm of the past. Pentecost was not a single outpouring. There are many Pentecosts. The Holy Ghost was not given once, or once only. He is constantly descending into all holy hearts. Our God is no sun that once shone and now has set; no, but He is always in the meridian. He is

> No ebbing tide that left
> Strewn with dead miracles those eldest shores
> For men to dry, and dryly lecture on,
> Himself henceforth *incapable* of flood.

No; but our God is a living God, and our Christ a living Christ, and the Holy Spirit is with us. Yea, except we be reprobates, He is *in* us now and for evermore.

VII. 144.

> O Light of Light eternal!
>   Sole Sun of every sphere!
> O gifts of life supernal!
>   The very God is here!
>
> . . . . . .
>
> I bask in light whose splendor
>   The farthest star-dust own;
> I feel strong arms and tender
>   That round the worlds are thrown.
>
> . . . . . .
>
> Deep after deep forever,
>   The gates of life unfold!
> Sing, happy heart! For never
>   Shall love and life grow old.

HORATIO NELSON POWERS.

MAY 25.

Know ye not that ye are the temple of God, and that the Spirit of God dwelleth in you?
I. COR. iii. 16.

NOR must we forget that it was through the temple of Christ's body . . . that the Spirit of God passed into the temple of every Christian heart. It was the promise wherewith our Lord had comforted His trembling disciples; and very soon after the temple of His mortal body had been taken up into heaven, was the new living temple filled with the Glory of the Presence, and the brows of the Apostles were mitred by the cloven tongues of the Pentecostal flame. . . . The true "Shechina, then, is man." . . . Let us try to realize the thought. God within us! — not only ever with us, unseen; not only watching us in our secret moments, and reading the very thoughts of our hearts; not only covering us with the shadow of His wings and lighting us with the light of His countenance; but within us, our bodies His temples, our hearts His home! . . . Oh, if we could but grasp the thought, we should live lives nobler and more beautiful; . . . from the cradle to the grave, the dark waters of life would be illuminated, and its dense clouds would be pierced through and through . . . with the unchangeable sunlight of that eternal life which is hid with Christ in God. XI. 261, 263.

> For man the living temple is,
> The mercy seat, the cherubim
> And all the holy mysteries
> He bears with him.
>
> WHITTIER.

MAY 26.

AND is there nothing for men who are filled with tne spirit of God to do now? Look at the universal worldliness around us, look at the passionate mammon worship, at the reckless competition, at the desecration of Sundays in the mere voluptuous wantonness of pleasure. Look at the curse of drink against which we have fought so many years utterly in vain; look at the dangerous increase in the guilty madness of betting and gambling, in every school, in every office, in every street, among our rich and among our poor. . . . Look at the rapid degradation of our journalism by the paltry flunkeyism of gossip and the evil malice of slander. . . . Oh, God, give us saints; oh, God, pour out the spirit of Thy might, were it but in the hearts of one or two, to slay these dragons and not to fear their poisonous breath! . . . Oh, Holy Ghost, the Comforter, fill one or two hearts once more with Thy rushing, mighty wind, and mitre one or two brows with Thy Pentecostal flame. Priests we have in plenty and Churchmen; but oh, send us men, send us saints, send us deeds! Yes, and so it shall be. We may not live to see it, yet . . .

IX. 125.

>Keeping the line of duty,
> Through good and evil report,
>They shall ride the storm out safely,
> Be the voyage long or short —
>For the ship that carries God's orders
> Shall anchor at last in port.

ADELINE D. T. WHITNEY.

MAY 27.

"God harden me against myself—
This traitor with pathetic voice
Who craves for ease and rest and joys;

Myself, arch-traitor to myself,
My hollowest friend, my deadly foe,
My clog whatever road I go.

One there is can curb myself,
Can roll this strangling load off me,
Break off my yoke and set me free."

THAT one is Christ. To lead you to Him; to teach you to place your souls in His keeping; that is the richest and most blessed boon your experience can confer on you. And it is happiness. Do not think that self-reverence and self-conquest will make you weak or sad; nay, the suppression of evil will be to you a forceful spring of good. Religion is no haggard and stern monitress waving you from enjoyment; she is a strong angel leading you to noble joy. The Bible is not a book of repressions and prohibitions; it is a book of kindling inspiration. God would not have you crouch, like a poor, timid, startled creature, torturing yourself with a terrified watch over your lower desires. He would see you stand erect and manly, like a victor, in heroic confidence, with these enemies beneath your feet. . . . He would make you run and not be weary, walk and not faint.   VII. 187.

MAY 28.

PERHAPS you will say as you set your faces hillwards for the steep straight path: "We will not take human rules for our guide, we will take the law of God. We will not take honor, but integrity. . . . We will summon to our aid our own manly resolution; on reason we will build resolve, 'that pillar of true majesty in man.' We will not say 'I might,' or 'I would;' but we will say, as a man should say, 'I am,' 'I ought,' 'I can,' 'I will.' . . . We do not pretend to be religious, but we are and will be moral and virtuous."

Ah! "that tune goes manly," no doubt, but if you try to please God in reliance on your own strength, you are doomed to humiliating failure. Most men, when they start, mean to be moral, mean to be virtuous. Adam never meant to eat the forbidden fruit. . . . The Prodigal never meant to become a hungry feeder of filthy swine. Judas never meant to be the seller of his Lord. The drunkard never meant to be a drunkard; nor the mammon worshipper a cheat; nor the sensualist a degraded and ruined slave. But temptation is strong; the heart is treacherous; the flesh is weak; Satan active; our own nature frail. The world's whole experience may be summed up in the confession that "we are not sufficient of ourselves to account anything as from ourselves;" and the Christian's, in the glad acknowledgment that our "sufficiency is from God."

V. 280, 281.

MAY 29.

Now the God of hope fill you with all joy and peace in believing . . . through the power of the Holy Ghost. — ROM. xv. 13.

WHATEVER Christianity may be, it is at least no narrow dogma, no evanescent influence. . . . It unites us to Nature, by whose conditions we are bounded, but whose forces we direct. It unites us to the Dead — all saints whom we reverence, all souls whom we commemorate; it unites us to the Living, all whom we love and know not, all whom we love and know; it unites us to Posterity, for which, sustained by Faith, inspired by Hope, we labor with patient unselfishness and active love; above all, and more than all, it unites us to the Infinite by making us the children of God and joint-heirs with Christ, if so be that we suffer with Him. . . . Is there anything, any religion or irreligion, any philosophy or any ignorance, which can in a greater degree than this

"Give grandeur to the beatings of the heart"?
XII. 193.

To have to do with nothing but the true,
The good, the eternal, — and these, not alone
In the main current of the general life,
But small experiences of every day, —
To learn not only by a comet's rush
But a rose's birth, — not by the grandeur, God,
But by the comfort, Christ.
BROWNING.

MAY 30.

Something there is in Death not all unkind:
  He hath a gentler aspect, looking back;
  For flowers may bloom in the dread thunder's track,
And even the cloud that struck with light was lined.
RICHARD WATSON GILDER.

IS it those only who are great, or those who are splendidly good, whose works do follow them? God forbid. . . . The general who is brave in the hour of danger does his duty, but then he knows that his shall be the glory of the battle : . . . is it not a greater thing when the common soldiers . . . do their heroic duty because it *is* their duty, and charge unflinchingly on the cannon that vomit on them a storm of fiery death, though they know that their names will be forgotten, their fate unnoticed ; — are not these the greater, "these unnamed demi-gods"? Yes, because they have done their obscure duty . . . because it is their duty, and have done it well. Nor is it otherwise on the battle-field of life.
XI. 209.

    Freedom lives, and Right shall stand;
    Blood of Faith is in the land.
SIDNEY LANIER.

MAY 31.

Holy, holy, holy, Lord God Almighty.

REV. iv. 8.

I believe in one God, the Father Almighty, Maker of heaven and earth:

And in one Lord Jesus Christ, the only-begotten Son of God:

And I believe in the Holy Ghost, the Lord and Giver of Life. Amen.

IT is well to ask ourselves if we indeed believe in this Triune God; — if we are loving the Father with all our heart and soul and strength; if we are believing in and following the example of His blessed Son; if we feel the quickening and sanctifying influences of the Holy Spirit? Might not an altar be built in many and many a Christian city to the Unknown God? Are not many of us living without God in the world? . . . Lay your hand upon your heart, and ask yourself whether you are indeed worshipping the Trinity of Heaven, or whether your lives show that your devotion is given to the World, the Flesh, and the Devil — rightly named "the great Anti-Trinity of Hell." Unhappy is he — unhappy and miserable, though he have rank and wealth and beauty . . . who knows not, and loves not, the living God. . . . And happy, though poor, and ill-favored, and ignorant, and despised, — happy alone is he who can say with fond yearning from his inmost heart, "This God is our God for ever and ever, He shall be our guide even unto death."

XI. 281, 283.

JUNE 1.

Unfathomable Sea!
All life is out of Thee,
And Thy life is Thy blissful Unity.

WHEN the great Father of the Christian Church was writing his discourse on the Trinity he wandered along the sea-shore lost in meditation, "when suddenly he beheld a child who, having dug a hole in the sand, appeared to be bringing water in a shell to fill it, and told Augustine that he intended to empty into this little hole all the water of the great deep. Impossible, said the saint. Not more impossible, oh Augustine, replied the child, than for thee to explain the mystery on which thou art now meditating." True, brethren; but the logic of the intellect is transcended by the logic of the heart. . . . In this case experience is the best learning, and Christianity is the best institution, and the Spirit of God is the best teacher, and holiness is the greatest wisdom; and he that sins most is the most ignorant, and the humble and obedient man is the best scholar. . . . Thanks be to God, we need not "dazzle ourselves blind by star-gazing at Omnipotence and Infinitude," but we may approach God in the likeness of ourselves. The Son of God . . . stands at His right hand . . . in our image.

XI. 272, 277.

The weakest hearts can lift their thoughts to Thee;
It makes us strong to think of Thine eternity.

FABER.

JUNE 2.

The natural man receiveth not the things of the Spirit of God: for they are foolishness unto him: neither can he know them, because they are spiritually discerned. — I. Cor. ii. 14.

JUST as to the blind eye light is invisible; just as to the deaf ear there is no melody in the harp; just as to the dead taste honey has no sweetness, so the truths of the Gospel are unreal, unintelligible, valueless to the natural heart. The ancient world was divided into two classes, Jews and Greeks. The Jews were great orthodox theologians, the Greeks were acute, subtle philosophers; yet how did the doctrine of the Cross appear to them? "We preach," says St. Paul, "Christ crucified; unto Jews, a stumbling-block, and unto Gentiles, foolishness; but, unto them that are called, both Jews and Greeks, Christ the power of God, and the wisdom of God." Now, in this respect we may still be as Jews and Greeks. We have been called; but we must have obeyed the call before the Cross and its meaning are to us the wisdom and the power of God. v. 305.

> The world sits at the feet of Christ,
> Unknowing, blind, and unconsoled;
> It yet shall touch His garment's fold,
> And feel the heavenly Alchemist
> Transform its very dust to gold.
>
> **Whittier.**

JUNE 3.

If ye have faith, and doubt not.
MATT. xxi. 21.

THE two things which prevent sinners from really crying to be delivered from the Evil One are the secret treachery which would fain keep both its sin and its Saviour; or the despairing apathy which drives men into the wretchedness of unclean living. Of that secret treachery which does not even really wish to be delivered, I shall say nothing. God alone can deal with it.

But of that other hindrance — men's despair: . . . To whom the answer is, O friend, O brother, O sinful soul, thou art thinking of thyself, and not of Christ; thou art looking to the place where the fiery serpent has bitten thee, and brooding over the venom in thy veins; not raising thine eyes to Him who was lifted up for thy healing, as Moses lifted up the brazen serpent in the wilderness. All that thou sayest of thyself is true. Thou art abject; thou art impotent; . . . of thyself thou canst do nothing. But thou art not asked to do it of thyself; and thou canst do all things through Him that strengtheneth thee. He can uplift; He can heal; He can inspire; He can even purify the unclean. It is to the helpless who feel themselves helpless, if with all their hearts they truly seek Him, that He will most surely come.

IV. 207, 209.

O Lord, I cannot plead my love of Thee:
I plead Thy love of me: —
The shallow conduit hails the unfathomed sea.

CHRISTINA ROSSETTI.

He hath delivered my soul in peace from the battle that was against me. — Ps. lv. 18.

IF the archangel be beautiful in all the grace and glory of youthful victory, who puts his foot on the conquered dragon, and has no speck of dust, no stain of blood upon his gleaming, invulnerable panoply — more pathetically beautiful it may be, in the sight of God, is that angel who is victorious, though it have only been after agonies and energies, only with sobbing breath and hacked sword and battered shield and soiled glory and trailing wing — and such is the angel of redeemed humanity. The best of us is scarcely saved. VIII. 58.

> We came not in with proud,
>   Firm, martial footstep, in a measured tread
> Slow pacing to the crash of music loud;
> No gorgeous trophies went before, no crowd
>   Of captives followed us with drooping head,
> No shining laurel sceptered us, nor crowned,
> Nor with its leaf our glittering lances bound. . . .
> With faces darkened in the battle flame,
>   With banners faded from their early pride,
> Through wind, and sun, and showers of bleaching rain.
>   Yet red in all our garments, doubly dyed,
> With many a wound upon us, many a stain,
> We came with steps that faltered — Yet we came!
>   DORA GREENWELL.

JUNE 5.

ALL through the Old Testament we read of what God *does;* in Nature, laying the beams of His chambers in the waters, making the clouds His chariot, walking upon the wings of the wind; in Creation, holding the waters in the hollow of His hand, and taking up the isles as a very little thing; in Providence, helping and loving us as an eagle stirreth up her nest, fluttereth over her young, spreadeth abroad her wings, taketh them, beareth them on her wings; in Individual Life, saying to each of us, "My son, give me thine heart."

But St. John alone tells us what God, in His own nature, *is.*

And he does not merely tell us this in vague abstractions — such, for instance, as that He is "the Supreme Existence," or "the Boundless," or "a stream of tendency," or "the something not ourselves which makes for righteousness;" nor yet in negations, such as that He is without body, parts, and passions; nor yet by properties, as that He is of infinite power, wisdom, and goodness; nor yet in acts, as that He is the Maker and Preserver of things. No; but he tells us what God *is*. He does so in three sentences, on which we shall do well to meditate: God is Spirit; God is Light; God is Love. Those three sentences give us the outline of all which we can rightly think respecting the Divine Majesty.

V. 32, 33.

JUNE 6.

God is light. — I. JOHN i. 5.

Give me a great truth that I may live on it.
HERDER.

TWO modern discoveries illustrate this deep truth that God is Light. Recently chemical researches have shown us that while the prism divides light into sevenfold elements of color, there are ultra-violet rays beyond the seven, which we cannot discover with the eye, ... so that even as light is but partially apprehensible to the eye, God is but partially apprehensible to our finite souls. And again, this age has discovered that light is ultimately the same thing as — in other words, is directly transformable into — heat, and force, and motion; so that all creation is but one act — the birth of Light. God is Light. The revelation sums up all that Christ was, all that Christ did; for He said, "I am the Light of the world." He is "the transitive energy of the immanent characteristic." In Him we see ... the Light of God transmitted in one continuous, undivided ray. In all human sainthood and holiness we see the same light, reflected indeed from Him, but broken up by its refractory media into all the imperfect yet lovely colors of the world, of the rainbow, and of the evening clouds.
V. 38.

God is Love. — I. John iv. 8.

DIVINEST, tenderest, most perfect of all divine, tender, perfect revelations; reserved, as it were, by inspiration for this Epistle of St. John, to be the last syllable of the apostolic witness. . . . "God is Spirit" in Himself; "God is Light" in His immanent diffusive character; "God is Love" in relation to you, and to me, and to all mankind. That is the ultimate, the most intelligible, the divinest utterance of God's own voice.

The correlative to that truth, which, in its excess of brightness, reduces love itself to silence, . . . is the lesson which the beloved disciple, too aged and too weak to preach, is said to have repeated in each church as he was carried thither in a litter, " Little children, love one another ! " It is the duty which of all others the world, both in the Church and out of it, most defiantly and flagrantly ignores. [Yet it] is the sole duty by which she can convert the world ; it is the source of the best we can do, and of all that we can hope. V. 39, 44.

What is the beginning? Love. What the course?
    Love still.
What the goal? The goal is Love on the happy hill.
Is there nothing then but love, search we sky or earth?
There is nothing out of Love hath perpetual worth.
CHRISTINA ROSSETTI.

JUNE 8.

> Well we know that all things move
> To the spheral rhythm of love.
> WHITTIER.

GOD makes us directly dependent on His mighty power; but to show that His power is all love, He stamps the gift with His own divine seal — He countersigns it with His own immediate autograph — of Beauty. This was the lesson — the love of God as shown in the loveliness of his work — which the Lord meant to emphasize when He pointed to the lilies of the field. In pointing to them once He points to them forever — to the poppy, robed in Solomonian purple, ... to the pink and fragrant snow of the apple-blossom and the May; . . . to the lily of the valley; to the soft green grass; to the rolling billows of golden corn. These, in their humbleness, in their joyful serenity, in their unimaginable fantasies of balm and bloom, say silently to us, We, like all things else, are God's gift to you; and we tell you, in multitudinous voices, that God is light; that God is love; that God is very good; that He maketh His sun to shine upon the evil and upon the good, and sendeth His rain upon the just and upon the unjust.
VIII. 8.

JUNE 9.

This God is our God forever and ever; He will be our guide even unto death. — Ps. xlviii. 14.

I KNOW not how it may be with others, but I confess, that to me, as life goes on, as I experience more and more how illusive is all that the world promises, and how empty is all that it bestows — I confess, I say, that I find even deeper comfort in these eternal verities which tower like mountain-peaks into the blue air of heaven. From squabbles over the infinitely little, we mount to a serener air when we fix our thoughts only on the love of God, the tenderness of Christ, the silver wings and the refreshing dew of the grace of the Comforter. The questions which whistle like empty winds and roar like brawling streams through the narrow banks of contemporary religion and contemporary politics, sink into a distant murmur when we take our stand by these eternal seas.

There is no truth more constantly reiterated, more emphatically insisted on throughout Scripture, than this — that "the Lord is King, be the people never so impatient; He sitteth between the Cherubim, be the earth never so unquiet."

IV. 216.

Time flies; it is his melancholy task
To bring, and bear away, delusive hopes,
And reproduce the trouble he destroys.
But, while his blindness thus is occupied,
Discerning mortal! do thou serve the will
Of Time's eternal Master; and that peace
Which the world wants, shall be for thee confirmed.

WORDSWORTH.

JUNE 10.

Oh that I had wings like a dove! for then would I fly away, and be at rest. — Ps. lv. 6.

THESE kings, heroes, prophets were just such men as ourselves; their hearts beating like our hearts; their joys and sorrows, their hopes and fears, even such as ours. This same sense of weariness, and discouragement, and willingness to die, we find in secular history: we find it in literature; we find it in our own souls. It is a part of our life. We get tired. We are tired of the daily sameness of life; . . . tired of the unrelenting past; of the dreary present; of the uncertain future. We are tired of the weary struggle in our own hearts; the to-and-fro conflicting waves of impulse and repression; the broad rejoicing tides of spiritual emotion, and the flat oozy shores of ebbing enthusiasm. . . . We feel inclined to cry with the sad thinker, at the end of another self-reproaching year, "Eternity, be thou my refuge!" . . . [Yet] no good and brave life will ever suffer itself to be crippled by conquerable melancholy. If we sigh for our own weaknesses and sins, we cannot indeed fly from ourselves, but we can by the grace of God amend ourselves. If we sigh for our surroundings, no wings of a dove indeed, can take us from these dwellings of Meshech, these tents of Kedar, but by God's grace we may help to make them better and happier places.

II. 132. 144.

JUNE 11.

That ye may know what is . . . the riches of the glory of His inheritance in the saints.
EPH. i. 18.

IF you would comfort your hearts, if you would strengthen your good resolutions, . . . make yourselves acquainted with Christian Biography, as an antidote to the degeneracy of these worldly and evil days. From our earthly mire and darkness lift your eyes to this starry path of great examples. . . . In laying down the laws of observation, the great philosopher of the Novum Organum describes what he calls "the prerogative of instances," and among them he speaks of instances which he calls *ostensivæ* or *elucescenies*, instances which show any quality in its purest exaltation, in its fullest vigor. Now the saints of God furnish us with just such *instantiæ elucescentes* of pure and possible human goodness. VII. 134, 135.

Are we weary, are we angered, are we discouraged? — then the high faith of these saints, their golden hope, their courage, their sweetness, their temperance, their magnanimity, restore to us our shaken faith in human nature; they show us what men may be by showing what they have been; they make us say to our souls: "The waves may seethe with mud, but be thou as the promontory on which they break." "Whatever any one does or says, thou must be good; just as if . . . the emerald were always saying: 'Whatever any one does or says, I must be emerald and keep my color.'"
VI. 341.

JUNE 12.

BECAUSE there are millions of roses we do not thank God for them, and yet the glory of creation is but as one rose flung down from the summer affluence of God. And as though this wealth of creation, as though this magnificence around us were too little, God gives, even to the poorest and least instructed of us, art, science, literature, appealing not only to the senses but to the soul. By the aid of those teachers of mankind we may, if we choose, build such houses and palaces within us as shall be proof against adversity — bright fancies, glad memories, noble histories, faithful sayings, treasure-houses of perfect and restful thoughts, which care cannot disturb, nor pain make gloomy, nor poverty take away from us. These He gives us as the foretastes of the many mansions which He has for us in His home above.

XI. 69.

There's not a single happy hour, —
  An hour that's ever worth the living, —
But holds the truth within its power,
  That happiness is God's own giving;

That He in whom all fulness dwells,
  Who gives to each of His good pleasure,
Reserves a bliss that far excels
  The compass of our finite measure.

My pleasant draught but makes me bold
  To taste a drop of Heaven's sweetness,
And find the tiniest flower doth hold
  An atom of the Lord's completeness.

A. W. A.

JUNE 13.

The work of righteousness shall be peace; and the effect of righteousness quietness and assurance for ever. — Is. xxxii. 17.

LET us aim at this tranquil, this sober happiness of quiet and confidence and peace in God. This is no chimæra. The possibility of winning this is no illusion. In our patience let us possess, let us acquire our souls. The world will still be the world. There will still be the pestilence which walketh in darkness and the arrow that flieth in the noon-day. The animalism of brutal passions will still crowd our streets with the infamy of its victims and the wretchedness which dogs their heels. There will still be envy and hatred and malice, and lies, and sickness, and poverty, and death; but the world in which our inmost souls shall live and move and have their being will even in this life become an anticipated fruition of the new heaven and the new earth. The outer world may still continue for many a long year, it may be for many a long century, to grope in Egyptian darkness, in darkness which may be felt; but our souls, like the children of Israel in Goshen, may have light in their dwellings.

VII. 29.

> Where light dwells pleasure dwells,
> And peace excels:
> Then rise and shine
> Thou shadowed soul of mine!

CHRISTINA ROSSETTI.

JUNE 14.

Why art thou cast down, O my soul?
                              Ps. xlii. 11.

IF we obstinately avert our hearts, how can they become vessels of grace? "The light of heaven," says the Chinese proverb, "cannot shine into an inverted bowl." Ah! if you would feel that you cannot be saved from the tyranny of your sins except by living the life in Christ, you must open your hearts to rays of heaven. The poet says:

> Sound, sound the clarion, shrill the fife,
> To all the sensual world proclaim,
> One crowded hour of glorious life
> Is worth an age without a name.

I translate that into Christian language, and I say that if . . . but for one day, you could personally experience the life in Christ, could feel the strength of it, could live in the light of it, could be dilated by its all-pervading happiness, could be thrilled with its illimitable consolations — then you would know more about it than a thousand sermons could teach you — you would set to your seal that God is true. If you will but wrestle with the angel and not let him go until he blesses you, then that wrestling would soon crowd eternity into an hour, and stretch an hour into eternity. V. 312.

> If only
> We give Him His royal seat,
> The earthly music will take its place,
> And tremble around His feet, —
> Sweeter than ever, because to our hearts
> The Master is still more sweet.
>   B. M.

JUNE 15.

Seek ye first the kingdom of God and His righteousness, and all these things shall be added unto you. — MATT. vi. 33.

THERE is nothing wrong in your trade, and your merchandise, and your daily work to earn your own living; so far from being a rival business to these, the seeking of the kingdom of heaven is a divine law, which should regulate, a divine temper which should pervade and transfigure them. Only for the sake of your own souls, for the sake of all that makes life life, for the sake alike of your temporal and eternal happiness, do not seek the dross of earth more, and love it better than the gold of heaven. . . . Do not let your daily necessities blunt the edge of your ideal aspirations. Do not sink into mere money-making machines. Man lives, indeed, by bread; but, oh! remember that he doth not live by bread alone. VIII. 12.

> The bread on which our bodies feed
> Is but the moiety of our need.
>
> The soul, the heart, must nurtured be,
> And share the daily urgency.
>
> And though it be but bitter bread
> On which these nobler parts are fed,
>
> No less we crave the daily dole,
> O Lord, of body and of soul.
> SUSAN COOLIDGE.

JUNE 16.

Work out your own salvation.—PHIL. ii. 12.

IS any other work worth doing until the initial work, ... the work of setting our own hearts right with God has been performed? He who would point others to the path which leads to their Saviour's feet, must first have found it himself. But how find it? Can it come to him in a dream? Can he stumble on it by accident? Can he yawn it into being by a wish? Or, does it not lie rather through a straight gate? and must not he struggle and agonize who would pass there-through?" ... In this respect, pre-eminently, work is a duty; the work of conscious, steady, self-improvement: the will, nay, the resolve; nay, the solemn vow; nay, the inflexible absorbing purpose, that each year shall see us better, holier, wiser than the last. And this work, too, must be with our might; it must be in penitence, and watchfulness, and self-denial. But *then* it must and will succeed; aye, succeed with that highest of all successes,—that success which includes and exceeds all others, and beside which all others shrink into insignificance—the prosperity of a heart at peace with God.   X. 177.

> But is my will alive, awake?
>   The one God will not heed,
> If in lips or hands I take
>   A half-word or half-deed.
>   GEORGE MACDONALD.

YOU may place the lamp upon its stand; you may fill it with fragrant oil; but unless the oil be perpetually renewed, it will soon go out in sickening fume, and leave the world in darkness. Why? Because God not only requires man's effort, but also his continuous efforts. In this rushing stream of time — the smoothness of the rapid ere it leaps in cataract — humanity can never afford for a moment to rest upon its oars. . . . When the influence of God's saints has spent its force, if the work pauses for a moment, everything falls into ruin and corruption. Christianity as a stereotyped system is nothing; Christianity as a human theology is nothing; only as a divine effort; only as an eternal progress; only as a living force; only as an inspiring, passionate, continuous energy can it regenerate the world. VIII. 211.

> Then bravely, comrades, to the fight,
>   With shout and song each other cheering;
> Strength not our own from heaven descends,
>   The sun breaks out, the clouds are clearing.
>
> On to the gates of Sion, on!
>   Break through the foe with fresh endeavor;
> We'll hang our colors up in heaven,
>   When peace shall be proclaimed forever.
>
> FABER.

JUNE 18.

MEN will be lofty or low according to the objects to which they direct their souls; according to the scale with which they measure their lives. If they think on things pure, and true, and lovely, they will reflect these qualities, even as the angels reflect the glory of God on their many-colored plumes. But if their ideal be dwarfed and miserable, their lives too will be small and mean. It is impossible to exaggerate the importance of having worthy ideals. Tell me whom you admire and I will tell you the drift of your character. Show me what your ideal is, and I will show you what you yet may be.
VII. 83.

The ideal, after all, is truer than the real: for the ideal is the eternal element in perishable things.
AMIEL.

> From dreams of bliss shall men awake
> One day, but not to weep:
> The dreams remain; they only break
> The mirror of the sleep.
GEORGE MACDONALD.

Let Him, our Lord, our Hope, our Saviour — let Him be our ideal, and not the ideal of the world; let His, and not the example of the world, be our example: so shall we attain the full height of our destiny.
XI. 101.

JUNE 19.

AND so, still believing in the ideal, let us strive after it. Do not let us be pessimists even in judging of ourselves. . . . Though we fail — though we fail seven times a day — yet let us never despair, never cease to try. God's promise is sure; and, if we strive, in faith and prayer, He will at last beat down Satan under our feet. It is not His way to do things by halves. He will not, for His love is infinite — He will not be tired of pardoning the returning prodigal.

"Oh God, how long?
Put forth indeed Thy powerful right hand
While time is yet,
Or never shall I reach the blissful land!"
Thus I. Then God, in pleasant speech and strong
(Which soon I shall forget),
"The man who, though his fights be all defeats,
Still fights,
Enters at last
The heavenly Jerusalem's rejoicing streets,
With glory more, and more triumphant rites,
Than always-conquering Joshua's, when his blast
The frighted walls of Jericho down cast;
And lo! the glad surprise
Of peace beyond surmise,
More than in common Saints, forever in his eyes!"

Yes, my brethren, cease not to aim at the glorious ideal of the life "in Christ;" cease not to strive after Him from faith to faith.   V. 364.

JUNE 20.

The Lord pondereth the hearts. — PROV. xxi. 2.

WE can see that some men have dared to be eminently good, and that other men have been conspicuously and infamously bad. But most men's lives and characters wear in our eyes a very mixed aspect. They show interchanging elements of good and evil, which run together like warp and woof in the varying web. We see human sin and weakness even in the good; we see here and there a gleam of saintliness even in the unsaintly. Only the balances of God are perfect. He alone, putting the just weights in the even scales, can pronounce on the whole life of most men that they "did that which was good," or "did that which was evil," in the sight of the Lord. VII. 131.

To Him be the glory forever! — We bear
To the Lord of the Harvest the wheat with the tare.
What we lack in our work may He find in our will,
And winnow in mercy the good from the ill!
WHITTIER.

JUNE 21.

I will seek that which was lost. — Ezek. xxxiv. 16.

THE woman who, having lost the coin, lights the candle and sweeps the house, and looks diligently till she finds it — who is she? She is perhaps meant for the Church of God. The Sheep wanders out of the fold; the Son goes into a far country; but the Coin is lost in the house itself. All that the woman can do is to repair, to her utmost, the consequences of her own neglect. It requires effort and trouble; the furniture must be moved; . . . the dust must fly about; but unless she neglect her duty altogether she must go on searching diligently till she find the coin. . . . And when I say the Church, I mean the whole Church. I mean the laity not only as much as the clergy, but more than the clergy, . . . seeing that they are the more in number. . . . Let not one among you all be content unless his conscience tells him that — apart from his mere selfish domesticity, and apart from his mere professional duties — . . . he is doing something, by pen, by voice, by personal effort, by the gift of his money, by the exertion of his energy, by the self-sacrifice of something at least of his own comfort and leisure, to search for, to recover, to brighten, to restore to its due place in the ruined symmetry, the lost coin — that coin which is the amalgam of every lost, of every neglected soul — in the bridal ornament of the Church of God. VIII. 123, 124.

JUNE 22.

Little children, keep yourselves from idols.
                                I. JOHN V. 21.

THE temptation to idolatry is no mere archaism. It is a very subtle thing. It lies at the root of all temptations; and men are often most in danger when they least expect it.

Not an idolater? alas! my brethren, every one of us is an idolater who has not God in all his thoughts, and who has cast away the laws of God from the governance of his life. I know not that it is a much worse idolatry to deny God altogether, and openly to deify the brute impulses of our lower nature, than it is in words to confess God, yet not to do, not to intend to do, never seriously to try to do what He commands, or to abandon what He forbids. . . . And if the love of pleasure, and the love of money, and the love of the world be idolatry, alas! how few of us have truly kept even that first commandment, "Thou shalt have none other God but Me"! VIII. 168, 172, 173.

    Ah, let me make no idols, Lord,
      To stand between my love and Thee!
    But if I do, then by Thy word
      Of power break them utterly;
    And grant that in their empty place
    I see the glory of Thy face.
                                J. L. M. W.

"Mammon, the least erected spirit that fell
   From heaven; for even in heaven his looks and
      thoughts
   Were ever downward bent, admiring more
   The riches of heaven's pavement, trodden gold,
   Than aught divine or holy else enjoyed
   In vision beatific."

MILTON.

IT is a fiend — this Mammon — which tries to wear a more respectable exterior than other fiends. He goes to church, and figures not seldom in the phylacteries of the Pharisee. Yet, this is he who taints with falsity so much of the trade and commerce of the world. . . . Who has not heard of — perhaps suffered from — swindling speculations, bubble companies, fraudulent bankrupts, defaulting trustees, cunning embezzlements, pious directors of unstable banks? Who does not see grasping luxury, which will not stretch out one of its fingers to the grinding poverty at its very doors? — Who does not know of "Wealth, a monster gorged, midst starving populations"? All these are the result of that universal love of money, which is the root of all evil; they are the works of Mammon. . . . And when you look over this dreary waste of avarice, — when you see myriads loving not God but gold — says not the voice of God to *thee* — *Is it nothing to you, all ye that pass by?*

II. 58, 59.

JUNE 24.

The voice of one crying in the wilderness.

MATT. iii. 3.

ASCETICISM may spring from very different motives. It may result from the arrogance of the cynic who wishes to stand apart from all men; or from the disgusted satiety of the epicurean who would fain find a refuge even for himself; or from the selfish terror of the fanatic, intent only on his own salvation. Far different and far nobler was the hard simplicity and noble self-denial of the Baptist. St. John was a dweller in the wilderness only that he might thereby become the prophet of the Highest. The light which was within him should be kindled, if need be, into a self-consuming flame, not for his own glory, but that it might illuminate the pathway of the coming King. . . . Men felt in him that power of mastery which is always granted to perfect self-denial. He who is superior to the common ambitions of man is superior also to their common timidities. If he have little to hope from the favor of his fellows he has little to fear from their dislike. . . . He sits as it were above his brethren, on a sunlit eminence of peace and purity, unblinded by the petty mists that dim their vision, untroubled by the petty influences that disturb their life.   XIII. 49.

Unite thyself to the One, cling to the One, for in the One all things consist.

Let others seek many and various things without, do thou seek the one inward Good, and it is sufficient.

THOMAS À KEMPIS.

JUNE 25.

The Lord shall be to thee an everlasting light, and thy God thy glory. — Is. lx. 19.

LET *us* too strive to be of those, into whom the Spirit of God entering in all ages, has made them Sons of God and Prophets. These are as the beacon-heights, which, from generation to generation, have caught and reflected back the risen light of the Sun of Righteousness; it is good to gaze upon their brightness; but it is better far to fix our eyes upon the source from which it sprang, and, " with open face, reflecting as in a glass the glory of the Lord, to be changed into the same image from glory to glory." So may we all — with willing self-abandonment, with long toil, with burning zeal, — through praise or blame, through success or failure, in peace or in agony of heart, — follow Christ now, that we may see His face hereafter, and, whithersoever He goeth, be not found absent from His side.   XI. 62.

O Thou the Life of living and of dead,
  Who givest more the more Thyself hast given,
Suffice us as Thy saints Thou hast sufficed,
  That, beautified, replenished, comforted,
Still gazing off from earth and up to heaven,
  We may pursue Thy steps, Lord Jesus Christ!
CHRISTINA ROSSETTI.

JUNE 26.

The heart knoweth his own bitterness.
PROV. xiv. 10.

WE are told that while yet the waters of the deluge weighed upon the drowning world, the dove flew back to the ark "and lo! in her mouth an olive leaf plucked off!" The olive leaf is bitter, but it is a sign of peace, and the Jewish legend tells that "the dove said before the Holy One, blessed be He! 'Lord of the Universe! let my food be bitter as an olive, delivered by Thy hands, rather than sweet as honey delivered by the hands of flesh and blood.'" My friends, however much the deluge may welter round us, that Holy Heavenly Dove of Peace —

"Sweet dove, the softest, steadiest plume,
  In all the sunbright sky ;
Brightening in ever changeful bloom,
  As breezes change on high," —

is ready to descend into our hearts and rest therein. And if the plucked leaf, which she bears to us from God in heaven, seem bitter to us, yet none the less is it a leaf of the Tree of Life, — a green leaf from that tree "whose leaves are for the healing of the nations."

II. 150.

Happy are they that learn, in Thee,
  Though patient suffering teach,
The secret of enduring strength,
  And praise too deep for speech —
Peace that no pressure from without,
  No strife within, can reach.

A. L. WARING.

JUNE 27.

Despise not thou the chastening of the Almighty; For He maketh sore, and bindeth up; He woundeth, and His hands make whole.

He shall deliver thee in six troubles: yea, in seven there shall no evil touch thee.

In famine He shall redeem thee from death; and in war from the power of the sword.

Thou shalt be hid from the scourge of the tongue; neither shalt thou be afraid of destruction when it cometh. — JOB V. 17–21.

GOD delivers us out of these evils by turning them into greater good. He chastens us *in* the world that we may not be condemned *with* the world. He turns the tears of sorrow into the pearls of a brighter crown. By weaning us from the transitory, He leads us to the eternal. By emptying us of the world, He fills us with Himself. He makes the *via crucis* the *via lucis*. He causes us, in the very fire, to thank Him that our light affliction, which is but for a moment, is working for us a far more exceeding and eternal weight of glory.   IV. 206.

> Yet had our pilgrimage bin free,
>   And smooth without a thorne,
> Pleasures had foiled eternitie,
>   And tares had choak'd the corne.
> Thus by the Crosse salvation runs,
>   Affliction is a mother,
> Whose painful throes yield many sons,
>   Each fairer than the other.
>   HENRY VAUGHAN.

JUNE 28.

Forgive, if ye have aught against any.
MARK xi. 25.

EVEN when we try to fulfil this duty, or think we do, we often deceive ourselves. Often our forgiveness is only semblable. . . .

"Forgive? How many will say forgive and find
 A sort of absolution in the sound
 To hate a little longer?"

And often our forgiveness is only skin deep, as when we say: "I forgive what you have done, but I can never forget it."

And how often our forgiveness is merely contemptuous and disdainful; as when the tyrant Dionysius sent to Plato and asked him not to abuse him at Athens for the wrongs he had inflicted, and Plato haughtily answered that "He had other things to do than to think of Dionysius." And how often our forgiveness is only quantitative. We ask, "How often must I forgive?" We say, "I cannot possibly forgive such repeated offences." Ah! God's forgiveness is not like that. We must forgive daily, as He forgives us daily; not seven times, but seventy times seven. We need daily cleansing from daily defilement by the spirit of hatred, as from all our other sins of word and deed.

IV. 132.

Good night, my foe! not all the wrong is thine.
 My share I own;
Forgive! we human know one word divine—
 The sun goes down!

HARRIET McEWEN KIMBALL.

JUNE 29.

Lord, if it be Thou, bid me come to Thee on the water. — And He said: Come. — MATT. xiv. 28, 29.

IF, like Peter, we fix our eyes on Jesus, we too may walk triumphantly over the swelling waves of disbelief, and unterrified amid the rising winds of doubt; but if we turn our eyes away from Him in whom we have believed — if, as it is so easy to do, and as we are so much tempted to do, we look rather at the power and fury of those terrible and destructive elements than at Him who can help and save, — then we too shall inevitably sink. Oh! if we feel, often and often that the water-floods threaten to drown us, and the deep to swallow up the tossed vessel of our Church and Faith, may it again and again be granted us to hear amid the storm and the darkness, and the voices prophesying war, those two sweetest of the Saviour's utterances —

"Fear not. Only believe."
"It is I. Be not afraid."   XIII. 192.

    If our love were but more simple,
      We should take Him at His word;
    And our lives would be all sunshine
      In the sweetness of the Lord.
                        FABER.

JUNE 30.

GOLDEN threads there are in the saddest life, but it is not of golden threads that the woof of any life is woven. To all of you pain must come, and inexorable weariness, and many frustrate hopes. All of you must weep over the graves of those you most dearly love; all of you suffer from man's meanness or man's malice. . . . But from one thing may God inHis great mercy save you, and that is "the meeting of calamity with an accusing conscience,"— the bitter punishment which comes of sin. This alone is to be really dreaded; though the natural calamities of life happen alike to all, they come differently to the wise and to the foolish, to the wicked and to the pure.

VI. 395.

> A Sower went forth to sow;
> His eyes were dark with woe;
> . . . . . .
> His seed was human blood,
> And tears of women and men.
> And I, who near him stood,
> Said: When the crop comes, then
> There will be sobbing and sighing,
> Weeping and wailing and crying.
> . . . . . .
> It was an autumn day
> When next I went that way.
> But a sea of sunlight flowed,
> A golden harvest glowed;
> And I said: Thou only art wise,
> God of the earth and skies!
> And I praise Thee again and again,
> For the Sower whose name is Pain.
>
> RICHARD WATSON GILDER.

JULY 1.

The lines are fallen unto me in pleasant places.
Ps. xvi. 6.

WE of this land, of this century, . . . are, by God's grace, heirs of the treasuries of the world. Nothing profound has been ever thought, nothing enchanting ever imagined, nothing noble ever uttered, nothing saintly or heroic ever done, which is not or may not be ours. For us Plato and Shakespeare thought; for us Dante and Milton sang; for us Bacon and Newton toiled; for us Angelo and Raphael painted; for us Benedict and Francis lived saintly lives; for the heritage of our liberty have myriads of heroes perished on the battle-field, and for the purity of our religion hundreds of martyrs sighed away their souls amid the flames. But let us not pride ourselves on this our glorious inheritance, or falsely dream that this alone will avail us anything, or that we are favorite children in the great family of God. Certainly since to us much has been given, from us much shall be required.
X. 13.

A sacred burthen is this life ye bear;
Look on it, lift it, bear it solemnly;
Stand up, and walk beneath it steadfastly.
F. A. KEMBLE.

IF pride and fashion have often been fatal conspirators against individual faith, so have wider but more specious evils wrought a certain atrophy in the spiritual life of nations and centuries. Ages of the most advanced refinement have not unfrequently been ages of the most open unbelief. At the zenith of their civilization nations have often been at the nadir of their faith: . . . amid the dust and glare of material interests, all heavenly hopes, all Godward aspirations have faded utterly away. The spectacle is full of warning for ourselves. It shows us that material advance may be moral retrogression, and that widely-extended comfort, rapidly-increasing knowledge, vast literary activity may co-exist in Philosophy with a dreary materialism, in morals with a corrupted selfishness, in religion with a blank negation. . . . It proves to us that not on refinement, but on spirituality; not on selfishness, but on sacrifice; not on knowledge, but on wisdom; not on intelligence, but on faith, rests the entire superstructure of national greatness and individual peace.

XII. 12.

In our doings and ambitions,
　Heaping gold and probing thought,
In crude science, worn traditions,
　Finds the spirit what it sought?
In the tumult of the nations,
　Surging shoreward like a sea,
Are Thy sundered congregations
　　Gathering unto Thee?

LUCY LARCOM.

JULY 3.

AMONG many perils which seem to lower like dark clouds on the horizon, the one hope for our age and nation lies in a faithful allegiance to the Living Christ. . . . I feel no misgivings as to the future of Christianity, if only Christ's sons abide in love, relying on His strength. Then the waves of the sea may rage horribly, but they will only roar and strike and be shattered into mist upon the shore. . . . But though Christianity can never be finally overthrown, . . . it may suffer an eclipse—disastrous, not indeed to any who love the Lord in sincerity and truth, but to the nations of a perplexed and groaning world. Can one of your white river-mists affect the sun? It cannot affect the sun, but it may grievously trouble our vision. . . . All the atheism of the world could not dethrone the Lord of Glory, . . . but atheism may hide God and His Christ from the hearts of men, and intercept the blessing of His grace. Even this it would, I am convinced, be powerless to do even for one brief and miserable day, except through our perversities or our faithlessness. Christianity can only be defeated by ourselves. It will never be condemned by the world, except because of our unworthiness, and of our shortcomings.

VIII. 29, 30.

Heaven doth with us as we with torches do,
Not light them for themselves; for if our virtues
Did not go forth of us, 'twere all alike
As if we had them not.
SHAKESPEARE.

JULY 4.

Land that we love! Thou Future of the World!
Thou refuge of the noble heart oppressed!
. . . .
Keep thou thy starry forehead as the dove
All white, and to the eternal Dawn inclined!
Thou art not for thyself, but for mankind!
RICHARD WATSON GILDER.

WHAT should be the one and only true ideal of each nation, if it would indeed be a wise and understanding people? Let the frivolous sneer and the faithless deride, but there is only one such ideal. It is duty. It is righteousness. It is the law of Sinai. It is the law of Christ. It is purity of life. It is honesty of trade. It is absolute allegiance to truth. It is the inviolable sanctity of the marriage law. There is a law above all the enactments of human gods, the same in all times. It is the law written by the finger of God upon the hearts of men. VIII. 933.

What constitutes a State?
Not high-raised battlement or labored mound,
Thick walls or moated gate;
Not cities proud, with spires and turrets crowned; . . .
No! Men — high-minded men;
Men who their duties know,
And know their rights, and, knowing, dare maintain; . . .
And sovereign Law that, with collected will,
On crowns and globes elate
Sits empress, crowning good, repressing ill.
SIR WILLIAM JONES.

Brethren, ye have been called unto liberty.
                              GAL. V. 13.
Jerusalem, which is above, is free, which is the mother of us all. — GAL. iv. 26.

THE Bible, rightly used, is eminently the book of freedom. All the noblest and most inspiring parts of its history tell of the struggles of a free people against colossal tyrannies. All the most glorious pages of its prophets are like the blasts of trumpets blown to awaken men from immoral acquiescence and apathetic sloth. Its spiritual law is a perfect law of liberty. The very spirit of its gospel is "Ye shall know the truth, and the truth shall make you free." . . . "Free from what?" you will ask. Free, I answer, from all things which enslave the body and the soul; free from morbid scrupulosities of conscience; free from morbid anxieties of service; . . . free from anything and everything but the law of faith, the law of grace, the royal law of liberty, the law of those who are not slaves, but sons; the law which is fulfilled in one word, even in this, "Thou shalt love thy neighbor as thyself."
But this freedom is "in Christ." I. 251, 253.

Stand fast in the liberty wherewith Christ hath made us free. — GAL. V. 1.

JULY 6.

WE are proud of our science. Will science save a people from demoralization?

"If we trod the deeps of ocean, if we struck the stars in rising,
  If we wrapped the globe intently in one hot electric breath,
'Twere but power within our tether, no new spirit-power comprising,
  And in life we are not greater men, nor bolder men in death."

We talk about our philanthropy. Will our philanthropy save us? I take a different view of it. I look on the vaunted charities not as the sign of our munificence, but as the demonstration of our meanness. We boast of our civilization. I recall how often in history civilization has proved itself to be but a film of iridescence over the corruption of a stagnant pool.

Periods of long prosperity are full of danger, and the attitude of moral watchfulness and the zeal of a noble discontent are better and safer than the vanity of self-congratulation. . . . Let us not dwell too much on the thought how religious, how orthodox, how progressive, how safe we are. Let us rather be very humble for our many sins and shortcomings.   VIII. 72, 73.

    Man now presides
In power where once he trembled in his weakness;
Science advances with gigantic strides:
But are we aught enriched in love and meekness?
Can aught in us be found of pure and wise
More than in humbler times graced human story?
That makes our hearts more apt to sympathize
With Heaven?   WORDSWORTH.

JULY 7.

TO all true Religion, as to all true Science, the Universe is an open book of revelation, whose divine hieroglyphics are decipherable by toil, and every fresh discovery is but a fresh fact to be recorded and coördinated with those which we already know. But Science and Faith must ever be united, they are the two wings whereby alone we can soar to the knowledge of God. And, believe me, if there be a theological, there is also such a thing as a scientific narrowness: there is a noble Science, and there is a Science inflated and ignorant, and, little as their authors knew of the sublimest laws of nature, yet this kind of Science is a thing as much lower than the Pentateuch or the Book of Psalms, as a treatise of Astronomy, however accurate, is a smaller thing than the midnight with all its stars.

XII. 188.

Beauty, loveliness, and awfulness have as good a right to be as logic and conclusive experiment have; and they are, in the fullest sense, as conversant with truth, law, order, and rational intelligence, as demonstration is. . . . The telescope is indeed a magnificent invention; all honor to it and to what it reveals! Yet I suspect that Night, star-tongued, though a very ancient orator, has lessons as inspiring, as uplifting, as expanding, as any that come through our modern optic glasses.

HENRY N. HUDSON.

JULY 8.

WE cannot love an awful uniformity of laws. "A stream of tendency flowing through the ages" may be a very philosophical conception of the God adopted by the insight or the criticism of the nineteenth century, but, unlike "our Father which is in heaven," it has "no ear for prayer, no heart for sympathy, no arm to save." This God is not our God, nor can *it* be our guide for ever and ever. And what follows? If God be not, . . . what then is man? What but a phantom, a vapor, . . . one unregarded raindrop in some immeasurable sea? And so, if life be but a semblance and death but an extinction, . . . —oh, dreary, dreary gospel of a darkness taking itself for exceptional enlightenment!—if God be nothing, and Man be nothing, what then is Virtue, and what is Truth? . . . If we sin, what does it matter to blind infinite Forces which may crush us, but cannot love? If we repent, what will the Æons and the Spaces care for our repentance?

X. 22, 23.

O World, what a fearful thing thou art,
    With no God at thy heart!
No watchful and tender Love to warm
    With a soul thy form!
No smallest place in thy whole vast scope
    For a deathless hope!
No word that gives us the vaguest key
    To thy mystery!
But with God and His Christ, what love and grace
    We find in thy face!

J. L. M. W.

JULY 9.

And this word, Yet once more, signifieth the removing of those things that are shaken, as of things that are made, that those things which cannot be shaken may remain. — HEB. xii. 27.

IN this remarkable verse the writer goes to the heart of the philosophy of religion and of history. He declares that through the ages runs one ever-increasing purpose, and that this purpose is the will of God. He tells us that, not by accident or by destiny, but by Heaven's own Providence,

" The old order changeth, giving place to new,
And God fulfils Himself in many ways,
Lest one good custom should corrupt the world."

. . . To cling to the old when the new demands our attention and our allegiance, has been a constant error and indolence of mankind. They look back to the east when the west is calling them. The noontide is approaching, and they linger amid the shadows of the dawn. . . . God Himself, as this text declares, is ever leading us onward, upward, forward. "The living sap of to-day outgrows the dead rind of yesterday." Therefore, in every true and living church there must be freedom and there must be progress. Freedom and progress are the law of true life.

VIII. 128, 129.

For He who worketh high and wise,
Nor pauses in His plan,
Will take the sun out of the skies,
Ere freedom out of man.

EMERSON.

JULY 10.

Yet once . . . I will shake the heavens, and the earth, and . . . all nations.

HAG. ii. 6, 7.

SOME things, in age after age, have been and they will be shaken; but there are some things real, solid, eternal, which cannot be shaken, and which for ever and ever will remain. . . . Shadows of theory, shadows of opinion, shadows of tradition, shadows of hierarchy and party may be shaken. Christ remains.

If we are Christians, if we are sincere and good men, there is nothing that can terrify us. There be many which say, "Who will show us any good?" Lord, lift Thou up the light of Thy countenance upon us. We believe in the Father who created, in the Son who redeemed, in the Holy Ghost who sanctifieth us! That faith is sufficient, is more than sufficient whereby to live, wherein to die. VIII. 145.

> Then 'gin I thinke on that which Nature said,
> Of that same time when no more change shall be,
> But steadfast rest of all things, firmly stayed
> Upon the pillars of Eternity,
> That is contrayr to Mutability:
> For all that moveth doth in change delight;
> But thenceforth all shall rest eternally
> With Him that is the God of Sabaoth hight:
> Oh, that great Sabaoth God, grant me that Sabbath's sight!

SPENSER.

JULY 11.

PEOPLE sometimes worry themselves because they cannot believe this or that. . . . You have doubts, it may be, about this or that form of church organization; . . . you feel uncertainties about parts of the Old Testament; about Balaam's ass, or the sun standing still, . . . or a thousand other things. Very well: study these questions humbly, reverently, impartially; but if nothing satisfies you, why, as brave old Martin Luther said, then let them go. "We cannot," he said, "prevent the birds of the air from flying about our heads; but no man need suffer them to build their nests in his beard." These questions have to do with criticism, with archæology, . . . and many other complex matters. To hold any particular view about them will not make you, by the millionth part of a scruple, a worse or a better man. . . . Turn from the non-essential things which can be shaken, or which for you *have* been shaken, to the things which cannot be shaken, and which remain. Spiritually, as well as intellectually and morally, turn from the shadow and face the sun.

The only real question of religion for you is, Am I sincere? Do I love the truth? Do I love the light? Am I striving ever more and more to live in the spirit of the beatitudes?

VIII. 134. 135. 136.

Unlovingness is unbelief;
Untruthful lives are heresies.
LUCY LARCOM.

JULY 12.

Ye stand this day all of you before the Lord your God. — DEUT. xxix. 10.

INTENSE in their significance—fresh in their solemnity—as when Moses uttered them to the listening multitudes on the farther shores of Jordan, the echo of those warning words rolls to us across the centuries. They express the formative principle, the regulating conception, the inspiring impulse of every greatly Christian life. The very differentia of such a life,—that is, its distinguishing feature,—is this, that it is spent always and consciously in the presence of God.

And in proportion to our faith is the vividness and reality wherewith, like Moses, we see God—like Enoch walk, like Abraham converse, like Jacob wrestle with Him, like Elijah thrill to the inward whisper of His still small voice. There are, indeed, some eyes so dim that they catch no gleam of His Presence; some ears so dull that they never hear the music or the thunder of His voice; and there are moments when even to the best of men He seems silent or far off.

VI. 2.

> Thrice blest is he to whom is given
> The instinct that can tell
> That God is on the field when He
> Is most invisible.
>
> FABER.

JULY 13.

Before I was afflicted, I went astray; but now have I kept Thy word. — Ps. cxix. 67.

THERE is such a thing as welcoming tribulation when we know that God only sends it for our good. When the wise slave Lokman was seen eating a bitter melon which his master had given him, and was asked how he could do it, he answered, "My master has given me multitudes of good things. Should I not eat one bitter melon if it comes from his hand?" . . . When we look at evil solely in the light of God, when that which seemed terrible, because it was so manifold, is condensed into "one thing only," and means nothing but opposition to God's will and transgression of His law, we shall regard no other evil as fatal. Our very sorrows will be beatitudes, for they will help to purge away the vile dross from us, and transmute us into purer gold.

IV. 184.

   Then, welcome each rebuff
   That turns earth's smoothness rough,
Each sting that bids nor sit nor stand but go!
   Be our joys three-parts pain!
   Strive, and hold cheap the strain!
Learn, nor account the pang; Dare, never grudge
   the throe!

BROWNING.

JULY 14.

And they shall look unto the earth, and behold trouble and darkness. —Is. viii. 22.

MOST of these our sufferings are self-inflicted. We are cruel to ourselves. We feather the arrows of our enemies, and make the wounds rankle, which otherwise they were powerless to inflict. We anticipate misfortunes which never come. We brood over injuries at which it would have been far wiser to smile. We neglect or despise the joys which God otherwise would freely give us. We will not know the things which make for our peace, and in things which we know naturally, like brute beasts made to be taken and destroyed, in these we corrupt ourselves. Ah, how true, how true it is that Heaven seems to be "everywhere if we would but enter it, and yet almost nowhere, because so few of us can." Alas, my brethren, all this might be otherwise, but as we ruin our bodies by excess and ignorance, so we ruin our minds by greed and care.

"O purblind race of miserable men,
How many among us at this very hour
Do forge a lifelong trouble for ourselves,
By taking true for false, or false for true,
Here through the feeble twilight of the world
Groping, how many, until we pass and reach
That other where we see as we are seen!"

II. 218.

JULY 15.

SEE all things, not in the blinding and deceitful glare of the world's noon, but as they will seem when the shadows of life are closing in. At evening the sun seems to loom large on the horizon, while the landscape gradually fades from view; and then the sunset reveals the infinitude of space crowded with unnumbered worlds, and the firmament glows with living sapphires. Even so, let the presence of God loom large upon the narrow horizon of your life, and the firmament of your souls glow with the living sapphires of holy thoughts.

Ah, try now to look at the world and its allurements as they will seem in the last hour; to look at unlawful pleasure as it shall then seem, not only a disappointing, but a depraving and an envenomed thing; to look at the small aims of ambition as they shall seem when they have dwindled into their true paltriness.
VII. 215, 217.

What matters it? — a few years more,
Life's surge so restless heretofore
Shall break upon the unknown shore!

In that far land shall disappear
The shadows which we follow here,
The mist-wreaths of our atmosphere.

Before no work of mortal hand,
Of human will or strength expand
The pearl gates of the Better Land;

Alone in that great Love which gave
Life to the sleeper of the grave,
Resteth the power to "seek and save."
WHITTIER.

JULY 16.

THERE are moments when the grace of God stirs sensibly in the human heart; when the soul seems to rise upon the eagle-wings of hope and prayer into the heaven of heavens; when caught up, as it were, into God's very presence, . . . we seem to know Him and be known of Him; and if it were possible for any man at such a moment to see into our souls, he would know all that is greatest and most immortal in our beings. . . . That such solitary musings — such penetrating, even in this life, "behind the vail" — such sudden kindlings of celestial lightning which seem to have fused all that is basest and meanest within us in an instant and forever — that these supreme crises are among the recorded experiences of the Christian life, rests upon indisputable testimony of evidence and of fact.

XIII. 73.

The lovely vision melts away,
. . . . . .
Duty is at the door.

But if I face with courage stout
 The labor and the din,
Thou, Lord, wilt let my mind go out,
 My heart with Thee stay in.

GEORGE MACDONALD.

Ask what I shall give thee. — 1 KINGS iii. 5.

HAD any man ever so splendid an opportunity? It is not only all the kingdoms of the world and the glory of them, but it is that at no price of iniquity; it is that with no concurrent sorrow; it is that with God's peace besides. . . . The tales of every land and age have imagined what man would desire if the powers of good, or the powers of evil, offered him a boundless choice. And it is one universal moral of all these tales that unless the choice come immediately from God, it were far better to make no such choice at all. Over and over again, in classic, in mediæval, in later stories men are supposed to sell themselves to the Evil Spirit, and it is the object of every one of those tales to show the crushing ruin and overwhelming bitterness of such an attempt to gain earth at the cost of heaven.

All gifts, save the spontaneous gifts of heaven, are like the fairy gold that turns to dust. It is God who weaves the little thread of our destinies, and He weaves it for our best happiness, unless our rude folly mars His plan. The granting of our prayers, even when they are not granted as they sometimes are, in anger, is not always for our immediate happiness.

VI. 160, 161.

We, ignorant of ourselves,
Beg often our own harm, which the Wise Powers
Deny us for our good: so find we profit
By losing of our prayers.

SHAKESPEARE.

JULY 18.

I LOVE happiness. I believe in happiness. I am sure that God meant us for happiness. think that we are all the better for happiness. I long that every one of you should be as happy as God gives it to any of His children to be. And though mere pleasure is a far lower thing, I do not even look with a dubious eye on pleasure. I know that many turn it into a Marah fountain, scorching and poisonous; but I know too that innocence can sweeten it. No good man can be a foe to happiness; no good man need be a foe to innocent pleasure. God meant us to have something of both; and the better we are, the more generous, the more pure, the more unselfish, the more we shall have of both. For there is but one form of happiness which can long satisfy the soul which God has made. It is when happiness is not sought at all for its own sake, but comes as the natural law of a noble existence; it is when duty and delight are synonymous and coincident; it is when peace is the reward of faithfulness, not the aim of self-indulgence; it is when gladness is found in the service of others, not in the satisfaction of self; it is when the psalm of life is, "Lo, I come to do Thy will, O my God. I am content to do it; yea, Thy law is within my heart."

"Who follows pleasure, pleasure slays,
  God's wrath upon himself he wreaks;
But all delights attend his days
  Who takes with thanks, but never seeks."

VI. 309.

JULY 19.

IT remains as true now as in the days of the Apostles that "the natural man receiveth not the things of the Spirit of God," and that "spiritual things must be spiritually discerned." . . . It was a poet who wrote, "*As are the inclinations so are the opinions,*" it was an idealizing philosopher who said "*that our system of thought was often only the history of our heart.*" Oh, my brethren, we may lose our faith in Christ from many causes, and from some which it is not for fallible man to denounce or to condemn; but it is well for us to know there is undoubtedly one path which leads with dangerous frequency from practical faithlessness to speculative infidelity; from the "Yea, hath God said?" to the "Ye shall not surely die." Let us then at least beware that in us unholiness do not cloud the spiritual eye and dull the spiritual ear; for the rank mists which reek upward from the sinful heart *do* tend most fatally to obliterate the Image, the Memory, the Life of Christ — they end by hiding from the human soul even the vision of its Creator in fold on fold of a more and more impenetrable night.   XII. 9.

As ye have yielded your members servants to uncleanness and to iniquity, unto iniquity; even so now yield your members servants to righteousness, unto righteousness. — ROM. vi. 19.

JULY 20.

Whatsoever a man soweth, that shall he also reap.—GAL. vi. 7.

LONG after a man has done with his sin, his sin has by no means done with him; his deeds live apart from him, and claim their fellowship with him long after he has grown ashamed of them; and he inherits them, for they are his. Look at the harvest rippling and bowing under the summer breeze with all its innumerable ears; innumerable as they seem, yet there is not one of them that did not spring from some seed which the sower sowed. Even so it is with the harvest of shame, of loneliness, of ruin, of agony which springs up in the lives of many men. "Nature," says one, "acts with fearful uniformity, . . . she has no ear for prayer, no heart for sympathy, no arm to save." And he who thus wrote believed not in God; but that which he called Nature is but the sum-total of God's laws — . . . laws which on every cloud of the stormy heavens, and every grave of the wrinkled earth, and on every gleam of that fiery Urim which is the awakened conscience of mankind, write with plainness unmistakable that the wages of sin is death. XI. 32.

We scatter seeds with careless hand,
  And dream we ne'er shall see them more:
    But for a thousand years
    Their fruit appears
  In weeds that mar the land or healthful store.
                                 KEBLE.

JULY 21.

Who for one morsel of meat sold his birthright.
HEB. xii. 16.

IT was done in a moment; but such moments cannot occur except as the epitome of years. There is a plant which is fabled to rush into crimson blossom once only in one hundred years; but even then all the one hundred years have been causing, have been maturing, that one crimson flower. So it is with every great sin. It is but the ripened fruit of hundreds of little tendencies. Esau's guilty moment was but the expression and heritage of all his past life.

And he thought nothing of what he had done. . . . He sold his birthright . . . because he despised it; and he despised it because it was not a thing which he could see, or eat, or drink, . . . because it was a glory and a blessing which pertained not to the body, but to the soul. That was his sin; that is why he — the gay, bright hunter, with his superficial virtues dragged down by the millstone of his vices — stands in Scripture as the eternal type of the sensual and the profane.

VII. 175, 177.

> Alas! how many, downward bowed,
> Their birthright have resigned!
> O God, how much of great and good,
> How much of fearful sin,
> Were gained, or gallantly withstood,
> If these their place would win!
>
> ROBERT LOWELL.

PLATO . . . compares men who have never tried to face the truth to prisoners in a deep underground cavern, who have been so chained . . . that they cannot turn their heads. In front of them is the rocky wall of their prison-house. Behind them and above them is a causeway, on which fires are burning, and along this causeway pass wayfarers singing and conversing and bearing burdens, whose shadows are thrown by the firelight on the cavern wall, and whose voices are reflected back from it. The imprisoned denizens of the dark cave, seeing only these flickering shadows, take them for substances and realities; and hearing only these vague echoes, take them for songs and voices. . . .

Imprisoned in self-chosen darkness, steeped in emptinesses, how few among living men even care for that wisdom which consists in seeing the things that are, and seeing them as they are! Let a man but once catch a glimpse of the true light and he learns utterly to despise the dim rush-light of this world's tinselled stage. Let one ray out of eternity shine down upon him, and for him the world and the things of the world shrivel into insignificance. IV. 259, 261

> Reality, reality,
> Lord Jesus Christ, Thou art to me!
> From the spectral mists and driving clouds,
> From the shifting shadows and phantom crowds;
> From unreal words and unreal lives,
> Where truth with falsehood feebly strives;
> From the passings away, the chance and change,
> Flickerings, vanishings, swift and strange,
> I turn to my glorious rest on Thee.
>
> FRANCES R. HAVERGAL.

JULY 23.

Awake, thou that sleepest. — EPH. v. 14.

NO doubt in buffetings of calamity, in prostrations of illness, in rude shocks of divine intimation — or again in spasms of agonizing disenchantment, when the Dead Sea apples have crumbled into bitterness, and the world itself has seemed at a touch to slip into dust, like the body of some exhumed king — men have been brought, in one moment, to recognize the things which, though unseen, are alone eternal. Having been blind, lo! at the touch of Christ they see! But is it not sad and strange that such penal dispensations should be so often necessary? Should not Reason and Conscience, and universal experience, suffice us for this end? The myrrh does not yield its fragrance unless it be incensed and crushed; the scented tree must be smitten by the axe before its perfume can flow forth; but why should life be only rendered holy and serious by pain and retribution? Ah! my friends, depend upon it that God does not willingly afflict us; that His afflictions are meant in saving mercy, because other means of arousing us have failed.

VII. 77.

> So oft the doing of God's will
>   Our foolish wills undoeth!
> And yet what idle dream breaks ill,
>   Which morning-light subdueth?
> And who would murmur or misdoubt
> When God's great sunrise finds him out?
>
> ELIZABETH BARRETT BROWNING.

JULY 24.

> We would be like Him whom we call our Lord;
> We would reflect the Image that we love.
> WHITTIER.

THE imitation of Christ is feasible in all conditions of life; . . . it can assume manifold forms. His example is too rich in its many-sidedness, . . . to place it within the reach of any man to achieve the sum, or complete the circle, of His infinite perfections. Saints have differed widely from each other in their manifestations of goodness. . . . Even angels have a beautiful diversity. The Seraphim of knowledge differ from the Cherubim of love; nor is Raphael the affable Archangel an exact counterpart of the herald Gabriel, or the warrior Michael. We must imitate Christ in the way open and possible to each of us, and according to the measure of our faith. . . . In Christ's body, which is the universal Church, there is the hand and the foot, as well as the eye and the ear. V. 133.

> Content to come, content to go,
>   Content to wrestle or to race,
> Content to know or not to know,
>   Each in his place.
>
> Lord, grant us grace to love Thee so
>   That glad of heart and glad of face,
> At last we may sit high or low,
>   Each in his place,
>
> Where pleasures flow as rivers flow,
>   And loss has left no barren trace,
> And all that are, are perfect so,
>   Each in his place.
> CHRISTINA ROSSETTI

They were stoned, they were sawn asunder, were tempted, were slain with the sword: they wandered about in sheepskins and goatskins, being destitute, afflicted, tormented (of whom the world was not worthy).— HEB. xi. 37, 38.

WE read the lives of the Saints of God, and we are perplexed at first and saddened to observe how one after another they may seem to have perished broken-hearted and despised, . . . but let us not also fail to notice that, one and all, they never lose the beatific vision and the transcendent hope: one and all they stretch forth their hands in glorious anticipation of the farther shore. Let us neither be deceived nor saddened: . . . each high ideal is a prophecy which, later if not sooner, brings about its own fulfilment. No good deed dies: be it a rejoicing river, be it but a tiny rill of human nobleness, yet, so it be pure and clean, never has it been lost in the poisonous marshes or choked in the muddy sands. It flows inevitably into that great river of the water of life which is not lost, save — if *that* be to be lost — in the infinite ocean of God's Eternal Love.
X. 73, 74.

Oh! how joyful are all the saints before the face of the Saint of saints,
Who is the cause and origin of their salvation.
To hold their faith, and to imitate their example, is the way to Everlasting Life.
THOMAS À KEMPIS.

JULY 26.

Gather up the fragments that remain, that nothing be lost.— JOHN vi. 12.

AS the miracles of Christ were more than mere acts of power, so the words of Christ reached farther than their direct significance. And I shall understand these words as warning us against other waste than the waste of food, — as bidding us to gather other fragments than the fragments of a feast. . . . If neither physically, nor morally, nor intellectually, you have been doing your duty, — if, instead of growing better and better, you are steadily and consciously growing worse and worse, — if over your soul is beginning to creep the chill of a fatal apathy, and the past-feelingness of a miserable despair, — then must we not to you *alter* the words of the text, not saying as Christ said to His faithful ones, "Gather up the fragments that remain, that nothing be lost," — but rather alas! with a more urgent insistency, "Gather up the fragments that remain, lest everything be lost"? . . . Make, by God's grace, now — even now and here — a higher purpose, and ask for grace to keep to that purpose; humbly remembering that you must take the difficulty of the upward path as grave punishment to be patiently borne for going downwards. So gather up the fragments that remain, lest all be lost. "Now is the accepted time, now is the day of salvation."

VI. 119, 124, 129.

JULY 27.

Casting all your care upon Him, for He careth for you. — I. PETER V. 7.

THE pestilent malaria does not creep with more certainty out of the stagnant swamp over the doomed city, than does that fatal blight which exhales over the soul from the undrained marshes of worldly care. O that we could all wring this black drop out of our souls. Then, if cares came, we could lay them all on Him who would bear for us their intolerable burden, and, after the very heaviest misfortune which could befall us, sorrowful it may be, but undebased,

> We might take up our burden of life again,
> Not saying even, It might have been.

Why should we be care-stricken? what business have we to be sad in the sunshine? we have nothing to do with the past, nothing to do with the future; we have to do with the present only, and that even in the hour of trial we are by God's grace strong enough to bear.

XI. 96.

> The happiest heart that ever beat
> Was in some quiet breast,
> That found the common daylight sweet,
> And left to Heaven the rest.

CHENEY.

JULY 28.

MY friends, do diligently and carefully the work of the common life, and you need not be over-careful, you need fear nothing. Do your duty, and God will provide for you. He will give you your daily bread, and He will give you something better — that bread which endureth unto eternal life. He will give you that water of which he that drinketh shall thirst never again; of that water which shall be within you a well of water springing up unto life eternal. Your Heavenly Father feedeth the fowls of the air, and the creatures of the field, and Christ's great lesson to us of the spectacle of the ceaseless providence is: Be not anxious about the morrow. Is not "life more than food, and the body than raiment? Seek God and you shall have life, and you shall have it more abundantly." IX. 157.

> Nurtured we all must be
>   By Thy sweet Word alone;
> Asking this bread of Thee,
>   Thou wilt not give a stone.
>
> . . . .
>
> With love for all around
>   Our days and hours to fill;
> Thus be it ever found
>   Our meat to do Thy will!
>
> . . . .
>
> Who seeks this bread shall be
>   Nor stinted, nor denied;
> Our hungry souls in Thee,
>   O Christ, are satisfied!
>
> LUCY LARCOM.

JULY 29.

Our fathers were under the cloud. — I. COR. x. 1.

THAT journey of the Israelites in the desert to which St. Paul alludes, furnishes a close emblem of our own. Before each one of us — a pillar of cloud by day, a pillar of fire by night — glides visibly the protecting providence of God. Wonderful deliverances are vouchsafed to us. Enemies pursue us, and we must fly from them. Enemies confront us, and we must fight with them. Vividly and distinctly, loudly and intelligibly, — as among the burning summits and thunder-beaten crags of Sinai, — blaze for us the revealing splendors, reverberate for us the majestic utterances of the moral law. Simple and sweet as virgin honey — if we will only live thereon — lies round us the angels' food; clear and crystalline — if we will but drink thereof — murmurs and shines about us the river of God's love. X. 129.

Leaning on Him, make with reverent meekness
    His own thy will;
And with strength from Him shall thy utter weakness
    Life's task fulfil.

And that cloud itself, which now before thee
    Lies dark in view,
Shall with beams of light from the inner glory
    Be stricken through.
                                    WHITTIER.

JULY 30.

WHEN we look up on some starlit evening and see the broad heavens . . . fading away into the intense void of systems and galaxies; . . . or when again we look into the mighty microcosm of a single water-drop, and see how, invisible yet infinitely divisible, the realms of being stretch down fathomlessly beneath us . . . never to be measured by the coarse and feeble calculus of our imperfect minds, — would not such great realities as this, — showing to us that we are but atoms, lost imperceptibly between two inconceivable infinities, — . . . would not such dread realities bewilder us into utter madness?
. . . But what then? are we but waifs of wreck tossed aimlessly, accidentally, hopelessly, on the shoreless, immeasurable ocean of being? . . . Ah, no! . . . this Awful and Supreme Majesty, — this invisible, unsearchable, incorruptible Spirit, — this immortal, immutable, Almighty God, is our Father . . . a Father taking us as the eagle taketh her young upon her wings; and, though human love may be sometimes found divine in its pureness and its intensity, loving us . . . with a tenderness yet more delicate, a love yet more divine.

XI. 275.

Love is the root of Creation; God's essence; worlds
   without number
Lie in His bosom like children; He made them for
   this purpose only —
Only to love and be loved again.

LONGFELLOW.

JULY 31.

Because he hath set his love upon me therefore will I deliver him. — Ps. xci. 14.

HERCULES, in the legend, while yet an infant in the cradle, strangles the serpents sent to slay him. He of whom the grace of God has taken early hold, and who has had early strength to conquer temptation, is not likely, later on, to lose his self-reverence and self-control. If in the flush of youth he has sat at the feet of law, he will be little likely to revolt afterwards. And these were the truths which the Greeks succinctly expressed by representing their hero in the invulnerable skin of the lion he has slain. It is in youth, in early youth, that men can most effectually win their victory — while yet they are uncontaminated by a corrupt present, unhampered by an unfaithful past. . . .

Let me add at once that it is never too late to fight, never impossible to slay that lion of evil within you, and to tread the young lion and the dragon under foot. If the grace of God shows exquisitely as a vernal rose in some soul, pure from its youth upward, growing like the Lord Jesus in wisdom and stature and favor with God and man, that grace shows yet more mightily in the case of those who, having fallen — having, as it were, lain prostrate in the bloody dust — having felt the fierce teeth and the merciless claws — spring up again, gather fresh strength, turn defeat into resistance, and resistance into victory.

VIII. 52, 53.

AUGUST 1.

THE voice of nature is none other than the voice of God. Our Lord Himself tried to teach us that God, of whom we speak as so far and so silent, is very near, and is speaking to us all day long. The word is very nigh thee — even in thy mouth and in thy heart. We think ourselves very pious, if, with narrow literalism and stupid superstition, we profess to worship the words of holy books written hundreds of years ago, as though they were the only voice in which God ever had spoken or could speak to us; and these books we too often use to show the sins and heresies of our neighbors; and all the while we lose the whole significance of our Saviour's lessons from that other book of God whose secret lies ever open to the eyes which will read it. VIII. 5.

Nature, in all its fulness, is the Lord's.
There are no Gentile oaks, no Pagan pines;
The grass beneath our feet is Christian grass;
The wayside weed is sacred unto Him.
Have we not groaned together, herbs and men,
Struggling through stifling earth-weights unto light,
Earnestly longing to be clothed upon
With our high possibility of bloom?
And He, He is the light, He is the sun
That draws us out of darkness . . .
Yea, makes us stand on some consummate day
A-bloom in white transfiguration robes.
LUCY LARCOM.

AUGUST 2.

NOT by singing "Lord, Lord," but by doing the will of Christ, shall you enjoy a foretaste of heaven. . . . Your Sabbaths may be to you a crystal river of unreproved enjoyment; they *may* become turbid and wearisome, an unprofitable burden, an idle form. But, for the heart which is cleansed and calm, not these only but life itself becomes a Sabbath, whose inward rest no agitations can disturb; a Service which no weariness can invade; . . . a Temple of God, about which indeed the clouds may roll, but of which no clouds can quench the Light of that Presence which shines within. Only through that heart can you see God. "Through the glass darkly," it has been said, "but except through the glass in no wise." A tremulous crystal, waved as water, poured out upon the ground: . . . despise it, pollute it, at your peril: for on the peace of those weak waves must all the heaven you shall ever gain be first seen: and through such purity as you can win for those dark waves must all the light of the risen Sun of Righteousness be bent down by faint refraction.

XI. 153.

O my soul!
God's blessèd day has dawned; partake!
Anoint thy head with oil and wine;
From the great sum, the mighty whole,
Thy little crumb and portion break,
And, giving thanks, arise and shine!

SUSAN COOLIDGE.

AUGUST 3.

And as the path of duty is made plain,
May grace be given that I walk therein
Not like the hireling for his selfish gain,
. . . .
But cheerful, in the light around me thrown,
Walking as one to pleasant service led,—
Doing God's will as if it were my own.

WHITTIER.

IF we look to our Great Example we shall see that even He was forced to sigh for the sad world of sin and death; but notice that the sigh had scarcely been uttered when once more He was engaged in works of mercy and thoughtful care. To sigh is sometimes natural; but to waste time in sighing, to suffer ourselves to be wholly absorbed in the dark side of life, to exclude ourselves from its many and simple gladnesses, is unthankful and useless. . . . If we sigh for our own weaknesses and sins, we cannot indeed fly from ourselves, but we can by the grace of God amend ourselves. If we sigh for our surroundings, no wings of a dove indeed, can take us from these dwellings of Meshech, these tents of Kedar, but by God's grace we may help to make them better and happier places. For, after all, at all times of our pilgrimage—

"The primal duties shine aloft like stars,
And charities that soothe, and heal, and bless,
Lie scattered at the feet of man like flowers."

II. 143.

AUGUST 4.

Thou hast but this, to set thy feet where Mine
Make prints, step after step, a track for thine.
MARGARET E. SANGSTER.

THE kindly deeds of this life, of every life which has trodden in the warm footsteps of our Saviour through this world's dinted snow, have had their mainspring in that sympathy which was expressed by the sigh of Jesus. We cannot all do as He did in the brief years of His Ministry, — "*go about* doing good;" but we can all live as He lived for His first thirty years of quiet, holy, strenuous duty, deliberately striving each day to *be* good; deliberately striving each day to *do* good; deliberately striving each day to abstain from evil, in order, so far as in us lies, in His name, and for His sake, to assuage the sorrows of the world.
II. 33.

So, when my Saviour calls, I rise,
  And calmly do my best;
Leaving to Him, with silent eyes
  Of hope and fear, the rest.

I step, I mount, where He has led; —
  Men count my haltings o'er; —
I know them; yet though self I dread,
  I love His precept more.
JOHN HENRY NEWMAN.

AUGUST 5.

Wash you, make you clean; put away the evil of your doings from before mine eyes. — Is. i. 16.

WE walk in a muddy world, and Satan will not suffer even the saints of God to reach heaven with stainless feet; but as the feet, even of apostles, must be washed before they could sit at the Supper of the Lord, so must every stain be constantly washed from our souls before we are in any way fit to come into the presence of God. . . . If we do not seek this constant repentance, this constant purification, if, habitually, even in what we dare to think light things, we go wrong, and make no use of God's appointed means of grace to get rid of these daily sins, how vast, how terrible in their aggregate do they become! Walk into the forest and learn this lesson from the falling autumn leaves. Dead leaves fall one by one: how small, how light a thing is a dead leaf. But when they lie together in putrescent multitudes, how dense, how miry do the forest paths become! . . . "If thou fearest not when thou weighest them," says St. Augustine, "at least fear them when thou numberest them!"
VI. 250.

> "Then, gracious Lord, prepare
> Our souls for that dread day;
> Oh, wash us in Thy precious blood
> And take our sins away."

AUGUST 6.

Jesus . . . leadeth them up into a high mountain apart. — MARK ix. 2.

HE knelt and prayed, and as He prayed, He was elevated far above the toil and misery of the world which rejected Him. He was transfigured before them; His countenance shone as the sun, . . . and He was enwrapped in such an aureole of glistering brilliance . . . that the light, the snow, the lightning are the only things to which the Evangelist can compare that celestial lustre. And, lo! two figures were by His side. "When, in the desert, He was girding Himself for the work of life, angels of life came and ministered unto Him; now, in the fair world, when He is girding Himself for the work of death, the ministrants come to Him from the grave — but from the conquered grave." . . . And when the prayer is ended, the task accepted, then the full glory falls upon Him from Heaven.

XIII. 242.

And Peter . . . said to Jesus, Master, it is good for us to be here. — MARK ix. 5.

Fountain of Life, in Thee alone is Light!
  Shine through our being, cleansing us of sin,
Till we grow lucid with Thy presence bright,
  The peace of God within.

If in our thoughts, by Thee made calm and clear,
  The brightening image of Thy face we see,
What hour of all our lives can be so dear
  As this still hour with Thee!

LUCY LARCOM.

AUGUST 7.

ALL that is essential in St. Paul's theology — the very heart and centre of his system — may be summed up in two words. Those two words are "in Christ." They are the very monogram of St. Paul. He uses them again and again; they occur thirty-five times at least in his thirteen short Epistles. It is the characteristic which a modern poet has seen in him —

"Christ! I am Christ's, and let the name suffice you,
  Aye for me too He greatly hath sufficed:
Lo! with no winning words I would entice you;
  Paul has no honor, and no friend but Christ.
Yea! through life, death, through sorrow and through sinning,
  He shall suffice me, for He hath sufficed;
Christ is the end, for Christ was the beginning,
  Christ the beginning, for the end is Christ."

But you and I will never learn the meaning of those words till we live up to them; and perhaps you say at once, "How can I live up to them? how can I ever be in Christ? how am I to get, where am I to find, this spiritual, this supernatural life?" Do we then forget, after all these eighteen centuries, do we forget that we are Christians? We are not to get, not to find it at all. It is given us; if we have not forfeited it, we have it. We have it: not of ourselves, but it is the gift of God.

V. 296, 297.

AUGUST 8.

WE visit the scenes of the Saviour's earthly life: The fair world is unaltered; the sky is there, the hill is there, the lake is there, the flowers are there, the birds are there, and Hermon still upheaves his shining shoulder into the blue air, and the farther snows of Lebanon are still crimson with the setting sun; — but where is He? To many of you, my brethren, if you will confess the truth, has not that awful, that gracious figure of the Son of Man, seated upon the mountain slope, faded away into a sea of darkness? Does not His voice sound to you like the dim-remembered story out of half-legendary days?

Alas! my friends, and why is this? Why has Christ seemed to vanish so far away? Why to so many is He a dead Christ, not a living Christ? Is it not chiefly because the world is ever with us? because it has got thoroughly into our hearts?

VIII. 4.

"The sun, the moon, the stars, the seas, the hills and the plains,—
Are not these, O soul, the vision of Him who reigns?

. . . .

Speak to Him thou, for He hears, and spirit with spirit can meet;
Closer is He than breathing, and nearer than hands and feet.

And the ear of man cannot hear, and the eye of man cannot see;
But if we could see and hear, this vision — were it not He?"

TENNYSON.

AUGUST 9.

If thou hadst known, even thou, at least in this thy day, the things which belong unto thy peace! but now they are hid from thine eyes.

LUKE xix. 42.

THERE, before the Saviour's gaze, lay a city, splendid apparently and in peace, and destined to enjoy another half century of existence. . . . The leaf of her national life was still glossy-green; the sun still shone on her; the rain fell; the dew stole down; but the fruit would grow on her no more, and therefore the fire was kindled for the burning. She was not spared for her beauty; she was not forgiven for her fame. And if it were so with the favored city, may it not be so with thee, and thee, and me? — . . . Yes, the lesson of the tears of Jesus over Jerusalem, as she gleamed before Him in the vernal sunshine, a gem upon her crown of hills, is this: . . . that, as for her, so for us, there may be a too-late; the door may be shut without a sound; life may be over before death comes. It is not — (oh, mark this!) — it is not that God loses His mercy, but that we lose our capacity for accepting it: it is not that God hath turned away from us, but that we have utterly paralyzed our own power of turning back to Him.

X. 216.

AUGUST 10.

If thou wilt enter into life, keep the commandments. — MATT. xix. 17.

AMID the minutiæ of controversial theology; amid the multiplication of ceremonies, rites, and forms; . . . amid the ambitious self-assertion of parties, their intrigues, their jealousies, their struggles, their ignoble warfare — it is most desirable . . . that all of us alike should constantly look back to the simplest and most primary elements of the revealed will of God. . . . Man cannot soar to the blue sky or storm heaven with angels' wings. Slowly and toilfully, and step by step, must he mount, as on a ladder, above his earthly and sensual tendencies, and never can he venture to scorn the low degrees by which he did ascend. Now the lowest step of the religious life is obedience to the moral law, and our time can never be lost when we are gazing at large duties based upon infinite, eternal sanctions. The plain Ten Commandments are to our Christian life as the primitive granite on which the world is built. VII. 110, 111.

> The rules to men made evident
> By Him who built the day;
> The columns of the firmament
> Not firmer based than they.
>
> EMERSON.

AUGUST 11.

IT is not without significance that week by week we stand at the holy table in our churches, and read the Ten Commandments, and usher them in with the mighty overture, "GOD SPAKE THESE WORDS AND SAID." . . . Whether the desert trembled and Sinai blazed or not, the great law of God, as expressed in those Ten Commandments, has to thee and me a sanction infinitely more transcendent, an origin indisputably more divine. That sanction is not derived from the mere historic record of the belief that more than thirty centuries ago a nation of slaves and fugitives heard a great Voice in the air which has been heard no more. . . . We do believe that by some mighty revelation which came to them as intensely as from the infolding flame, those commandments were stamped upon the heart of Israel; but if we believe that "God spake these words and said," it is mainly because we also believe (and would that we could put that utterance in the thunder's mouth!) that here and now, . . . to every heart, whether innocent or guilty, to every conscience, whether slumbering or awakened, to every intellect, whether humble or defiant, God *speaks* these words and *says*. III. 39. 43.

AUGUST 12.

Thou shalt have none other Gods before Me. — EXOD. xx. 3.

THERE is a . . . nominal belief which is practical atheism. There is the belief of rebellion, which defies God. There is the belief of worldliness, which ignores God. There is . . . "a practical atheism, orthodox in language and reverent in bearing, which can enter a Christian church, and charm the conscience to rest with shadowy traditions." Our danger is, not to worship other gods, and so to break this first commandment, but rather to have no God, like those Israelites of whom God said, "This people draweth nigh unto Me with their mouth, and honoreth Me with their lips, but their heart is far from Me."

But, in reality, to have no God, is, in one form or another, to worship other gods. . . . In the hearts of thousands greed and gold and custom and selfishness are gods; . . . and we have not learnt the meaning of either the first or the second commandment: "Thou shalt love the Lord thy God with all thy heart, and thy neighbor as thyself."   III. 98, 105.

From worshipping and serving the creature more than the Creator; from striving to serve two masters; Deliver us, Lord Jesus.

CHRISTINA ROSSETTI.

Thou shalt not make unto thee any graven image. — Exod. xx. 4.

THE first commandment bids us worship the one God exclusively, the second bids us to worship Him spiritually. The first commandment forbids us to worship false gods; the second forbids us to worship the true God under false forms. . . . We cannot have a visible God; or a God materialized under any outward form whatever. . . . The kingdom of Heaven is within you. God dwells unseen in the holy heart. He cannot be seen, tasted, or held in the hollow of the hand. . . . His presence is not a material, it is a spiritual presence.

Seek for God in Christ; . . . seek Him in His own word; seek Him in loving lives; seek Him in sincere hearts; . . . seek Him in the revelation of Himself which He gives to all who, by walking in His ways, see His face, and have His name written on their foreheads; and so will you be able to keep that admonition of the last word of all the New Testament revelation, "Little children, keep yourselves from idols."   III. 113, 118, 128.

Cease to seek for many, unite thyself to the One;
Cling to the One, for in the One all things consist. . . .
Let others seek the many and various things without;
Do thou seek the one inward Good, and it is sufficient.
      THOMAS À KEMPIS.

AUGUST 14.

Thou shalt not take the name of the Lord thy God in vain. — EXOD. xx. 7.

THE Lord Jesus taught His disciples to pray, "Hallowed be Thy name." In that name lay the essence of the Gospel. It was the name of the Father, of whom every fatherhood in the Heaven and the earth is named. . . . If we are rather dishallowing His name, hindering the spread of His kingdom, . . . are we not at once convicted of taking His name in vain ? . . . Let us search ourselves with candles, and see whether, amid all our self-satisfaction, our own lives are not falling short. . . . If by profanity, falsity, malice, sloth, self-indulgence, lust, wordliness, greed, or merely nominal profession, we, in our whole lives, have hitherto been taking God's name in vain, . . . let us grasp the proffered hand of Christ, our sinless Elder Brother in the great sinful family, and suffer Him to lead us, as weeping prodigals, to the Father, who will receive us graciously, who will forgive us freely.

III. 136, 144, 145.

Blessed be the Name of the Lord
From this time forth for evermore.
From the rising of the sun unto the going down of the same
The Lord's Name is to be praised:
The Lord is high above all nations,
And His glory above the heavens. . . .
Praise ye the Lord !

Ps. 113, 2, 3, 4.

AUGUST 15.

Remember the Sabbath day, to keep it holy.
EXOD. xx. 8.

"THERE are," it has been truly said, "three things to which man is born: labor, and sorrow, and joy. . . . Nor can any life be right that has not all three." . . . Now you will observe that the fourth commandment is a twofold commandment of labor and of rest, and was also meant to give us joy in both. There is nothing limited, nothing Judaic here. It is a command for the whole race of man. "Six days shalt thou labor;" but that the labor may not be degradingly and exhaustingly wearisome; that the man may not become a mere machine, "worn out by the dust of its own grinding;" that the thread of sorrow, which runs through all labor, may never wholly blacken into despair; that the thread of joy, thinly and rarely intertwined with it, may be brightened into spiritual intensity and permanence — therefore, "the seventh day is the Sabbath of the Lord thy God; in it thou shalt do no manner of work."

III. 151.

To rest from weary work one day in seven;
  One day to turn our backs upon the world,
  Its soil wash from us, and strive on to Heaven,—
  Whereto we daily climb, but quick are hurled
Down to the deep of human pride and sin.
  Help me, ye powers celestial! to come nigh;
  Ah, let me catch one little glimpse within
The Heavenly City, lest my spirit die.

RICHARD WATSON GILDER.

AUGUST 16.

Honor thy father and thy mother. — Exod. xx. 12.

THE fifth commandment applies to every one of us, whether our parents be living or dead. It is the sanctification of all social life. It involves for each one of us the enforcement of the truth that man is not meant to live alone, but in families and communities. It is the corrective of each man's insolent tendency to make himself, regardless of all others, the centre of the universe. It is the surest basis of all righteous government. . . . "The cornerstone of the commonwealth is the hearthstone." The nation which produces bad sons will assuredly not have good citizens. . . . Obedient sons make unflinching patriots; and it was because honor to parents means honor to our country's cause, that those three hundred Spartans stood against the vast hosts of the Persians at Thermopylæ.

Oh, may it never be your lot to cry with the poet to some dead father or mother:

"Ah! would that I could see thee in thy heaven
For one brief hour, and know I was forgiven!"

God's prodigals — prodigals to that Heavenly Father to whom His Son on earth gave such loving and awful obedience — God's prodigals are we all! . . . Deep need there is for every one of us to say, "I will arise, and go to my Father, and say unto Him: Father, I have sinned . . . and am no more worthy to be called Thy son."

III. 172, 182, 187.

AUGUST 17.

Thou shalt not kill. — Exod. xx. 13.

CHRIST warned us that the sixth commandment touches many a highly respectable person, who hardly thinks that a murderer is of the same flesh and blood with himself. . . . "I say unto you, that whosoever is angry with his brother is in danger of the judgment." . . . Into what an abyss of crime has base anger hurried many a miserable man! How often has a life been poisoned by one angry letter, and the wedded calm and golden peace of homes shattered by one hasty word! . . . But there may be murderers in other ways. . . . To put stumbling blocks in the way of innocence; to tempt the weak into the paths of vice; . . . to destroy the souls for whom Christ died — these are the deadliest sins which man can commit. . . . Again, all selfish, all oppressive trade is murder in God's sight; . . . and all who, loving gold more than God, have any share in thus destroying the lives and souls of their brethren . . . shall stand at the last day as murderers before the awful eyes of Him who sees the things that are, and sees them as they are. . . . There is even a sort of murder in cold indifference and callousness to human misery.

Ah, my brethren, is not this commandment "exceeding broad"? But . . . in keeping of it there is great reward. We cannot obey even this one law in its fulness without gaining Christ's peace in our hearts. May Almighty God give us grace to read our lives by the light of it!

III. 202, 207, 210.

AUGUST 18.

Thou shalt not commit adultery. — EXOD. xx. 14.

"CHASTITY is a delicate, tender grace, and can scarcely endure the naming of itself, far less of that which is contrary to it." . . . To sensual sin the Scripture warning applies especially: "Avoid it; pass not by it; turn from it, and pass away." . . . As the prophets and apostles alike tell us, impurity takes away the understanding; darkens it; brings upon it a penal blindness. . . . It is a sin against mankind, for it adds virulence to man's heaviest curse, and undoes the influence of his purest sympathies. It is a sin against the commonwealth, for uncleanness has ever been the deadliest canker-worm at the root of kingdoms. It is a sin against the family, for it undermines the holy bases on which it rests. . . . It is a sin against God and His image upon us; . . . it is a sin against Christ and His members — against the Holy Spirit and His indwelling presence. It is the worst form of sacrilege, because it defiles the temple of the Most High.

Blessed are the pure in heart, for they shall see God! Lord, grant to us, Thy children, this Thy most divine beatitude, that following Thee with pure hearts and minds, we may see Thy face and Thy name be written on our foreheads.

III. 213, 223, 231.

> Thou judgest us; Thy purity
> Doth all our lusts condemn;
> The love that draws us nearer Thee
> Is hot with wrath to them.
>
> WHITTIER.

AUGUST 19.

Thou shalt not steal. — EXOD. xx. 15.

ALAS! the very meaning of the word honesty has been degraded. It now means doing nothing which is technically illegal; but once it meant the honor, the nobleness which preferred equity to self-interest, and would rather suffer from guileless simplicity than profit by the mean cleverness which takes advantage of the ignorance of others. When St. Paul said, "Provide things honest in the sight of all men," he did not mean merely that his converts were not to be thieves or cheats. The Greek word, καλὸς, which he uses, implies all moral beauty, all spiritual nobleness. The καλὸς κἀγαθὸς in Greek meant a man as he should be, a perfect man and an upright. . . . The negative abstention from acts of wrongdoing, and the hard legal performance of right acts, are of very little value apart from a noble motive. The general truths to which the eighth commandment leads us affect our whole life. . . . It disavows all base acquisition and all unhallowed ownership. It condemns the idler, . . . the spendthrift, and the prodigal.

The lesson of the eighth commandment is the lesson of Christ, "Set your affections on things above." III. 235, 250, 253.

> Man is his own star, and that soul that can
> Be honest is the only perfect man.
> FLETCHER.

AUGUST 20.

Thou shalt not bear false witness against thy neighbor. — EXOD. xx. 16.

CHARITY is the one sovereign remedy and antidote for this heinous transgression of injuring our neighbors with false tongues. If you would see detraction in all its leprous ugliness, contrast it with the sovereign beauty, the heavenly lustre of charity as St. Paul depicts it to the Corinthians. Look on that picture — so soft, so radiant, so angelically winning, so bathed in airs of Heaven, so full of enchanting colors; and then look at this picture of calumny, so foul and noisome, so weltering with the venom of every base passion; so lurid with the light of hell, which speaks and can speak no language but that of the devil, whose very name means the slanderer. Consider those two pictures; and lest you sink into this devilish spirit, . . . lay aside all malice, guile, hypocrisy, and all evil speaking.

We should all perhaps feel a sense of deeper responsibility if we bore in mind our Lord's warning, "By thy words thou shalt be justified, and by thy words thou shalt be condemned."
III. 273, 270.

Is it worth while to jostle a brother,
  Bearing his load on the rough road of life?
Is it worth while that we jeer at each other,
  In blackness of heart that we war to the knife?
God pity us all in our pitiful strife!
JOAQUIN MILLER.

AUGUST 21.

Thou shalt not covet. — EXOD. xx. 17.

HUMAN laws can only prohibit those crimes of which human eyes can take cognizance; the thoughts of men are beyond their reach. . . . The command which prohibits not only commission but concupiscence, can be uttered by God alone. . . . It is a commandment preëminently spiritual. . . . It reveals to us, as with a flash out of eternity, where and how the one work of our life has to be done. It says to us, as the prophet said to Jerusalem, "O Jerusalem, wash thine heart from wickedness, that thou mayest be saved."

Perhaps you think, What harm can a mere desire do? What wrong can there be in an airy nothing, an impalpable thought? . . . First, that airy nothing, that impalpable desire, as you call it, is, with God, a real thing. It is seen in Heaven; it is heard in Heaven; in Heaven it needs forgiveness. And, secondly, that thought will be, if dwelt upon, the prolific mother of all sins — it is the cockatrice's egg from which breaks forth the fiery flying serpent. . . . He who would win the easiest, the happiest, and the securest victory, must win it in the thoughts of the heart. III. 277, 279, 281.

> True dignity abides with him alone
> Who, in the silent hour of inward thought,
> Can still suspect, and still revere himself
> In lowliness of heart.
> WORDSWORTH.

AUGUST 22.

Thou shalt NOT. — Exod. xx. 4.

THAT "not" should remind us that we are warned against sin by the terrible voice of God's most just judgment. . . . That "everlasting No" of God should be to us as the flaming sword of a cherub, to keep us from the tree of the knowledge of good and evil. It should be a ray out of eternity to disenchant our earthly senses from the foul glamour of the world, the flesh, and the devil. But, if there be this significance of warning in the "NOT," is there no significance of blessing and helpfulness, as well as of warning, in the "THOU"?

It was in the Gospel that men first learned to realize the grandeur and preciousness of the individual soul; it was the Gospel which took the brief beatings of the heart and added to them infinitude. Yet even at Sinai men were taught that, in the ultimate deeps of personality, there remain "but two certain and self-luminous entities" — the soul and God. . . . If the "Thou" thus spoken may well terrify the sinner, it may also well inspire the saint. . . . The "Thou" of God has in it the accent, not of wrath — for His prohibitions are in mercy, not in menace — but of a Father's love.

III. 299, 300, 306.

I who saw power, see love now perfect too.
Perfect I call Thy plan:
Thanks that I was a man!
Maker, remake, complete, — I trust what Thou shalt do!
BROWNING.

AUGUST 23.

And looking up to heaven, He sighed, and saith unto him, Ephphatha! that is, "Be opened." — MARK vii. 34.

Who went about doing good. — ACTS x. 38.

OUR strength must fail. Our youth must vanish like the morning dew. Our joys must make themselves wings and fly away. Our intellect must grow feebler, our mortal powers decay, our dearest die. "To each his suffering; all are men condemned alike to groan." But what is the lesson? *Not* unmanly complaining; *not* idle speculation; *not* the selfish attempt to secure ourselves alone; — No! but help; no! but sympathy. Not ignorant of misery, we learn, or ought to learn, to help the miserable. Our Lord looked up to Heaven indeed and sighed, because He was a High Priest who can be touched with the feeling of our infirmities; but the sorrow which wrung that sigh from Him did but make Him more earnest day by day in doing good. . . . His was no feeble sympathy, but an active ministration.

What a divine example, what a stimulus, what an encouragement, have we here! Our Lord saw all the sorrow; He did not ignore it; He sighed for it; He wept for it; He prayed for it; — but not for one moment did He despair of it; — nay, He worked to lighten it, leaving us thereby, as in all things, an ensample that we should follow His steps. II. 29.

AUGUST 24.

Blameless and harmless, the sons of God, without rebuke. — PHIL. ii. 15.

WE read of many of these high saints . . . nor have only read of them: we have known them, we have loved them, we have seen their faces, and not in dreams; our souls have been refreshed by their unselfish sorrow, their unaffected delicacy, their spontaneous charity, their ingenuous self-reproach. Cedars were they in God's fair garden — constellations in the firmament of Christian nobleness. Clean hands had they and pure hearts; and they spake the truth, and did the thing that was right, and never slandered, and did not think much of themselves, but were lowly in their own eyes; and therefore they did not fall. . . . And when, from this low smoke and stir, and contact with so much that is mean and vile, we raise our eyes to the sunlit heights whereon they sit in their "solemn choirs and sweet societies," is there any but the very deadest heart which feels no more beauty in the picture, "Blameless and harmless, the sons of God, without rebuke"? — no more force in the encouragement, "Oh, serve the Lord in the beauty of holiness"?

VI. 321, 322.

Lord, bring me low,
For Thou wert lowly in Thy blessed heart:
Lord, keep me so!
CHRISTINA ROSSETTI.

OF all the glorious aspects of that holy faith which we profess — of all those points of spiritual elevation and moral beauty which, to the world's end, shall give it such infinite charm for every generous and unselfish soul — there is none more noticeable than the fact that it allied itself with the world's feebleness, not its strength. It was with "the irresistible might of weakness" that it shook the nations. Herod sat in his golden palace at Tiberias in dissolute splendor; . . . the Pharisees swept through the Temple courts . . . in all the haughtiness of a sacerdotal clique; and for them Christ had no words but . . . the scathing flame of His indignation and rebuke. . . . For pride, for cruelty, for scornful laughter, for insolent lust, He had nothing but thunder; but for all that suffers, for all that is humble . . . faithful . . . oppressed, He had an infinite, unfathomable, all-embracing love. . . . He loved the poor: He loved the sick: He loved the ignorant: He loved children: He loved sinners; and among sinners, He, the friend of sinners, loved most those who had suffered most.
VI. 61.

>Who hath trod the ways of pain
>Hath not met Him in the gloom,
>Coming swiftly through the rain?
>Hath not prayed to see Him come?
>Many a weary head hath lain
>On His breast and found it home.
>
> KATHERINE TYNAN HINKSON.

AUGUST 26.

Then they that feared the Lord spake often to one another: and the Lord hearkened, and heard it, and a book of remembrance was written before Him for them that feared the Lord and thought upon His name. — MAL. iii. 16.

AND is there no other book of remembrance, a book of remembrance which must also be a book of condemnation? Do you think that those who have willingly defied God's laws, even if they die splendid and prosperous in the scarlet fruitage of their sins, do you think that they have escaped the Divine justice? Ah, no; there is many a word of thine written on those awful pages, and by thy words thou shalt be justified, and by thy words thou shalt be condemned.

"Words, words, words," it has been exclaimed, "good and bad, loud and soft, millions in the hour, innumerable in the day, unimaginable in the year: — what then in the life? What in the history of a nation? What in that of the world? And not one of them is ever forgotten. There is a book where they are all set down." Oh, let the thought add dignity, add solemnity, add truthfulness, add absolute and perfect purity, add sacred and illimitable charity to all we say!   VI. 32.

Govern the lips
As they were palace-doors, the King within:
Tranquil and fair and courteous be all words
Which from that presence win.

SIR EDWIN ARNOLD.

AUGUST 27.

LET us take for our brief meditation the glory and the blessing of little faithfulnesses. . . . We praise the high, the splendid, the heroic: we dwell on the great deeds—on the glorious sacrifices. When you read how the lady of the house of Douglas thrust her own arm through the bolt grooves of the door and let the murderers break it while her king had time to hide; or how the pilot of Lake Erie stood undaunted upon the burning deck, and, reckless of the intense agony, steered the crew safe to the jetty, and then fell dead among the crackling flames; . . . whose soul is so leaden that it does not thrill with admiration at deeds like these? But think you, that these brave men and women sprang, as it were, full-sized into their heroic stature? Nay; but, like the gorgeous blossom of the aloe, elaborated through long years of silent and unnoticed growth, so these deeds were but the bright consummate flower borne by lives of quiet, faithful, unrecorded service; and no one, be sure, has ever greatly done or gloriously dared who has not been familiar with the grand unselfishness of little duties. VI. 13.

> We build the ladder by which we rise
> From the lowly earth to the vaulted skies,
> And we mount to its summit round by round.
>
> J. G. HOLLAND.

AUGUST 28.

LITTLE faithfulnesses are not only the *preparation* for great ones, but little faithfulnesses are in themselves the great ones. Observe the striking fact that our Lord does not say, "He that is faithful in that which is least *will be* faithful also in much," but "He that is faithful in that which is least *is* faithful also in much." The essential fidelity of the heart is the same whether it be exercised in two mites or in a regal treasury; the genuine faithfulness of the life is equally beautiful whether it be displayed in governing an empire or in writing an exercise. It has been quaintly said that if God were to send two angels to earth, the one to occupy a throne, and the other to clean a road, they would each regard their employments as equally distinguished and equally happy. In the poem of *Theocrite*, the Archangel Gabriel takes the poor boy's place: —

> "Then to his poor trade he turned,
> By which the daily bread was earned;
>
> And ever o'er the trade he bent,
> And ever lived on earth content;
>
> He did God's will: to him all one
> If on the earth, or in the sun."

VI. 16.

AUGUST 29.

My God, wilt Thou accept, and will not we
    Give aught to Thee?
The kept we lose, the offered we retain,
    Or find again.
Christina Rossetti.

WE are often doubtless exhorted to Christian liberality. Yet when we notice the urgency with which St. Paul in letter after letter pleads for the poor saints at Jerusalem, we may well doubt whether this great duty is pressed home to us so plainly, so fearlessly, and so decisively as is desirable. Out of the circle of our own immediate families, beyond the edge of what may be called a somewhat selfish domesticity, over the verge of the slightly expanded egotism of the private home, how many of us do anything appreciable to alleviate the distresses, to lessen the misery, to heal the open sores of the world, to visit Christ in His sickness, to relieve Christ in His hunger, to comfort Him in His imprisonment, or clothe Him in His nakedness? And if this be so, if it be not ours to visit the fatherless and widows in their affliction, or to discharge in person the high duties of Christian charity, we can only fulfil these duties at all by generous giving. I. 302.

Whoso hath this world's goods, and seeth his brother have need, and shutteth up his bowels of compassion from him, how dwelleth the love of God in him? — I. John iii. 17.

AUGUST 30.

> "Daily with souls that cringe and plot
> We Sinais climb and know it not;
> Over our manhood bend the skies;
> Against our fallen and traitor lives
> The great winds utter prophecies;
> With our faint hearts the mountain strives."

AND when this has indeed been brought home to us, when the law, which is the will of God, has also become the mirror of ourselves, and we see the unfathomable gulf which yawns between a God of infinite holiness and a heart of desperate corruption, then cometh the midnight. But after that midnight, to the faithful soul there shall be light. With the personal conviction that the law worketh wrath, comes also the personal experience that Christ hath delivered us from the curse. . . . We are guilty, and He offers us a free forgiveness; we are weary, and He bids us come to Him for rest; we are helpless, and He sends the Strengthener to "turn our rout into resistance, and our resistance into victory." And thus by love, and gratitude, and hope, and help He gives us a new impulse, a new inspiration — and this is Christianity; and this Christianity has ennobled, has regenerated the world. To them who receive it in the heart, to them fear is abolished, and

> "Love is an unerring light,
> And joy its own security."

And then for us the law has done its work, . . . it has driven us to Christ.

III. 49.

AUGUST 31.

ARE you even trying to save your own soul, or are you drowning it in the mud of pleasure and the siftings of gold? And ah! if you *are* trying to save your own soul, does it content you to save it alone? Is the whole world of "men, your brothers," nothing to you? does the sigh of Jesus wake no echo in your heart? Are you content to clutch for your bare self one plank amid the fiery deluge of universal ruin? Do you think that selfishness for Time is a sin, but that if it be spun out to Eternity it is a Celestial Prudence? Or will you rather cry: O Lord, let me not live in vain! let me not live only for my own miserable, shivering, hungry self! Thou hast work to do, oh let me do it! Lord! what wouldst Thou have me to do?
II. 89.

. . . I make with one of old
This fervent prayer: Do Thou enlarge my coast
And o'er it rule Thyself! Where Thou art most
    Beloved is room for all! The heart grows wide
That holdeth Thee!—a heaven where none doth press
Upon the other; none of more or less
Doth ask solicitous; for ever there
Is bread enough, and fulness still to spare;
    And none that come depart unsatisfied.
DORA GREENWELL.

SEPTEMBER 1.

Thou art not far from the kingdom of God.
MARK xii. 34.

TO such a nature as that of the Scribe — a nature not ungenerous, if very faulty, . . . how precious, how healing, would these words have been. Oh! let us not be all so afraid of words of hearty encouragement and honest praise. They reinspire the failing effort; they fall like the dew of heaven upon the fainting soul. The sunbeam touches the mountain, and at its touch the heavy load of winter which the hurricane could not dislodge melts and slips insensibly away, and where but yesterday was snow, to-day is green grass and gentian flower. It is even so with words of sympathy, which are so rare, alas! while they can cheer or bless, but which only, when they are useless, fall thick as a dust over the buried dust. . . . It is something to abstain from slander, and censoriousness, and the hard luxury of injustice; something to be like that good man who passed everything which he had to say of others through the three sieves: Is it just? Is it necessary? Is it kind? But it is more to be like Christ, to be generous and cordial, to have "the glow of sympathy" with "the bloom of modesty;" not to be too vain to appreciate; not to be too envious to help and cheer. VI. 267.

> Should a brother workman dear
> Falter for a word of cheer?
> > I. H. BROWN.

SEPTEMBER 2.

IT is a solemn thought that a man may perform his duties, and yet not be a holy man; he may be apparently upright, not really innocent; outwardly conscientious, not inwardly sincere. It is one thing to be "not far from the kingdom of God," another to be a member thereof; one thing to be near the gate of heaven, another thing to be therein. I do not mean that men are open and conscious hypocrites. These, I believe, are very rare. But it is mostly some cherished idol, some wilful reservation, some favorite temptation, in a word, some besetting sin, that makes men fall short of that truth in the inward parts which God requires, and which, to those who seek for it and love it, He will give For God says— tenderly indeed, yet absolutely—"My son, give Me thine heart." He says, "Be ye holy, for I am holy." He forbids us, not only to seek our own pleasure, or do our own ways, but even to think our own thoughts; He requires not only duty, but holiness; He searcheth the spirits; He discerneth the very reins and hearts.

VI. 7.

From cleaving to anything apart from Thee; from loving anything incompatible with Thee;
    Deliver us, Lord Jesus.
Until the day break and the shadows flee away; until we wake up in Thy likeness, and are satisfied therewith;
    Deliver us, Lord Jesus. Amen.

CHRISTINA ROSSETTI.

SEPTEMBER 3.

GOD is a God of laws, not of exceptions. God is a God of justice, not of favoritism. Whatever charge of folly may justly attach to the saying, "There is no God," that folly is prouder, deeper, and less pardonable which says God will deal differently with me than with others. Because you are you, because you fancy that your temptations have been exceptional, which is not true; because you think that your passions have been strong, which means only that your reason has been weak; because you think you have so many virtues, and amiable qualities; . . . shall God, because of this self-love, because of these filthy rags of your own righteousness, break, in your case, and yours alone, the adamantine rivet that links punishment to unrepented crime?

VIII. 177.

"She is fair as the earth after showers,
   When the Spring and the Summer first meet;
She is queen of all seasons and hours,
She is crowned with a crown of glad flowers,
   And princes have knelt at her feet.
     With tears and sharp anguish hereafter
       Shall my wine-press of anger be trod,
      When for glory she reaps scorn and laughter,
       Saith the Lord God."

SEPTEMBER 4.

Before I was afflicted I went astray, but now have I kept Thy word. — Ps. cxix. 67.

THE sorrows of life come to all, though they seem to come in very different measure; but the point for us to observe is how differently they affect the wise and the foolish. Some men murmur against God's dealings, and even against His just punishments; they resent His chastisements with an unsubmissive anger as mad as it is impotent. Others accept all God's dealings with them, knowing that what He doth is well. They accept them, it may be, with bowed head and weeping eyes, yet with the heart of a weaned child. To these the miseries which God sends come as a healing medicine: to the others they come as a maddening draught.

IX. 175.

> Bitter? Quaff and call it good!
> Though by thee not understood,
> 'Tis a tonic for thy blood.
>
> He who drinketh, looking up
> For a blessing on his cup,
> Doth with God and angels sup.
>
> EMILY E. BRADDOCK.

SEPTEMBER 5.

THAT must be a very dull heart, or a very sleepy conscience, or a very shallow experience, that finds no cause for sorrow in "thinking of the days that are no more." . . . Yet, if even the best man must feel sorrow and shame in remembering how little worthy his life has been, how far he has fallen short of his own ideal, how often he has swerved from the high laws of duty to God and charity to man, — if, I say, even the best man may feel sorrow, let not even the lowest feel despair. . . . It is Christ's own Voice which says to us, "Let the dead bury their dead, follow thou me." Let the time past of our lives suffice for folly and for sin. "Forgetting that which is behind," not indeed forgetting its mercies, for they may be remembered with eternal thankfulness, but forgetting its sinful allurements, because they have been displaced by nobler thoughts — forgetting its failures, because they may be still repaired — forgetting its guilt, because in Christ's blood it can be washed away — forgetting even its successes, because the goal of yesterday should be but our starting-point to-day.   VI. 55, 56.

The victory of to-day, that seems so passing bright,
Is but a hamlet rude where thou shalt rest to-night.
To-morrow up and on ! . . .
Thou hast done well thy part, if thou hast done thy best:
As sure as I am God, I answer for the rest.
JOHN W. CHADWICK.

SEPTEMBER 6.

> A day to seek
> Eternity in time; the steps by which
> We climb above all ages; lamps that light
> Man through his heap of dark days; and the rich
> And full redemption of the whole week's flight!
> HENRY VAUGHAN.

THE Christian Sunday, like the Jewish Sabbath, is God's gift to us of rest and joy. We need both. Blessed indeed is work; but blessed, too, is rest when work is done. God did not mean us to be drudges, to spend all our lives in grim, sordid, worldly toil.

But if Sunday is to be a day of rest, . . . it must be a holy, not an ignoble rest. . . . Let not ours be the Puritanic Sunday of gloomy strictness, for God meant us to be glad sons, not groaning slaves; nor the Parisian Sunday of frivolous pleasure-seeking, for we are children of immortality, not butterflies of a summer season; nor yet the Pharisaical Sunday of petty rules and restrictions, for God bids us stand fast in the liberty wherewith He has made us free. He who has felt that the consecration of the Sabbath is not a bondage, but a beatitude, will hardly worry himself with little shivering scrupulosities and abject alarms, asking, May I do this? ought I not to do that?

Bishop Hackett was contented with the wise, beautiful, manly rule: "Serve God, and be cheerful."
III. 155, 157.

SEPTEMBER 7.

Know ye not that they which run in a race, run all, but one receiveth the prize? — I. COR. ix. 24.

IT is so, alas! in most of earth's too numerous competitions; the success of one means the failure of many; and men, it has been said, grow by degrees each to deem himself "as only one among the myriad of horses set to drag on the chariot of Time — to deem that his only pleasure is to snatch what provender he can as he rushes along the way — that his only glory is to surpass his yoke-fellows in speed — and that, anon, when his strength fails, the chariot will pass over him, and millions of hoofs will trample him to dust." But, thank God! so it is not in our heavenly race. . . . None who enter that race are defeated; no rivalries can enter into it; no failure embitter. Like the sweet air, like the summer sunshine, the glories and rewards of it may be enjoyed to the very full by all who truly seek them: . . . and so far from envy at what this man is famed for, or for what another is preferred — the individual happiness is so thoroughly the general happiness — that, like the common light reflected from within a globe of crystal, the radiances of each pure spirit are but multiplied and made intense by myriads of reflections. Run only in the Christian race, and the prize is yours.

VI. 278.

SEPTEMBER 8.

Is not this the carpenter? — MARK vi. 3.

IN all ages there has been an exaggerated desire for wealth, . . . an exaggerated belief in its influence in producing or increasing the happiness of life; and from these errors a flood of cares and jealousies and meannesses have devastated the life of man. And therefore Jesus chose voluntarily the "low estate of the poor — not, indeed, an absorbing, degrading, grinding poverty, . . . but that commonest lot of honest poverty, which, though it necessitates self-denial, can provide with ease for the necessities of a simple life. . . . Again, there has ever been, in the unenlightened mind, . . . a desire to delegate labor to the lower and weaker, and to brand it with the stigma of inferiority and contempt. But our Lord wished to show that labor is a pure and noble thing; it is the salt of life; it is the girdle of manliness; it saves the body from effeminate languor, and the soul from polluting thoughts. And therefore Christ labored, working with His own hands.

XIII. 37.

A blessing now, a curse no more,
Since He, whose name we name with awe,
The coarse mechanic vesture wore, —
A poor man toiling with the poor,
In labor, as in prayer, fulfilling the same law.

WHITTIER.

SEPTEMBER 9.

BUT while you work, you must remember that you are not, or ought not, to be working for yourselves, or your own selfish interests alone, but also, and mainly, for the good of others. If all the law be summed up in those two commandments, "Thou shalt love the Lord God with all thy heart," and "Thou shalt love thy neighbor as thyself," then, assuredly, that work for others should begin here and now. We are not alone in this world. In communities like these it is emphatically true that no man liveth, no man dieth to himself. . . . [He] does, and must, and cannot help, in some way, and to some degree, influencing others. Not more surely does every word you speak make a tremulous ripple on the surrounding air than it makes a ripple in the hearts of those around: but with this difference, that, whereas the pulse of articulated air seems soon to die away, on the other hand —

> "*Our* echoes roll from soul to soul,
> And live for ever and for ever."
>
> X. 173.

— No stream from its source
Flows seaward, how lonely soever its course,
But what some land is gladdened. No star ever rose
And set, without influence somewhere. Who knows
What earth needs from earth's lowest creature? No life
Can be pure in its purpose and strong in its strife,
And all life not be purer and stronger thereby.

OWEN MEREDITH.

SEPTEMBER 10.

Redeeming the time. — Col. iv. 5.

CONSIDER that awful mystery of Time,— the Future not to be anticipated, the Past not to be recalled, only the Present ours; and that Present, what is it? An island ever encroached upon by the dark and swelling waves —a quicksand which ever swallows the place where last we trod—the flowing water of a river which is already far upon its way to the great sea. Even while we speak, it was and is not. For ever—never. It passes away with every ticking of the clock; with every beating of the heart; with every breath of articulated air. Yet how priceless! In it alone we live. With it alone can we purchase eternity. It perishes and is recorded.

VI. 125.

      Our part be, then,
Thee only to adore, true Infinite!
Thee only, true Eternal! Father, Son,
And Spirit ever-blest! And oh, vouchsafe
That here by Thine all-perfect ordinance
Established in this sublunary state,
We may so estimate and duly measure
Thy sacred gift of time, our golden treasure,
That every hour to Thy pure glory spending,
We may acquire in glory never ending
A life all time, all space, all measurement transcending!

EDWARD CASWALL.

SEPTEMBER 11.

> . . . "Every man God made
> Is different, has some work to do,
> Some deed to work: be undismayed;
> Though thine be humble, do it too."

ALL have something entrusted to their care; all, in that something, possess means whereby they may happily serve their God, and their brother here, and enter into His joy hereafter. Is not the lesson a lesson of hopefulness and comfort? Look up to the sky this evening, and you will see some stars preëminent in magnitude, while others, set in the galaxy, are lost in one white undistinguishable haze. Yet though, as the great apostle says, one star differeth from another star in glory, all are of the same pure essence, all of the same divine origin:

> "All are the undying offspring of one sire."

And, therefore, if — as is indeed the case —

> "If thou indeed derive thy light from heaven,"

then, whether it be the most immeasurable radiance or the tiniest and feeblest gleam, still

> "To the measure of that heaven-born light,
> Shine, Christian, in thy place and be content."

VI. 65.

SEPTEMBER 12.

"HE was born a man," said a French epitaph, "and died a grocer." In other words, he merged the sacredness of his manhood in the pursuits of his shop. His heart had been so ossified by the benumbing pursuits of his trade, that men had ceased to think of him as a man at all. . . . How many a business man, how many a clerk, spending day after day, year after year, at the same desk, over the same ledgers, at the same accounts, till the frame is bent and the brow wrinkled, runs the same risks! His soul is liable to be "subdued to what it works in, like the dyer's hand."

Now the weekly recurrent Sunday is the one thing which God designs "to keep us from being drawn into this great whirlpool of time and sense." It reminds us that behind . . . the toiler stands the *man* who is something transcendently greater, the man made in God's image, the heir of immortality. And by helping us always to remain conscious of this high nobleness, . . . Sunday lends its own eternal dignity even to the common routine. "He that brings much of the week with him into the Sabbath will have the sure Nemesis of taking little of the Sabbath back with him into the week."

III. 166.

SEPTEMBER 13.

Behold the fowls of the air, for they sow not, neither do they reap, . . . yet your Heavenly Father feedeth them. — MATT. vi. 26.

MIGHT not this exquisite illustration have furnished its own antidote against misrepresentation? God feedeth them; but do they do nothing for themselves? Why, the whole joy of the life of the birds of heaven is in its eager industry! Did Jesus then point to the birds of the air as if they set us an example of greedy dependence or lazy sloth? Nay, not so.
VIII. 11.

Lord, according to Thy words,
I have considered the birds;
And I find their life good,
And better the better understood: . . .
A hungry bird has a free mind;
He is hungry to-day, not to-morrow;
Steals no comfort, no grief doth borrow;
This moment is hid, Thy will hath said it,
The next is nothing till Thou hast made it. . . .
When cold and hunger and harm betide him,
He gathers them not to stuff inside him;
Content with the day's ill he hath got,
He waits just, nor haggles with his lot.

It cometh, therefore, to this, Lord;
I have considered Thy word,
And henceforth will be Thy bird.
GEORGE MACDONALD.

SEPTEMBER 14.

I bear in my body the marks of the Lord Jesus.
                                GAL. vi. 17.

WHEREVER there is any form of self-conquest, sternly achieved, for conscience' sake—there is one of the marks of Jesus. Is there one here, who, being naturally proud, has schooled himself to the sweet virtue of humility in love of Christ? Is there one here, who, having been prone to passion and sarcasm, has yet tutored his lips to gentleness and his heart to calm? Is there one who, being of a jealous and envious spirit, has grown to rejoice honestly at the success, not only of his rivals, but even of his inferiors? Is there one who, being full of earthly ambition, has learnt of Him who refused all the kingdoms of the world and the glory of them, that there is no noble ambition save that of eminently serving God? Is there one who, having been indolent and self-indulgent, has learnt "the dignity of work, the innocence of work, the holiness of work, the happiness of work," for God and man? . . . — then there — even if there have been no bitter sorrow, no rending conflict — there, even upon that soul, are marks — marks, however faint, of the Lord Jesus. . . .

Oh, let us strive with all our energy that, upon the souls of every one of us, we may bear the marks of the Lord Jesus, visible to His tenderness, however faint to the eye of man.

VII. 293.

SEPTEMBER 15.

ALL sins committed leave their own scar on earth, even after the wound is healed; but when, after prayer and penitence, sins have been forgiven through the atoning blood of Christ, then the very scars they leave are — as Bossuet said of the wounds of the immortal Condé — "Proofs of the protection of heaven." If we can take with us no saintly self-denials, no noble services, no rich spiritual gifts, when we stand before the judgment-seat of Christ, let us at least take the traces of wounds which His grace has closed : proofs of recovery ; scars touched into healing by His hand of love. It was for this — it was for the forgiveness of sins — that Christ died and rose again, and ever liveth to make intercession for us; and these, even these, shall be marks of the Lord Jesus in such as we.   VII. 296.

>Thine was the chastisement, with no release,
>>That mine might be the peace ;
>The bruising and the cruel stripes were Thine,
>>That healing might be mine ;
>Thine was the sentence and the condemnation,
>Mine the acquittal and the full salvation.
>>>FRANCES R. HAVERGAL.

SEPTEMBER 16.

But these things are written that ye may believe that Jesus is the Christ, the Son of God; and that believing ye may have life in His name.— JOHN xx. 31. (Revised Version.)

"JESUS." The name means Saviour. He was a Saviour *by teaching*. How could we live in these days without all those words of His which are spirit and which are life? Without those Beatitudes which divinely reversed all the world's estimates of what is good? Without that last High-priestly prayer, so "rarely mixed of sorrows and joys, and studded with mysteries as with emeralds"?

Jesus — He was the Saviour also *by self-sacrifice*, even unto death. Who else could have taught us the lesson — so hard, so very hard to learn — that we must bear our cross, that he who would save his life must be ready to lose it amid the hatred and falsehood of the world? V. 7, 8.

> Yes, for Thy sake, O God Most High,
> O Man Most Meek, we too can die:
> Die to the death which Thou hast slain,
> Die to the deepest source of pain,
> And walk, by Love's sustaining store,
> As seekers of our own no more.
>
> ANNA L. WARING.

SEPTEMBER 17.

As He hath chosen us in Him . . . that we should be holy and without blame before Him in love. — EPH. i. 4.

THE sorrows of the world are caused mainly by its sins; and in the warfare against those sins, the very first condition is sincerity and whole-heartedness in ourselves — the struggle at least after personal innocence and personal holiness. . . . For no mean benefactor of the world is he, who, even in the humblest and most private capacity, has been able to show — were it but by his obscure example in one quiet home — that his soul breathes a purer atmosphere than that which floats in the corrupted currents of the world.

II. 84.

>What life art thou living?
>   A life of giving —
> Not of mere golden store,
>   But more — much more?
> Is it a simple life,
>   Soft to the touch, —
> Not one of many words,
>   But of "love much"?
> Sounding an echo meek
>   (Heard through the strife —
> Trembling, indeed, and weak)
>   Of the Great Life?
> If so, thy Life may be
>   Humble, unknown:
> Yet it is leading thee
>   Up to a throne.
>
> ANNA E. HAMILTON.

SEPTEMBER 18.

The kingdom of heaven is like to a grain of mustard seed, . . . which is indeed the least of all seeds; but when it is grown, it is the greatest of herbs, . . . so that the birds of the air come and lodge in the branches thereof. — MATT. xiii. 31, 32.

IF you would test whether, even but as a grain of mustard seed, the kingdom of God is within you, you may do so decisively by telling whether you feel a deepening dislike for . . . the sin which most easily besetteth you. If you hate the sin less than you did when you were first tempted, . . . then look to it, for evil is before you. He who says I will struggle against sin hereafter, instead of saying I will struggle with it now; he who is content to fight with it in *fancy* " in the green avenues of the future," not in *fact* in the hot plains of to-day — will proceed to make excuses for it, will come at last not even to feel its horror. To put off repentance is to court ruin; to postpone the season is to perpetuate the sin. Even to hesitate is to yield; even to deliberate is to be lost.

VI. 86.

> To-morrow, and to-morrow, and to-morrow
> Creeps in this petty pace from day to day
> To the last syllable of recorded time;
> And all our yesterdays have lighted fools
> The way to dusty death.
> SHAKESPEARE

OUT of the darkness, out of the great deep we all came; into the darkness, into the great deep we all are going. . . . No gleam comes, no whisper thrills from the other side of that curtain, "impenetrable as midnight, yet thin as a spider's thread," through which we all must shortly pass. Only two or three broad elementary facts are clear to us—that God made us; that our bodies are not ourselves; that when we die we do not die; that our well-being, here and hereafter, depends only on obeying the will of God; that all else is, in comparison, less than nothing. The bridge of three-score and ten arches, and one or two broken ones beyond it, with a black cloud at either end of it, and many trap-doors through which multitudes are dropping every moment into the rolling waters of that prodigious tide— yes, that remains a most true picture of human life!

And should we not expect that men would at least be serious in this short journey, and do justly, and love mercy, and walk humbly with their God? We live for a moment; we shall live for ever and ever. Yet how are we occupying ourselves? Multitudes of us in chasing bubbles.

"Things needful we have thought on; but the thing
Of all most needful — that which Scripture terms,
As if alone it merited regard,
The one thing needful — that's yet unconsidered."

IV. 243.

SEPTEMBER 20.

I desire that ye faint not at my tribulations for you, which is your glory. — EPH. iii. 13.

[ST. PAUL'S] gallant spirit could transmute even its trials into gold, as the sunbeams fire the sullen pines. Is he chained to a Roman soldier? — the sword and the breastplate and the helm inspire him with the immortal imagery of the armor of righteousness; does he hear the rattle of chariots in the shouting course? in his wretched prison, a weary and decrepit prisoner, awaiting his doom of death, he yet remembers that he too is running a mighty race, at which the angels are spectators, and the Agonothetes is God, and in that glorious contest for a crown of amaranth he hangs over his winged and immortal steeds. Be it so with us! Life is but one passing "now," until with one last "*now!*" like a clap of thunder, the hour of judgment comes. And, therefore, oh, give the present moment wholly, heartily to your Father in Heaven, now, and at yonder holy table, offering yourselves, your souls, and bodies, a reasonable lively sacrifice, — now, in silent prayer consecrating your hearts to God. Oh, buy your eternity with this little hour. *Ex hoc momento,* says the famous sundial, and there is deep truth in its eloquence of warning, *pendet æternitas!* VI. 57.

SEPTEMBER 21.

He saw a man, named Matthew, sitting at the receipt of custom : And He saith unto him, Follow me. And he arose and followed Him.—MATT. ix. 9.

IF you follow Christ, what shall be your reward ? And here let us not be mistaken ; Christianity is no far-sighted prudence, no vulgar aiming at a mere absence of disappointment and of pain; if you serve with a selfish eye to the reward your service will not be accepted ; you must love the battle, not the victory; the work, not the success ; you must be prepared to perish, the forlorn hope of humanity, in the yet unconquered breach ; you must be prepared, again and again, "to give up your broken sword to Fate the conqueror with a humble and a manly heart." As the world goes, your reward shall be nothing—not the palace or the equipage, not the marble monument or the wreath of fame ; — these may be won by "intense selfishness, intense worldliness, intense hardness of heart," but *your* nobler reward shall be the bleeding feet which yet are beautiful upon the mountains, and the aching brow which shall have an aureole for crown.

XI. 59.

Who serves for gain, a slave, by thankless pelf
  Is paid ; who gives himself is priceless, free.
  I give myself, a man, to God : lo, He
Renders me back, a saint, unto myself !

OWEN MEREDITH.

PETER said: "Lo, we have forsaken all, and followed Thee," and either added or implied: In what respect, then, shall we be gainers? The answer of Jesus was at once a magnificent encouragement and a solemn warning. The encouragement was that there was no instance of self-sacrifice which would not, even in this world, . . . receive its hundred-fold increase in the harvest of spiritual blessings, and would in the world to come be rewarded by the infinite recompense of eternal life; the warning was . . . that many of the last should be first and the first last. And to impress them still more deeply that the kingdom of heaven is not a mere matter of mercenary calculation or exact equivalent . . . He told them the memorable Parable of the Laborers in the Vineyard.

That parable . . . involved the truth that, while all who serve God should not be deprived of their . . . rich reward, there could be in heaven no murmuring, no envyings, no base strugglings for precedency, no miserable disputings as to who had performed the maximum of service or who had received the minimum of grace. XIII. 313.

> The stars have a differing brightness,
>   Yet all upon each do shine;
> All joy in the wide resplendence,
>   None thinketh of "thine" or "mine;" —
> All know that the source of their glory,
>   O Sun of the Kingdom, is Thine!
>
> J. L. M. W.

SEPTEMBER 23.

THE insignificance of our wordly rank affects in nowise our membership of the spiritual aristocracy. The thing really important is, not the trust committed to us, but the loyalty wherewith we fulfil it. All of us may be, in St. Paul's high language, fellow-laborers with God; and he who is that, be he slave or angel, can be nothing better or greater. The mountains cease to be colossal, the ocean tides lose their majesty, if you see what an atom our earth is in the starry space. Even so, turn the telescope of faith to heaven, and see how at once earth's grandeurs dwindle into nothingness, and Heaven's least interests dilate into eternal breadth. Yes, to be a faithful Christian is greater in God's sight than to be a triumphant statesman or a victorious emperor. "God's heroes may be the world's helots." "God's prophets, best or worst, are we—there is no last or first."

VI. 17.

One who never turned his back, but marched breast forward,
    Never doubted clouds would break,
Never dreamed, though right were worsted, wrong would triumph,
    Held we fall to rise again, are baffled to fight better,
        Sleep, to wake!

BROWNING.

SEPTEMBER 24.

But God, who is rich in mercy, . . . hath quickened us together with Christ, . . . and made us sit together in heavenly places in Christ Jesus. — EPH. ii. 4, 5, 6.

DO you want "to go to heaven"? as they phrase it. . . . "Go to heaven"! My friends, heaven is a temper, not a place. What do you pray for, when you pray for heaven? What was the reward for which the saints have looked? A white robe? a golden harp? a house of gems? to be praised by all men? to be avenged on their enemies? . . . Did not David say, "Thou, O God, art the thing that I long for"? "Whom have I in heaven but Thee; and there is none upon earth that I desire in comparison of Thee"? Are our souls thus athirst for God? Amid the eager competition of business, amid the mad desire for pleasure and for gold, how many of you are seeking first the kingdom of God and His righteousness? Ah! my friends, if God and His righteousness be our conception of heaven, we may attain thereto — ay, without money, without price; . . . for us, even here and now, "the path to heaven lies through heaven, and all the way to heaven is heaven." VII. 35.

"We need not die to go to God!
  See how the daily prayer is given, —
'Tis not across a gulf we cry,
  'Our Father who dost dwell in heaven!'

"And 'Let Thy will on earth be done,
  As in Thy heaven, by this Thy child!'
What is it but all prayers in one,
  That soul and sense be reconciled?"

SEPTEMBER 25.

YES, the Eternal is not opposite to the Temporal, but to the Visible; it is not a period, but a condition; not a locality, but a state; not a thing of the future, but of the for-ever. Let us live with the sense of it about us now, and then we cannot live those utterly dreary, empty, idle, unprofitable, vicious lives which we sometimes see. The eternal things are all around us. Let us then live in purity, knowing that no step that defileth can pass over the golden streets. Let us live in love, lest we blush, with burning shame, to find that God honors, and the Lamb of God receives into His bosom, those whom we coldly neglected or wickedly despised. Let us live in humility, lest God punish our pride and leave us in horrible dispraise. So will Eternity unveil itself to us more and more in our daily walk. XI. 69.

The eternal life is not the future life; it is life in harmony with the true order of things — life in God. We must learn to look upon time as a movement of eternity, as an undulation in the ocean of being. To live so as to keep this consciousness of ours in perpetual relation with the eternal, is to be wise; to live so as to personify and embody the eternal, is to be religious.

AMIEL.

SEPTEMBER 26.

Deal courageously, and the Lord shall be with the good. — II. CHR. xix. 11.

RESULTS are not in our hands, efforts are; and what God requires of all of us is effort, not result; and the very best efforts of the very greatest and holiest men have often been exactly those which, from the Cross of Christ downwards, have often seemed to fail the most; so that all we have to do is to work on always, undiscouraged, in the unalterable conviction that, in the course of duty, failure can never be more than apparent, and that to the end of time, because God is God, evil things shall perish, but "good deeds cannot die."

VI. 190.

> It may not be our lot to wield
> The sickle in the ripened field;
> Nor ours to hear, on summer eves,
> The reaper's song among the sheaves;
>
> Yet where our duty's task is wrought
> In unison with God's great thought,
> The near and future blend in one,
> And whatsoe'er is willed, is done!

WHITTIER

SEPTEMBER 27.

I therefore . . . beseech you that ye walk worthy of the vocation wherewith ye are called.
                                        EPH. iv. 1.

BE an act ever so unimportant, the *principle* involved in our acts is not unimportant. You say that there is very little harm in this or that; if there is even a little harm in it then there is great harm in it. A feather will show you the direction of the wind ; a straw will prove the set of a current. And this is why Christ says, "Be ye perfect." It is a precept intensely practical. No day passes but what we can put it into action. Not to speak of the weightier matters of the law, little punctualities, little self-denials, little honesties, little passing words of sympathy, little nameless acts of kindness, little silent victories over favorite temptations —these are the little threads of gold, which, when woven together, gleam out so brightly in the pattern of a life that God approves. VI. 19.

Since trifles make the sum of human things,
And half our misery from our foibles springs ;
Since life's best joys consist in peace and ease,
And though but few can serve, yet all may please,
Then let the ungentle spirit learn from hence —
A small unkindness is a great offence.
                                        HANNAH MORE.

SEPTEMBER 28.

> He that of greatest works is finisher
> Oft does them by the weakest minister.
> **SHAKESPEARE.**

THE imitation of Christ standeth not at all in outward things. In wealth or in deepest want, in rank or in utter lowliness, in a palace or a squalid garret, with ten talents or with but one, we may walk in His steps; nor is there any place, from the desert to the city, from the cathedral to the log hut on the prairie, nor any condition of life, from that of St. Louis the King to that of Santa Zita the maid-of-all-work, which has not been rendered more lovely by the lives of the Saints of God. Their footsteps have illuminated life's deepest valleys, as well as shone upon its loftiest hills. V. 131.

There dwells in this wide world no man or woman or child but either is, or is not, of the number of God's saints. We in Christendom, if we belong not to that illustrious company, yet abide within sight of it. God grant that the shining lights may shine, glow, radiate, more and more, and that the lookers-on, glorifying the Father of all, may catch fire.
CHRISTINA ROSSETTI.

SEPTEMBER 29.

And he said, I will not let thee go, except thou bless me. — GEN. xxxii. 26.

THOUGH no vision is vouchsafed to our mortal eyes, — although the darkness does not move and flash around us with bright faces and glorious plumes, — yet angels of God are with us oftener than we know, and to the pure heart every home is a Bethel, and every path of life a Penuel and a Mahanaim. In the outer world and the inner world do we see and meet continually these messengers of God. In the outer world God maketh the winds His angels, and the flames of fire His messengers; the sun and the moon utter His knowledge, and the morning stars shout His praise. And in the inner world there are angels too, — the angels of youth, and of innocence, and of opportunity; — the angels of prayer, and of time, and of death;

"*Our acts our angels are* — or good or ill,
Our fatal shadows that walk by us still."

These too are God's messengers; these are even more to us for practical consideration than Saint Michael and all Angels; they encircle us continually with a curse or a blessing, — a blessing for those of the girded loin and the burning lamp, but a curse for the idle and the wicked, a curse for the heart of the sensual and the life of the sluggard. To those who wrestle with them in faith and prayer, they are angels with hands full of immortal gifts; — to those who neglect or use them ill, they are angels with drawn sword and scathing flame.

XI. 187.

SEPTEMBER 30.

Are they not all ministering spirits, sent forth to minister for them who shall be heirs of salvation?
HEB. i. 14.

From Care and Grief
She parted first: "Companions sworn and true
Have ye been ever to me, but for Friends
I knew ye not till later, and did miss
Much solace through that error; let this kiss,
Late-known and prized, be taken for amends:
Thou, too, kind, constant Patience, with thy slow,
Sweet counsels aiding me; I did not know
That ye were Angels, until ye displayed
Your wings for flight; now bless me!" But they said,
"We blest thee long ago."
DORA GREENWELL.

WHAT are the angels themselves, even, in respect of Christ? What but "sparks from the unemptiable fountain of His glory"? What but "dewdrops on the head of the Bridegroom, lost in the splendor of his hair"? They may help us, the thought of them may ennoble us, their glittering faces may look down on us from the lucent cloud of witnesses, compassionate and pure. They may be to us as our "high-born kinsmen;" we may see their waving robes in the flash of the sunlight; we may hear their voices in the music of the wind: but their glory is but an effulgence of Christ's glory; they are but ministering spirits of that Lord of whom it is written, "And let all the Angels of God worship Him!"
VII. 92.

IT is wiser to think of our possible exaltation than of our actual fall. It is better to bear in mind the glory we might bear with us, and the divine altar from whose brightness the flame of our souls was lit, than to conceive of ourselves as a mean, a worthless, and a ruined herd; — it is better with David to lift up our eyes, undaunted, even to the starry vault of heaven, and to believe that on the very throne of the Omnipotent is the likeness of a human form, than to regard ourselves with the diseased and anguished Job, as the valueless playthings of a divine irony, and the scorned slaves of an unmerciful decree. For as our thoughts are we shall be; and if they are fixed on glory and immortality, with Christ in heavenly places, there is more hope that we too shall in heart and mind thither ascend. XI. 93.

> We share in what is infinite: 'tis ours,
>   For we and it alike are thine;
> What I enjoy, great God! by right of Thee,
>   Is more than doubly mine.
>
> Thus doth Thy hospitable greatness lie
>   Outside us like a boundless sea;
> We cannot lose ourselves where all is home,
>   Nor drift away from Thee.
>
> . . . .
>
> Then on Thy grandeur I will lay me down;
>   Already life is heaven for me;
> No cradled child more softly lies than I:
>   Come soon, Eternity!

FABER.

After this manner pray ye. — MATT. vi. 9.

THE voice of God in the heart of man imperiously bids him to make known his requests unto God. . . . "Every time, place, posture, is easy. Talent is not needful; eloquence is out of place; dignity is no recommendation. . . . The whole function is simply this: a child, a wandering child, comes to its Father, and pleads for grace and pity, for forgiveness and help." . . . Long prayers, even repeated prayers, may have their place. . . . But the moment a prayer becomes a mechanical weariness, the moment the lips repeat it but the heart cannot follow, it ceases to be a prayer, and becomes a mockery. . . . Far better that our prayers should only occupy five minutes and be sincere, rising like incense through the golden censer of our one and only Priest, Christ Jesus, than that they should be a spiritless mummery, or that they should resemble the idle vaunt of the Pharisee.

IV. 12, 15, 18.

> When the Soul, growing clearer,
>   Sees God no nearer;
> When the Soul, mounting higher,
>   To God comes no nigher;
> When the Arch-fiend, Pride,
>   Mounts at her side,
>
> . . . .
>
> Changing the pure emotion
> Of her high devotion
> To a skin-deep sense
> Of her own eloquence,
> Strong to deceive, strong to enslave —
>   *Save, oh! save.*

MATTHEW ARNOLD.

OCTOBER 3.

Our Father, which art in heaven. — MATT. vi. 9.

HOW deep is the meaning in this prayer! Its first word, "Our," is a plea for the universal brotherhood of our race. . . . The word "Father" is the appeal of love, reminding us, not only of our creation, but also of our re-creation, of our brotherhood with the incarnate Christ, of His Spirit shed abroad in our hearts, whereby we cry, "Abba, Father." The words "which art in heaven" temper with humility and solemn reverence our new friendship and filial relation with God.

Is it, then, too high, too deep for creatures such as we are? Would you have it otherwise? Would you have a prayer which you can fathom? Nay; such a prayer could never have come from the lips of the Son of God. Its absolute simplicity, its fathomless meaning, its all-embracing charity, are the stamp of its divine origin. This is why it has "shallows which the lamb may ford, and depths which the elephant must swim." To pride and Pharisaism, to selfishness and hatred, it will remain forever a dead and empty formula. But it will tremble into angelic music to the ear of humility, and glow and breathe with all its celestial ardor to the heart of gentleness and love.   IV. 36, 37.

> I can touch
> This border of Thy garment: now I know
> I love Thee, Lord, I will not let Thee go!
> DORA GREENWELL.

Hallowed be Thy name. — MATT. vi. 9.

THE first star is the most lustrous of all the night. May not this first prayer, "Hallowed be Thy name," be the brightest of all; the most radiant Pleiad of the seven petitions? I think that it is, and oh! that God would give us this evening star!

For observe, "Hallowed be Thy name" is almost the last thing that we should think of putting into our prayers. Least of all should we be inclined to put this prayer before all the rest, because we are essentially and supremely selfish, and this prayer is absolutely and supremely unselfish.

Ah! if we would only remember the principle that to *become* and not to *get* should be more the motive of our prayers, that the true tone of prayer is the "Hallowed be Thy name" of the adoring child, not the "Give, give," of the daughters of the horse-leech — neither our prayers nor our lives would be so poor.

IV. 41, 44.

Our Father, Thy promise we earnestly claim —
The sanctified heart that shall hallow Thy Name:
In ourselves, in our dear ones, throughout the wide world,
Be Thy Name as a banner of glory unfurled;
Let it triumph o'er evil and darkness and guilt,
We know Thou canst do it, we know that Thou wilt,
    For Thine is the Power!

FRANCES R. HAVERGAL.

Thy kingdom come. — MATT. vi. 10.

HOW can we pray this prayer who aim no higher than slothful contentment with the life of the animal, — the multitudes who eat, and drink, and sleep, and live in self-indulgent comfort, but have yet never struck one blow, never lifted one finger, never suffered one loss, never dared even to brave one taunt for the cause of God, nor can show one scar of a single wound in even the lightest of His battles? If we pray "Thy kingdom come," we are bound to fight for it and fight hard; to strike for it and strike home; to wrestle mightily, and shoulder to shoulder, and at all costs, against the corruption of its truth and the adversaries of its holiness!

In one of the battles during the American Civil War, a young officer stood at a battery which had dwindled down to a single gun. That single gun he loaded again and again, and fired it into the thick darkness *with an aim that had been given him in the light*. At last the bugles rang out the victory of his army; and, said he, "Then I knew that whatever others did, for me a victory meant keeping my own gun loaded and fired." Work in that spirit. Remember that "in God's war slackness is infamy," and in your lives or on your lips there shall be power and healing in the prayer "Thy kingdom come."

IV. 65, 67.

OCTOBER 6.

Thy will be done on earth, as it is in heaven.
                                    MATT. vi. 10.

THOUGH in nature and the issues of destiny God's will is always done, there is another and terribly real sense in which the will of God is not done. . . . Look into our own hearts! Which of us does not daily and grievously do that which we ought not to have done, and leave undone that which we ought to do?

This prayer is an appeal to give up our own wills altogether, . . . and it also sets before us an example as to how we should do it. . . . God's angels, we know, . . . do God's will, not only unquestioningly, cheerfully, but zealously, swift as the hurricane, vividly as the lightning. . . . And they do it harmoniously. There are no jealousies among the angels; no cut-throat combinations; no base rivalries. . . . Yet God has given us a nearer, dearer, truer example even than that of the angels. He has given us His Son as a divine and perfect ensample, that we should walk in His steps. His life and death are the eternal model of how God's work should be done, alike on earth and in heaven. For that will is best done when we kill in us all the desires of self, and lose ourselves in Him.

IV. 74, 76, 81, 84.

Teach me, my God and King,
 In all things Thee to see,
And what I do in anything
 To do it as for Thee.
                                    GEORGE HERBERT.

OCTOBER 7.

Give us this day our daily bread. — MATT. vi. 11.

OUT of seven petitions — three for God's glory and three for our souls — there is this one for earthly things; yet every word of this one rebukes our earthliness.

"Give us, O Father": what a lovely prayer it is, thus simply uttered; what a world of gratitude, of filial dependence, of devout acknowledgment, lies in it! The prayer is broad and simple. . . . We will not say — Christ would not have us say — give *me*. . . . We will not ask anything for ourselves alone. All our prayers shall be in the spirit of that large and lovely petition, "That it may please Thee to have mercy upon all men." . . . And give us *this day*. We are but creatures of a day; we will not be troubled and anxious about the morrow. Sufficient for the day its want, its good, its evil. To-day is ours; to-morrow is Thine, as yesterday is Thine. We will ask for no accumulations. If Thou hast given us much, we will no more trust in ourselves than if we had nothing; and if we have nothing for to-morrow, we will trust Thee still. . . . Give us this day our *daily* bread: that only which pertains to us, which is convenient for us, which is sufficient for our sustenance. . . . Give us this day our daily *bread:* day by day the bread for this life; the living bread, the bread which came down from heaven, even the Son of Man who is in heaven, which if any eat he shall live forever.

IV. 92, 95, 96, 102.

OCTOBER 8.

"*FORGIVE us our trespasses.*" St. Matthew has the word "debts": St. Luke says "sins." . . . All sin is of the nature of a debt. It is a vast threefold debt, against which there are no assets, which man incurs to himself, to his neighbor, and to his God. . . . Who shall measure it? Do not our lives often look to us like one black night of sins of omission, lightened through by sins of commission? . . . Yet sin can be forgiven, always; can be forgiven, utterly; supernaturally, not naturally; in Christ, not in ourselves. Is sin a debt? It shall be cancelled. Is it a handwriting against us? It shall be annulled, torn across, blotted out. . . . Why was there, and why is there, and why has there ever been, this forgiveness so large, so full, so free, but because Christ bore for us the crushing burden, and paid for us the immeasurable debt?

"I stood amazed, and whispered, 'Can it be
That He hath granted all the boon I sought?
How wonderful that He for me hath wrought!
How wonderful that He hath answered me!'
O faithless heart! He *said* that He would hear
And answer thy poor prayer; and He *hath* heard,
And proved his promise! Wherefore didst thou fear?
Why marvel that thy Lord hath kept His word?
More wonderful if He should fail to bless
Expectant faith and prayer with good success!"

IV. 109, 110, 114, 117.

"*As we forgive those who trespass against us.*" Are we then to set up ourselves as an example to God? Do we bid Him to copy us, and not to be harder or worse than we are? Nay, that might be a quite impossible blasphemy; and yet, in the sense of a dumb, blind, helpless appeal, God does permit something like it. . . . Our forgiveness is at the best but a dewdrop; yet even a dewdrop may reflect the blue infinite heaven and the glory of the risen sun. . . . Our forgiveness must be real; it must be *ex animo;* it must reserve no spite nor grudge; it must utterly clear itself of all ill-will and desire for revenge. . . . I know how bitter a man must feel it to receive wrongs at the hands of others which might fairly be regarded as intolerable; to be thwarted, to be undermined, to be basely and systematically misrepresented; yet, even under these circumstances, . . . the duty of magnanimity, of returning good for evil, of ungrudging forgiveness, is blessedly inexorable. . . . If there be bliss, if there be peace on earth, it is when we rise above earth's sulphurous fogs and chilling mists to the sunlit hills of the charity which suffereth long, and is kind, and is not easily provoked, and thinketh no evil.   IV. 127, 128, 134.

> 'Tis not enough to weep my sins,
> 'Tis but one step to heaven:
> When I am kind to others, then
> I know myself forgiven.
>
> FABER.

And lead us not into temptation. — MATT. vi. 13.

BUT does God ever lead us into temptation? . . . The explanation lies in the two senses of the word "temptation." It means "trial," the conditions meant to test our faithfulness; and it means actual incitement, allurement in the direction of wrongdoing. Now, in the first sense, God does tempt us; He tries us as gold in the fire is tried. . . . Man achieves his utmost nobleness by victory over temptation. . . . If there were no temptation to sin, there would be no glory in righteousness. Were virtue a thing compulsory and inevitable in us, then virtue itself would be valueless. And so St. James says, "Brethren, count it all joy when ye fall into divers temptations."

God, then, *tries* us, but He does not tempt; and our prayer is that we may not turn His trials into Satan's allurements, His fire, which purges, into Satan's, which consumes.

Be sure of this: he who tampers with temptation is lost. There is but one rule about it; namely,

"Think it as a serpent's egg,
Which, hatched, would, as his kind, grow mischievous,
And kill it in the shell."

It is *fugiendo pugnare.* Like the Parthian warriors, we must overcome by flight.

IV. 142, 145, 150.

OCTOBER 11.

Deliver us from evil. — MATT. vi. 13.

IS it not true that when we offer this prayer, we think most often of those earthly conditions which men count evil, but which are to God's children but blessings in disguise ? If so, we utterly miss the spirit of this prayer, and the spirit of all Christ's teaching. What Christ meant by evil, what alone in its ultimate essence is evil, lies far behind these things. Wealth, rank, power, popularity, ease, pleasure, success — with blind folly we pursue these things and take them for good, but they do not constitute good ; the combination of them all may be coincident with deadliest evil. Sickness, obscurity, failure, abuse, hardship, poverty, do not constitute evil ; the combination of them all may be coincident with the most glorious good. IV. 178.

> I remember best
> The good time when we were unhappy; then
> When we were full of sorrows and unrest,
> Without a friend among the sons of men,
> We found the Comforter, we found the Light,
> We found the Strength beyond our doubts and fears ;
> We met with Angels both by day and night,
> And touched the Hand that wiped away our tears.
> AMELIA E. BARR.

OCTOBER 12.

For Thine is the kingdom. — MATT. vi. 13.

WITH what deeper awe, with what grander aspirations, can we, as citizens, enter on the duties which from time to time claim all our energy than with those inspired by the sense of this mighty truth? And it is everywhere around you if you will notice it. It is written on the heavens above and on the earth beneath; now in autographs of love and beauty, and now in blood, and fire, and vapor of smoke. Will you not see God because He is so near you? Will you not recognize His kingdom because of its familiarity?

"'Oh where is the sea?' the fishes cried,
  As they swam the crystal waters through;
'We've heard from of old, of the ocean's tide,
  And we long to look on the waters blue.
The wise ones tell of an infinite sea:
  Oh! who can tell us if such there be?'"

Shall we men be like those ignorant fishes? We are members of God's kingdom: in it we live, and move, and have our being; it lies around us in the atmosphere we breathe. Shall we ignore it? Shall we live as though it were not? Shall we violate its conditions, defy its laws? . . . Ah! if we acknowledge the truth of Christ's kingdom on our lips, let us acknowledge it in our lives.

IV. 323.

O wondrous New Jerusalem,
  From Heaven thou art come down!
On earth thy firm foundations are,
  Here weareth Christ His crown.

DENIS WORTMAN.

OCTOBER 13.

For Thine . . . is the power. — MATT. vi. 13.

WE talk of space, we live in space; and yet space is a thing not only absolutely indefinable, but absolutely unthinkable. It is a circle, of which the centre is everywhere, the circumference nowhere. We cannot imagine it as limited by any conceivable boundary, nor can we in any way grasp its "endless extension." . . . We can but confess that we are creatures of a day, . . . that man in himself is but "a shadow less than a shade," . . . and that "power belongeth unto God."

And, as Pascal pointed out, we stand between two infinitudes. There is another infinity beneath us. . . . The least of God's works is as infinitely beyond the reach of our cognizance as the greatest.

Is there no lesson but curiosity in all this? There is this lesson, that there can be no effort so futile as the attempt to resist the will of God, and no infatuation so insensate as to kindle His displeasure. . . . *Thine is the power!* — and therefore it is utter madness for man, an ephemeris, in these æons, to do anything but walk humbly with his God, in that obedience in which alone lies for any man the path of happiness, the path of safety.

IV. 232, 233, 234.

O Majesty unspeakable and dread!
  Wert Thou less mighty than Thou art,
Thou wert, O Lord, too great for our belief,
  Too little for our heart.

FABER.

OCTOBER 14.

For Thine is . . . the glory. — MATT. vi. 13.

GOD is so infinite that nothing which we call human glory can furnish us with any analogy to His. We must go back again to the primary idea of the word glory, which is light and splendor. And not only does God "cover Himself with light as with a garment," but "God *is* light." When we say "Thine is the glory" we mean that without God the physical world would sink into a chaos of darkness, the moral world into an abyss of crime. In a starless night all is black; but from the moment that the dawn has kindled its first beacon-light of vivid crimson on the ice-clad mountain-peak, it fires — summit after summit — the splendor of the hills, and flows down their sides in rivers of molten gold. The streams flash into silver; the sea burns beneath the flood of radiance; the fields burst into color; the forest leaves and dewy flowers gleam with millions of diamonds; the whole world thrills and burns with lustre and with life. Like that is the glory of God. God is Light; He is that light, bodiless and impalpable, from whose unemptiable fountain our earthly light is but a faint spark, or a dim shadow. IV. 234.

> Around Thee all is light,
> And rest of perfect love,
> And glory full and bright,
> All human thought above.
>
> F. R. HAVERGAL.

OCTOBER 15.

For ever and ever. — MATT. vi. 13.

THE imagination which can enter into the meaning of those words reels before them. There is something awfully pathetic and mysterious in the interminable procession of mankind over our earth. There are at this moment some fifteen hundred millions of human beings passing for their brief span across its surface. A few years past and they were not; a few years hence and their place will know them no more. The commonest things we use outlast us. . . . Nature is full of death. The leaf falls, the tree dies, the gray earth is wrinkled with the graves of her children. . . . The air is tremulous with knells; there are vacant places in our homes; the dust is strewn over the faces that we loved. What is man, whose breath is in his nostrils? Behold, we die, we perish, we all perish! . . . Why, then, do we forsake the living fountains for our broken cisterns? He who eateth of this bread shall hunger, he who drinketh of this water shall thirst again; but he who eateth the bread of life, and drinketh of the water which Christ shall give him, shall hunger and thirst no more. Lord, give us that water! Lord, evermore give us that bread from heaven, which is Thyself! . . . Give it to us now and for ever.

IV. 242, 245, 253.

Then what this earth to thee, my heart?
Its gifts nor feed thee, nor can bless.
Thou hast no owner's part
In all its fleetingness.

JOHN HENRY NEWMAN.

OCTOBER 16.

These things saith the Amen, the faithful and true witness. — Rev. iii. 14.

He who blesseth himself in the earth shall bless himself in the God of Amen, and he who sweareth in the earth shall swear by the God of Amen. — Is. lxv. 16.

All the promises of God in Him are yea, and in Him Amen. — I. Cor. 20.

IN the Gospel of St. John alone, no less than twenty-five times our Lord Jesus Christ introduces his deepest asseverations with " Amen, Amen " — translated in our version, " Verily, verily — I say unto you."

What, then, is the meaning of this solemn and sacred word? It means Truth; it means Reality. Every time we use it we should be reminded that God is not the God of fantasies and shams, but that He is the God of reality and of truth.

Earnestly, then, I would invite you to base yourselves on the Amen, on the solid and ultimate reality of life, by denying ungodliness and worldly lusts, and living soberly, righteously, and godly in this present world; and to base your lives on the Amen of true religion; on those things which cannot be shaken, but remain. In these days, as in all days, a great deal is mixed up with religion . . . which is not religion, and has nothing whatever to do with the God of Amen, with the Christ who is the Amen, the faithful and true witness. . . . Seek truth, and you will find it, because God is the God of truth.

IV. 259, 264.

> "We pray for mercy,
> And that same prayer doth teach us all to render
> The deeds of mercy."

LET the Lord's Prayer teach us that by Christ's own lesson, the condition of all prayer is action. Prayer, which we deem so easy, which we perform so perfunctorily, is, when it is real prayer, the passion of an effort, the wrestling of a life. Prayers which are not uttered from the heart are but forms and functions and idle breaths of articulated air.

A Christian who does not pray is a dead Christian. He is not — he cannot be — a true Christian at all. For he violates the most imperious instinct, and flings away the chiefest blessing of the Christian life. IV. 125, 14.

> To pray, to do —
> To pray, to do according to the prayer,
> Are both to worship Alla; but the prayers
> Which have no successors in deed are faint
> And pale in Alla's eyes, — fair mothers they,
> Dying in childbirth of dead sons.
> TENNYSON.

OCTOBER 18.

ST. Luke's Gospel is dominated throughout by a spirit large and sweet and wise. It is full of tears and songs and laughter; it is the hymn of the new people, the hosanna of the little ones and of the humble introduced into the kingdom. . . . It is preëminently the Gospel of the poor. . . . He felt it to be his duty to warn all who were tempted — as the rich in all ages are tempted — to trust in uncertain riches, instead of being rich towards God. It is not that he holds poverty in itself to be a beatitude, but only that kind of poverty which is "not voluntary nor proud, but only accepted and submissive; . . . too laborious to be thoughtful, too innocent to be conscious, too long-experienced in sorrow to be hopeful; waiting in its peaceful darkness for the unconceived dawn, yet not without its sweet, complete, untainted happiness, like intermittent notes of birds before the daybreak, or the first gleams of heaven's amber in the eastern gray." Which is there of us all who does not need this lesson?
I. 76, 83.

Honest love, honest sorrow,
Honest work for the day, honest hope for the morrow, —
Are these worth nothing more than the hand they make weary,
The heart they have saddened, the life they leave dreary?
Hush! the sevenfold heavens to the voice of the Spirit
Echo: He that o'ercometh shall all things inherit.

OWEN MEREDITH.

I counsel thee to buy of me gold tried in the fire, that thou mayest be rich. — REV. iii. 18.

THE sorest poverty is not poverty of gold, but poverty of good will; it is caused, not by distress, but by avarice; it is due, not to lack of means, but to the alarming growth of that grasping and grinding spirit of accumulation which I much fear is seizing upon the upper and middle classes. . . . To amass, to lay by, to invest for ourselves and for our children, so that we will not spare anything for the good of the nation or the Church — is that what our prosperity has come to? . . . Ah, let us rise above this sordidness, and learn to believe that it may be better sometimes to invest in deeds of mercy than in the best of securities, that works of love may bring us in something better than fifteen per cent., and that life, which may be clad, as it were, with white robes and angel wings and sent forth to bless the world, is fairer and more blessed so than when it is used for selfish luxury, for family aggrandizement, or for personal display!

IX. 35.

> Is Honor gone into his grave?
> Hath Faith become a caitiff knave,
> And Selfhood turned into a slave,
>   To work in Mammon's cave?
> . . . .
> Will Truth's long blade ne'er gleam again?
> Hath Giant Trade in dungeons slain
> All great contempts of mean-got gain,
>   And hates of inward stain?
>   SIDNEY LANIER.

OCTOBER 20.

WHAT does that "empty, swept, and garnished" mean? It means that if your heart is not preoccupied with good, it will be invaded by evil. Oh, beware of idleness in its every form, idle procrastinations, idle talk, idle habits, idle thoughts, these are the certain ruin of the soul. The laborer who stands idle in the marketplace is ever ready to be hired in the devil's service. The worm of sin gnaws deepest into the idle heart. Never will it be known, till the last great day, how many souls have been shipwrecked on the rock of an idle hour. But preoccupy your heart with good; preoccupy your time with honest industry, and you are safe. . . . When the air is filled with sunlight there is no opportunity for the deeds of darkness. Where the soul has tasted of the bread of life, it cannot hunger for the stones of the wilderness. Where God is all to us, the world is nothing.

VI. 145.

Unveil, O Lord, and on us shine
  In glory and in grace;
This gaudy world grows pale before
  The brightness of Thy face.

Till Thou art seen, it seems to be
  A sort of fairy ground,
Where suns unsetting light the sky,
  And flowers and fruits abound.

But when Thy keener, purer beam
  Is poured upon our sight,
It loses all its power to charm,
  And what was day is night.

JOHN HENRY NEWMAN.

OCTOBER 21.

THERE are, alas! many who have lost their faith in God. . . . Knowing how terrible, how irreparable, would be the loss of such faith to us, we regret their loss; and we pray that they, no less than we, may be folded at last in the arms of God's infinite mercy, and led into the radiance of His Eternal Light. But seeing that the faith of their childhood has suffered shipwreck; seeing that they think, or think that they think, that there is no God, and that we die as the beasts of the field, we cannot wonder that they ask themselves if life be at all worth living. Nay, we are glad that they should discuss such questions; because the deeper their bark sinks, the more sure we are that they must at last reach that bed on which the ocean rests, — that God, whose offspring we all are, and in whom, whether we deny Him or have faith in Him, we all live, and move, and have our being.

XIV. 30.

The World that puts Thee by,
That opens not to greet Thee with Thy train,
That sendeth after Thee the sullen cry,
"We will not have Thee over us to reign,"
Itself doth testify, through searchings vain,
Of Thee and of Its need.

DORA GREENWELL.

OCTOBER 22.

IS then life worth living? Life, I mean, regarded by itself; life on this earth; life apart from God; your life, my life, human life in general, considered under its purely earthly aspects and relationships. . . . Ask the atheist, and if he tells you his real thought, it must be that of the Greek poet, "That it were best never to have been born, and next best to depart as soon as possible." . . . But ask the Christian, "Is life worth living?" and he will answer: Ay, indeed, life is infinitely worth living, and death is infinitely more worth dying; for to live is Christ, and to die is gain; to live is to have faith in God, and to die is to be with Him for evermore.

> "Death is the veil which they who live call life;
> We sleep, and it is lifted."
>
> XIV. 33. 47.

Because the Perfect, evermore postponed,
   Yet ever beckoning, is our only goal;
Because the deathless Love that sits enthroned
   On changeless Truth, holds us in firm control;
Because within God's Heart our pulses beat;
Because His Law is holy, life is sweet!

Because it is of Him, His infinite gift;
   Lost, but restored by One who came to share
His riches with our poverty, and lift
   The human to the heavenly, everywhere;
Because in Christ we breathe immortal breath,
Sweet, sweet is life! He hath abolished death!

LUCY LARCOM.

OCTOBER 23.

All that is in the world, the lust of the flesh, and the lust of the eyes, and the pride of life, is not of the Father. — I. JOHN ii. 16.

BY the lust of the flesh we mean every sinful indulgence of the appetites of the lower nature; — the man who so loves the world is dead while he lives. . . . And the lust of the eyes — what is it? It is covetousness, which is idolatry; it is immoral content with things comfortable; it is fastidious indifference and slothful æstheticism. . . . It is the spirit of desire engendered by the sight of all things which, apart from our duty to God and man, attract the imagination or fascinate the sense. And the pride of life . . . is the spirit of puff and push; of inflation and pomposity; of fastidious contempt and domineering cynicism.

Now "it is the law of equilibrium that nothing can rise higher than its source." If the springs of our action flow from such molehill altitudes, our life will but dribble through meanness like some wretched gutter of the street, instead of leaping upwards like some strong, pure fountain whose source is in the eternal hills. V. 158, 159, 162.

Happy, I thought, that which can draw its life
    Deep from the nether springs, —
Safe 'neath the pressure, tranquil 'mid the strife
    Of surface things, —
Safe — for the sources of the nether springs
    Up in the far hill lie;
Calm — for their life its power and freshness brings
    Down from the sky.
JOHN KERR.

OCTOBER 24.

CHRIST is the life, and the eternal life; and He came that we might have life, and have it more abundantly. It is not only the death of the body which He has conquered. That which is terrible to the guilty and the worldling, is to the Christian only a step into the sunlight from the sun-illumined tent; but He came to thrill new life into the spirit entombed in vice and vanity, into the soul dead in trespasses and sins. V. 14.

Let me not dwell so much within
  My bounded heart, with anxious heed—
Where all my searches meet with sin,
  And nothing satisfies my need,—
It shuts me from the sound and sight
Of that pure world of life and light,
Which has no breadth, or length, or height.

Let me Thy power, Thy beauty, see;
  So shall the hopeless labor cease,
And my free heart shall follow Thee
  Through paths of everlasting peace.
My strength Thy gift,—my life Thy care,—
I shall forget to seek elsewhere
The wealth to which my soul is heir.

ANNA L. WARING.

OCTOBER 25.

See then that ye walk circumspectly. — EPH. v. 15.

GODLINESS is possible; . . . it is not possible without effort. Be sure of this — nothing worth anything can ever be gained without paying the price which nature, and man, and God have ordained. If you want physical success, you must work for it. If you want intellectual success, you must work for it. If you would conquer your bad habits, if you would resist your besetting sins, if you would save your souls from sin, and hell, and the death that cannot die, you must work for it. For not, as Dante says —

> "Not on flowery beds, or under shade
> Of canopy reposing, heaven is won."

It stands written in the Koran that, "Under the shadow of the crossing scimitars Paradise is prefigured": the prophet meant it of the sword by which he propagated his faith; but we may understand it of the spiritual armor. Yes, under the shadow of the crossing scimitars — yes, in the battlefield against sin and death, — yes, where the fiery darts of the wicked one fly fast and thick . . . there for us lies the only safety. If you would win the saint's glory, you must fight the saint's fight:

> "*They* climbed the steep ascent of heaven,
> 'Mid peril, toil, and pain:
> Oh God, to us may grace be given
> To follow in their train!"

OCTOBER 26.

Thine ears shall hear a word behind thee, saying, This is the way, walk ye in it, when ye turn to the right hand, and when ye turn to the left.

Is. xxx. 21.

TWO classes of interests daily appeal to us with intense persistence — the lower and the higher; the earthly and the divine; those of the animal and those of the spiritual nature. On the one side money, self-importance, power, comfort, pleasure, grasp us with the attraction of their nearness, and of their coarse reality; on the other hand, calling to us as with sweet, far voices from the invisible world, are grace, contentment, trust, duty, thankfulness for undeserved mercies, a desire to give rather than to receive, the holy readiness to spend and be spent for the good of others, not our own.

VIII. 12.

> Leave ye your flesh-pots! Turn from filthy greed
>   Of gain that doth the hungry spirit mock;
> And heaven shall drop sweet manna for your need,
>   And rain clear rivers from the unhewn rock.
> Thus saith the Lord! And Moses, meek, unshod,
> Within the cloud stands hearkening to his God.

ADELINE D. T. WHITNEY.

THE history of mankind, whether secular or religious, resolves itself ultimately into the history of a few individuals. It is not that all the rest do not live their own lives or can shirk their own eternal responsibilities, but it is that the march and movement of the many is as surely influenced by the genius of the few, as is the swing of the tide by the law of gravitation. . . . The hope of the world is in those rarer souls which, becoming themselves magnetic with knowledge or with nobleness, flash into the deathful sloth or deep corruption of their age and nation the force of their own convictions, the passion of their own resolves.

VIII. 202, 204.

> Whene'er a noble deed is wrought,
> Whene'er is spoken a noble thought,
>   Our hearts, in glad surprise,
>   To higher levels rise.
>
> The tidal wave of deeper souls
> Into our inmost being rolls,
>   And lifts us unawares
>   Out of all meaner cares.
>
> Honor to those whose words or deeds
> Thus help us in our daily needs,
>   And by their overflow
>   Raise us from what is low!
>
> LONGFELLOW.

OCTOBER 28.

THE love of God to man is beautifully manifested in the sunset, in the blue sky, in the morning and evening star; but nowhere is it mirrored with such winning loveliness as in a holy soul. The world could do without great heroes, even without great discoverers; it could not do without the saints of God. They are the salt of the earth; they are the kindled light on a golden candlestick; they are a city set upon a hill. They alone have proved to us that virtue is possible, that it is possible, by the grace of God, to reach the noblest of ideals. They have shown that life may be grand and happy and divine —

> "Till e'en the witless Gadarene,
> Preferring Christ to swine, can feel
> That life is sweetest when 'tis clean.
> And all the saints that hear their word
> Say: Lo! the clouds begin to shine
> About the coming of the Lord."

It is on the lives of these alone that we can look with unmingled happiness; in these alone can we see how Christians may be like their Lord.

V. 239.

> Thy lovely saints do bring Thee love,
>   Incense and joy and gold;
> . . . .
> Love kindling faith and pure desire,
>   Love following on to bliss,
> A spark, O Jesus, from Thy fire,
>   A drop from Thine abyss.

CHRISTINA ROSSETTI.

OCTOBER 29.

THERE are, thank God, myriads of saints which the world never heard of. Their names are in no calendar; their graves are never visited; yet, in the midst of all this sin and sorrow, has God, in every society, preserved him His seven thousand who have not bowed the knee to Baal. Strive we to be of these, the faithful who were not famous; and then our lives, however insignificant, will not have been in vain. . . . Each drop in the rain-shower helps to fertilize the soil; each grain of sand upon the shore is taken up upon the wings of the wind to do its part as a barrier against the raging of the sea. If in life we can neither be saints nor heroes, yet we can delight in these and help them in carrying on God's work; the work of the very humblest among us may be necessary to make it clearer to all that come after us, . . . that good and not evil is, and is to be, the law of our being; and that, if the course of all mankind as it sweeps across the universe from the great deep of nothing to the great deep of death, be a course from mystery to mystery, it is also a course from God to God.   VIII. 215.

> All the forms are fugitive,
> But the substances survive.
> Ever fresh the broad creation —
> A divine improvisation —
> From the heart of God proceeds,
> A single will, a million deeds.
>
> EMERSON.

OCTOBER 30.

He answered and said, It is written, Man shall not live by bread alone, but by every word that proceedeth out of the mouth of God. — MATT. iv. 4.

AND what a lesson lies herein for us . . . that we are not to be guided by the wants of our lower nature; that we may not misuse that lower nature for the purposes of our own sustenance or enjoyment; that we are not our own, and may not do what we will with that which we imagine to be our own; that even those things which may seem lawful are yet not all expedient; that man has higher principles of life than material sustenance, as he is a higher existence than his material frame. He who thinks that we live by bread alone will make the securing of bread the chief object of his life — will determine to have it at whatever cost, . . . and because he seeks no diviner food will inevitably starve with hunger in the midst of it. But he who knows that man does *not* live by bread alone will not thus, for the sake of living, lose all that makes life dear, — will, when he has done his duty, trust God to preserve with all things needful the body He has made, — will seek with more earnest endeavor the bread from heaven, and that living water whereof he who drinketh shall thirst no more.   XIII. 60.

OCTOBER 31.

As with external food, O Lord,
  Thou feed'st our bodies now;
E'en so, Thy blest incarnate Word
  Upon our souls bestow.
And whilst the flesh her nourishment
  From Thy good creatures takes,
Let not into our souls be sent
  What there a leanness makes.

GEORGE WITHER, 1641.

"CARNAL men," it has been said, "are like swine, which ravin upon the acorns, but look not up to the oak whence they drop." I hope that none of you neglect the good old simple, beautiful practice of "grace before meat," and that, by teaching the significance of it to your children, you save them from the "inexpressible calamity" of living lives which do not habitually look upwards to their source. Why should we live in the world as orphans, by not knowing our Heavenly Father, or strut through it in silly disregard of Him? . . . Let us rather know the filial joy of humble thankfulness, while, like those early Christians, breaking our bread at home, we take our food with gladness and singleness of heart, praising God. Otherwise we do but bar God out of our hearts with His own gifts, and make our life like

    "The pleachèd bower
Where honeysuckles, ripened by the sun,
Forbid the sun to enter."

IV. 92, 95.

NOVEMBER 1.

IT was ardor for His service which kindled the glorious devotions of those saints who shine like a river of stars athwart the Church's firmament. They are the glory of Christendom—*lucentes et ardentes*—the Cherubim of knowledge, and the Seraphim of love. . . . And if, as many tell us, in our refinement and perplexities—if in our luxury and mammon-worship—if in our despair and faithlessness—the race of these hero souls be past, yet at least the race of the humbler children in God's great family abides. They, thank God, can be counted in their myriads still, and henceforth as well as heretofore shall the world for which Christ died abound with these beautiful and holy souls. And as the moon can shine only by reflection of the sun, so do these, as they borrow their light from the Sun of Righteousness, become the clearest evidence, the predestined issue, the living illustration of their Saviour's work. And while these remain it shall always be believed. Yea, Lord, the enemy may reproach, and the foolish people blaspheme Thy Name, but that Name shall be exalted for ever above every name, for:

"The glorious company of the Apostles praise Thee.
"The goodly fellowship of the Prophets praise Thee.
"The noble army of Martyrs praise Thee.
"The Holy Church throughout all the world doth acknowledge Thee.
"Thou art the King of Glory, O Christ; Thou art the everlasting Son of the Father."

XII. 162.

NOVEMBER 2.

IN past centuries the second of November was set apart in honor of "All Souls." . . . Our finite imagination may grow dizzy at the thought of these infinite multitudes, — the tribes, the generations, the centuries, the milleniums, the æons of the dead; all of which are but the leaves — green or fallen — of the mighty Tree of Existence. . . . To us, inevitably, in this infinitude, all individuality is lost; human numerations reel at it. But it is not so with Him to whom is known the number of the stars of heaven, and the sands of the sea. . . . And knowing this, we are not appalled at the thought of these vast multitudes, whose bodies are now the dust of the solid earth, even though so many millions of them passed away in sin and sorrow, because we can say with the holy Psalmist of Israel: "O let the sorrowful sighing of the prisoners come before Thee; according to the greatness of Thy power, save Thou those that are appointed to die." XIV. 26, 28.

Great Universe — what dost thou with thy dead!
. . . .
In vain to question — save the heart of man,
  The throbbing human heart, that still doth keep
  Its truth, love, hope, its high and quenchless faith.
By day, by night, when all else faints in sleep,
  "Naught is but life," it cries; "there is no death;
  Life, Life doth only live, since Life began."
RICHARD WATSON GILDER.

NOVEMBER 3.

Blessed are the dead, . . . that they may rest from their labors. —REV. xiv. 13.

THIS verse calls us to consider the dead, not in their new condition, but in their immortal memory; not as what they are in death, but as what they were in life. . . . It does not contemplate the possibility of any dead, *i.e.*, of any *blessed* dead, who have not labored. He whose sweet voice fell from heaven, bearing comfort to the mourning souls of earth, He knew of none such. There are none such. "Sweet is rest when work is done." But if there have been no work, there can be no rest. It was the first law that God gave in Eden: Work; it is the last blessing that He utters: Enter, now that thy work is over, into thy rest. . . . Work till death release thee; then shalt thou have earned, thus only canst thou obtain, thus only couldst thou enjoy, thy rest. For the idle, for the useless, for the self-indulgent, there is no place in heaven. . . .

O how pitiful, how dreary, how unutterably despicable will appear, when the end cometh, a life spent in doing nothing;—how dreary, when the end cometh, will appear the life of the worldling and the sluggard, the life of the unlit lamp and the ungirded loin, the life of the buried talent and the neglected vine! XI. 203.

> No fate, save by the victim's fault, is low,
> For God hath writ all dooms magnificent,
> So guilt not traverses His tender will.
>   EMERSON.

NOVEMBER 4.

And their works do follow them. — REV. xiv. 13.

WHAT works? Not those, which, if you were to judge from men's lives alone, you might suppose. Not, for instance, the gold and silver which they toiled for, which shall perhaps be squandered after they are gone; not the idle voice of praise and fame, . . . nor the stately houses which they shall abandon for the damp and narrow grave. . . . It is not these works that will follow them, — for they are valueless, perishing, and corruptible, — but their love, their truth, their purity, their generosity, the hearts they comforted, the souls they saved. . . .

"Thy works, and alms, and all thy good endeavor
   Stayed not behind, nor in the grave were trod;
   But as Faith pointed with her golden rod,
Followed thee up to joy and bliss for ever.
Love led them on, and Faith, who knew them best,
   Thy handmaids, clad them o'er with purple beams
   And azure wings, that up they flew so drest,
   And spake the truth of thee on glorious themes
Before the Judge: who henceforth bade thee rest,
   And drink thy fill of pure immortal streams."

XI. 204.

NOVEMBER 5.

THE true education of life — and, for all we know, it may go on even beyond the grave — is never attained until the awful, eternal difference between right and wrong is fully, finally, personally, practically, irrevocably learned. Alas! the experience of every day teaches us that the lesson, which looks so simple, is in reality very difficult; we get easily confused in our judgments about wrong-doing; easily blunted in the edge of our moral sense; easily apt to estimate the seriousness of sin only by the gravity of its consequences, not by the fatality of its nature. "I saw in Rome," says a modern writer, "an old coin, a silver denarius, all coated and crusted with green and purple rust. I called it rust, but I was told that it was copper; the alloy thrown out from the silver until there was none left within, the silver was all pure. It takes ages to do it, but it does get done. Souls are like that. Something moves in them slowly, till the debasement is all thrown out. Some day perhaps the very tarnish shall be taken off." Well, there is this alloy, this tarnish in all of us, and the education of life is to purge it all away — by sorrows, by disappointments, by failures, by judgments,

"By fires far fiercer than are blown to prove
And purge the silver ore adulterate."
VI. 310.

And He shall . . . purge them as gold and silver, that they may offer unto the Lord an offering in righteousness. — MAL. iv. 3.

NOVEMBER 6.

Thou therefore endure hardness, as a good soldier of Jesus Christ. — II. TIM. ii. 3.

> This is the happy Warrior — this is he
> Whom every man in arms should wish to be.
> WORDSWORTH.

WHEN God in bad times has good soldiers, He places them in the thick of the battle, and they have fallen under a monument of darts. Near Him, they have been near the fire. . . . See how they have sunk to the ground with bleeding feet on the world's highway, whereon often till death they have walked well-nigh alone! But what happens? They have never failed — never ultimately failed; they have startled the deep slumber of false opinions; they have thrilled a pang of noble shame through callous consciences; they become magnetic. Into the next age, if not into their own, "they flash an epidemic of nobleness."

> "They utter but a thought,
> And it becomes a proverb for the state;
> They write a sentence in a studious mood:
> It is a saying for a hemisphere."
>
> II. 96.

NOVEMBER 7.

Do not be dazzled by the world's false judgments. The common soldier is often nobler than the general. . . . Nor is it otherwise on the battle-field of life. There is a yet harder and higher heroism — to live well in the quiet routine of life; to fill a little space because God wills it; to go on cheerfully with a petty round of little duties, little vocations; to accept unmurmuringly a low position; to smile for the joys of others when the heart is aching; to banish all ambition, all pride, and all restlessness, in a single regard to our Saviour's work. To do this for a lifetime is a greater effort, and he who does this is a greater hero than he who for one hour stems a breach, or for one day rushes onward undaunted in the flaming front of shot and shell. His works will follow him. He may not be a hero to the world, but he is one of God's heroes, and though the builders of Nineveh and Babylon be forgotten and unknown, his memory shall live and shall be blessed.

XI. 210.

To be exultant, good, or strong,
When praised or flattered by the throng —
When circumstance and men conspire
To raise us to a level higher —
This were not hard: but if through long
Prosaic years we do not tire,
Can in small things be tried yet true —
This is to live as heroes do.

JOSEPH W. SUTPHEN.

NOVEMBER 8.

This I pray, that your love may abound yet more and more. — PHIL. i. 9.

LOVE — an all-embracing charity — was the new light which Christ had introduced into human life. The moral darkness of the world consisted in the fact that hatred, not love, had been the principle of life. Already the new glory of unselfishness had begun to shine; Christ had risen in thousands of holy hearts. And, as century after century passed by, that principle of love saved the gladiator from the arena; emancipated the slave; mitigated the doom of the captive; reared the hospital; tended the leper; rescued the fallen; elevated the destiny of trampled womanhood; kindled the holy light of Christian homes; flung, with a millstone round his neck, into the sea, the offender against the innocence of the child. Love was the one best evidence of Christianity, and love is the one truest sign of individual sincerity.

V. 139.

>   Lord, make us all love all; that when we meet
>   Even myriads of earth's myriads at Thy Bar,
>   We may be glad as all true lovers are
>   Who, having parted, count reunion sweet;
>   Safe gathered home around Thy blessèd feet,
>   Come home by different roads from near or far.
>
>   CHRISTINA ROSSETTI.

NOVEMBER 9.

Rejoice evermore. — I. THESS. v. 16.
Be sober, be vigilant. — I. PET. v. 8.

LET not the Evil One, or those who do his work, let them not persuade you that seriousness is sadness, or righteousness depression. Religion is no "haggard necromancer" to be driven away, but a noble and loving friend, to be nobly welcomed. . . . In bidding you be serious, God does not forbid you to be bright. Let the web of your days be shot through with gold, and woven, an God will, of crimson in the grain.

[But] make time for serious thoughts. Let no day pass without some memory of solemn things. Each morning as you rise, remind yourselves that "God spake these words and said;" each evening as you lie down to rest, let God's angels close the door of your heart on thoughts of purity and peace. The soul that has never lived face to face with eternity is a vulgar soul ; the life that has never learnt the high law of holiness is a ruined and a wasted life.

"Who never ate with tears his bread,
　Nor through the long-drawn midnight hours
Sate weeping on his lonely bed,
　He knows ye not, ye heavenly powers."

VI. 257, 259.

NOVEMBER 10.

Fear not, little flock; for it is your Father's good pleasure to give you the kingdom. — LUKE xii. 32.

TIMID, indeed, must they be who are driven into alarm and anxiety when some man of science, or some lady who writes a novel, professes himself or herself an agnostic or an atheist. Again and again Christianity, in the days of utmost feebleness, had opponents as strong or stronger than any she is likely to encounter in future, and for the most part their very names are forgotten : philosophy has done its worst from the days of Celsus to the days of Schopenhauer, yet Christians have multiplied by millions. . . . Again and again in the seventeenth and eighteenth centuries has the roar of Antichrist been heard, and again and again when the scoffers have been driven back in disastrous rout, the archangel of the Church has been standing on the prostrate body, his sword unhacked, no blood-stains upon his armor, not one plume ruffled in his azure wings. From no armies which the world can raise against her has Christianity anything to fear.

IX. 149.

If e'er when faith had fallen asleep
I heard a voice, "Believe no more,"
And heard an ever-breaking shore
That tumbled in the godless deep;

A warmth within the breast would melt
The freezing reason's colder part,
And like a man in wrath the heart
Stood up and answered, "I have *felt*."

TENNYSON.

NOVEMBER 11.

Thou madest him to have dominion over the works of Thy hands; Thou hast put all things under his feet. — Ps. viii. 6.

ARE we, after all, so very helpless before the aggregate of [Nature's] mighty forces, as materialism loves to represent? Not so! "Replenish the earth, and subdue, and have dominion," said the first utterance of God to man. And what is this but an equivalent of the latest utterances of science, that "the order of nature is ascertainable by our faculties to an extent which is practically unlimited, and that our volition counts for something in the course of events"? Man has done much to make the world in all senses a worse place for himself, but he has also, thank God, done much to make it better, and he may, to an almost unspeakable extent, remedy for himself and for his race the throes and agonies of the groaning universe.

II. 170.

In His vast work, for good or ill,
　The undone and the done He blends:
With whatsoever woof we fill,
　To our weak hands His might He lends,
And gives the threads beneath His eye
The texture of eternity.

LUCY LARCOM.

NOVEMBER 12.

These things have I written unto you that believe on the name of the Son of God, that ye may know that ye have eternal life. — I. JOHN v. 13.

WHERE faith is, there is life : where it is not, there is death. This metaphor of life and death runs all through Scripture from its first page to its last. Would that we grasped it! The busy scenes of guilty crowded cities ; the rush and moil and care of business; the gayety and fascination of what men call pleasure ; the lust of the flesh, the lust of the eyes, and the pride of life ; the glamour of wealth, the fury of ambition, the gratified egotism of success — this is what men call "life."

It is not life, it is death ; death in its hollowness ; death in its anguish of retribution ; death in its initiation ; death in its issues; the death of the body in its pollution and corruption ; the death of the soul in its paralysis and stupefaction ; the death of the spirit in its extinction and obliteration. V. 12, 13.

> Ah, then, I pray Thee, gracious Lord,
>   By that eternal love
> Which brought Thee down, for my poor sake,
>   From Thy bright throne above ;
>
> At every risk, at every cost,
>   Whatever pain it be,
> To break and bruise without remorse
>   These germs of death in me.
>
> EDWARD CASWALL.

Whatsoever he saith unto you, do it. — JOHN ii. 5.

THE will of God, in these lower regions of distortion and perversion, does not work automatically. It is His will that all work *for* man should, with the help of His grace, be done *by* man. "Well, God mend all!" said Lord Rea, in 1630. "Nay," impatiently exclaimed Sir David Ramsay, "nay, Donald, we must help Him to mend it."

> "God cannot make man's best
> Without best men to help Him."
>
> IV. 83.

Let us lay it down as an unalterable law of the Divine economy that God never does for man what man can do for himself. Why it is so we cannot tell; why God should leave it to men so feeble and so faithless as ourselves to further His Kingdom we cannot tell, but so it is. Remember, then, that the cause of God rests in the hands of every single soul among you.   IX. 98.

> I must not fail
> Nor be discouraged. In the work of God
> No man may turn or falter: I am His,
> Not mine, . . . when God hath need of Me.
>
> B. M.

NOVEMBER 14.

Do not yield to over-anxiety. Fevered work, flurried work, anxious work, restless work, is always bad work. . . . Do your best loyally and cheerfully, and suffer yourself to feel no anxiety or fear. Your times are in God's hands. He has assigned you your place. . . . He will accept your efforts if they be faithful. He will bless your aims if they be for your soul's good. Regard your present life — the present conditions of your life — as His assignment and His boon; regard the present hours — yea, the very moments of your life — as no less important, as no less certain to enjoy God's blessing of innocent happiness and cheerful hope — perhaps far more so — than any of the moments which are yet to come. Do your best then in quietness, not in feverish impulse; do your best with confidence, — not confidence in your poor, ignorant, feeble self, but in a merciful and tender God, and be quite sure that whatever else may happen to you, or not happen, this at least will happen — which is greater than all earthly blessing — that His loving Spirit will lead you into the land of righteousness.

VI. 78.

> "He doeth well who doeth his best;
> He doeth well who strives;
> Noblest efforts may sometimes fail,
> Never noble lives:
> Work the six days, pray all seven;
> Trust the rest to the grace of Heaven."

NOVEMBER 15.

That ye might be filled with the knowledge of His will in all wisdom and spiritual understanding. — COL. i. 9.

KNOWLEDGE without wisdom is, as even a corrupt and worldly poet has expressed it,

"Dim as the borrowed beams of moon or stars
To lonely, weary, wandering travellers;
And as their twinkling tapers disappear
When day's bright lord ascends the hemisphere,
So pale grows Reason at Religion's sight,
So dies and so dissolves in supernatural light."

Wisdom then is the principal thing, therefore get wisdom. But what is wisdom? The world gives the name to many higher and lower manifestations of intellectual foresight and practical sense, but Scripture sees in it nothing save one single law of life. X. 152.

But where shall wisdom be found? . . .
The depth saith, It is not in me:
And the sea saith, It is not with me.
It cannot be gotten for gold,
Neither shall silver be weighed for the price thereof. . . .
Destruction and Death say,
We have heard the fame thereof with our ears.
God understandeth the way thereof,
And He knoweth the place thereof. . . .
And unto man He said,
Behold, the fear of the Lord, that is wisdom;
And to depart from evil, that is understanding.
JOB xxviii. 12, 14, 15, 22, 23, 28.

NOVEMBER 16.

GOD helps those who help themselves. Were it not so, if vice could, with a wish, yawn into being the rewards of virtue; if sluggishness could, at a touch, appropriate to itself the gifts of toil: then prayer would corrupt the world. But God will not listen to a prayer that is not a prayer; nor will He regard as a prayer the drawling formula of the sluggard or the sly falsehood of the hypocrite. Action, effort, perseverance: these are the touchstones that test the pure gold of sincerity. Pagans saw something of the truth. "To the persevering man," says the Persian poet, "the blessed immortals are swift;" and one of the most vigorous of the Roman emperors died with the grand word "*laboremus*" on his lips. And labor may do much; but if we add the *oremus* to the *laboremus,* then the two are simply irresistible. The race is not to the swift, nor the battle to the strong, but to the diligent and to the prayerful.

VI. 164.

>Faith is a grasping of Almighty power;
>The hand of man laid on the arm of God, —
> The grand and blessed hour
>In which the things impossible to me
>Become the possible, O Lord, through Thee.
>
>ANNA E. HAMILTON.

NOVEMBER 17.

Truly our fellowship is with the Father, and with His Son Jesus Christ. — I. JOHN i. 3.

"OUR fellowship is *with the Father.*" Ah! if we could but grasp that one truth, how would all life be elevated and inspired! how would it cease to look dim, and mean, and not worth living! how would it catch and reflect the glory of its encircling heaven! For this fellowship is eternal life. Half the systems of human philosophy and religion have been devised to rear up some ladder, of endless rounds, between earth and heaven; to bridge, by some intermediate agencies, the fathomless cleft which seemed to separate man from God. There is but one ladder: it is the Son of man, on whom angels ascended and descended. There is but one bridge: it is that bridge of the Divine Humanity, with its one vast span flung by God Himself over the immeasurable void. When we separate ourselves from God by wilful sin we may well despair; for then we are the most deplorable and miserable of all the creatures which God has made: but when we attain, as we may attain, to fellowship with Him, then we may feel that there is a "grandeur in the beatings of the heart," for then life is immortality.

V. 21.

> And when I sit and think of this
>   I am so glad,
> That half it seems that nevermore
>   Can I be sad!
>
> JOHN W. CHADWICK.

NOVEMBER 18.

"*AND with His Son Jesus Christ.*" Fellowship with God is not possible without fellowship with the man Christ Jesus. It is not a different fellowship, but one nearer, more tender, more capable of realization. In Christ we see a God whom we can imagine, whom we can know; who does not hide Himself; who has a face like our own face; who still wears the glorified body of humanity; who speaks to us in that still small voice, of which the accents stir our inmost souls. That Jesus, whose blessed feet walked by the lake of Galilee — that Christ of whom all the prophets prophesied — is God in the form of man, the God-man, who condescended for us men and for our salvation to be a living personal friend. Do not, I entreat you, take this for a mere conventional formula, a mere theological phrase; it represents a reality wherein alone lies the secret of eternal life.

V. 22.

Is the way long? Meseems not so.
No way is long where friends do go
   In converse low, and sweet, and deep, —
And all the way I have with me
   My Lord's dear companie.

Is the way hard? But, surely, nay!
For "Lean on me," His voice doth say;
   And scarce I know the path grows steep,
So wondrously it heartens me,
   My Lord's dear companie.

J. L. M. W.

NOVEMBER 19.

That which we have seen and heard declare we unto you also, that ye also may have fellowship with us. . . . And these things we write that your joy may be full.—I. JOHN i. 3, 4.

GOD has no favorites. He did not give to the first disciples an infinitely exceptional privilege which He denied to the countless millions of mankind. . . . It is not such bodily nearness to our Lord which could have been of the least help to us. Do not let us cheat ourselves as if we were ruined for lack of a mere "might have been." We are better off, not worse off, than the poor disciples of Galilee. Christ Himself said to them that His bodily absence meant His nearer spiritual presence. . . . And did He not pronounce a distinct beatitude on those who have not seen, yet believe? If we think the Apostles so specially blessed, let us remember that the very object of their preaching, the one reason why the New Testament was written, was that we might have fellowship with them; that all which they had enjoyed might, in richer fulness of fruition, belong to all who love the Lord Jesus Christ. . . . This unity in love, is the essence of Christ's kingdom. V. 17, 19.

    So search we, Lord, not for some rare
      Far visions of Thy face;
    In present loves and joys and toils
      Let us Thy presence trace;
    In brave contentions for the right,
      Forgivenesses of wrong,
    The fears that hope, the tears that smile,
      Weak lives by faith made strong.
                      DENIS WORTMAN.

NOVEMBER 20.

WHO are we, creatures so slight and so transient, things so ordinary and so ignoble, that we should have fellowship with God? And yet this is the very meaning of the Incarnation; it is the sole and immense reality, and without it all life is a fatal shipwreck or a hollow dream. Let us, then, with the deepest reverence and solemnity, try to understand something of what God is. You will ask, "How can we do so?" Can the finite compass the infinite? Can a dewdrop measure all the oceans? No; but I answer that it is the very meaning of the Gospel that Christ has taken up the Finite into the Infinite, so that two whole and perfect natures— that is to say, the Godhead and the Manhood— are joined together in the one Person never to be divided; and I answer that the dewdrop, no less than the ocean, can mirror the blue depth of heaven. And thus, in its measure, the finite mortal being of man *can* apprehend—nay, can even be changed into—the image of the infinite eternal God.

V. 31.

> Thou art a sea without a shore;
> Awful, immense Thou art;
> A sea which can contract itself
> Within my narrow heart.
>
> And yet Thou art a haven too
> Out on the shoreless sea,
> A harbor that can hold full well
> Shipwrecked Humanity.

FABER.

NOVEMBER 21.

THE terms of our fellowship of love should be Catholic, as the Church of God. The railing restrictions which fence in as with razors and pitchforks the narrow wicket of parties, and would fain make the portal of the Church itself bristle with anathemas, are unevangelic, unapostolic, unchristian. The more we are Christians the more will our faith "be broad with the breadth of the charity of Almighty God, and narrow only with the narrowness of His righteousness." To those who tried at Corinth to foster party spirit, and draw party distinctions, St. Paul addressed the indignant question, μεμέρισται ὁ Χριστός; "Has Christ been parcelled into fragments?" . . . Partisans are ever ready to say with the Sons of Thunder, "We forbade him because he followeth not after us;" but Christ's answer was, "Forbid him not." Fatal will it be to any Church to prefer the Elijah spirit which calls down fire from heaven to the Christ spirit which forbears and forgives.

"The true religion sprung from God above,
  Is like its fountain, full of charity;
  Embracing all things with a tender love,
    Full of good-will, and meek expectancy;
    Full of true justice and sure verity;
  In voice and heart free, large, ev'n infinite;
    Not wedged in strait particularity,
  But grasping all things in her free, active spirit.
  Bright lamp of God! Oh! that all men could joy
    In thy pure light!"

VIII. 273.

NOVEMBER 22.

Gather up the fragments that remain, that nothing be lost. — JOHN vi. 12.

IN giving us time, God gives us all. Still, morning by morning, He causes another day — a day unstained — to dawn for us out of His eternity; still, morning by morning, His hand holds forth to us a green leaf out of the tree of life. Such a day is this. Oh, waste it not! Is there a good impression that you have suffered to grow faint? Is there a holy practice that you have long neglected? Have you an offended friend who is still unreconciled? a temper still unchecked? a besetting sin still unresisted? — oh, here is work for you to-day! "Watch against that which, in your better heart, with your truer self, you desire not to do; watch for the thing which you feel you ought to do;" and . . . so gather up the fragments that remain, lest *all* be lost.

VI. 127.

The time for sowin' seed, it is wearin', wearin' dune;
An the time for winnin' souls will be ower verra sune:
Then let us a' be active, if a fruitfu' sheaf we'd bring
To adorn the royal table i' the palace of the King.

WILLIAM MORRIS.

NOVEMBER 23.

Ask, and it shall be given you; seek, and ye shall find. — MATT. vii. 7.

IF any of you cared to make to-day so poor a vow, as that you would die rich, there is no doubt that you could die rich. If any of you willed to-day to force your path to power and distinction, there is no doubt that you could so force on to power and distinction. Nature will give you nothing for nothing. She offers you her gifts clenched tight in a granite hand, and before you can have them you must force that hand open by sheer labor. Say what you will have, pay the price, and she will give it you; she will give it you, although she warns you beforehand, that if rank, and wealth, and fame, and ease, are what you long for, these, without God's blessing, are apples of Sodom filled with bitter dust. . . . And though this be true of earthly things, it is ten times more indisputably true of the better and the heavenly. Oh, covet earnestly the best gifts, and you shall have them. Here God says to you with yet more earnest insistency, "Ask what I shall give thee." Dost thou love uprightness? Ask it, *will* it, and thou shalt be upright. Dost thou love purity? Ask it, will it, and thou shalt be pure. Dost thou feel the high ideal of moral nobleness? Ask for it, will it, and thou shalt be noble.

VI. 165, 167.

Be boundless in thy faith, for not misspent
Is confidence unto the Father lent:
Thy need is sowed and rooted for His rain.
GEORGE MACDONALD.

NOVEMBER 24.

He that is unjust in the least is unjust also in much. — LUKE xvi. 10.

WHAT a world of warning lies in those words! The little foxes that spoil the vines — the little canker that slays the oak — the little leak which ever gains upon the vessel till it sinks — the little fissure in the mountain-side, out of which the lava pours — the little rift within the lute that, slowly widening, makes the music mute — what are all these, in their ruinous influence, but a fit emblem of the sinfulness of little sins? how do they illustrate that old proverb that the mother of mischief is no bigger than a midge's wing! Yes, my brethren, small injustices are but the wet and slippery stepping-stones down into deeper waters. He who is unjust in a penny now may be so in thousands of pounds hereafter. He who is not perfectly honest in trifles now, may, if unchecked, develop, in later life, a character radically untrustworthy — fundamentally unsound.

VI. 12.

It was only a seed that fell,
  A downy and tiny seed;
And few that saw it could tell
  What an evil and pestilent weed
Would spring from that little sphere,
  With power to spread at the root
Till it choked out all blossoms of cheer,
  And cut off all promise of fruit.

J. L. M. W.

NOVEMBER 25.

EVERY day of your life repeats the question, "Ask what I shall give thee." Every day comes to you like the Sibyl of old to the incredulous king, offering you priceless opportunities of wisdom, and, as they are rejected, tossing them into the flame, and passing away in sorrow or contempt.

"Muffled and dumb, the hypocritic days,
And marching single in an endless file,
Bring diadems or fagots in their hands.
To each they offer gifts after his will —
Bread, kingdoms, stars, and heaven that holds them all.
I, in my pleachëd garden, watched the pomp,
Forgot my morning wishes, hastily
Took a few herbs and apples, and the day
Turned and departed silent: I too late
Under her solemn fillet saw the scorn."

Of course you will see at a glance that asking God for these gifts at the hands of time or opportunity does not mean *mere* asking; that he who asks must, if his prayer is to be listened to, be sincere in his petition, and if he be sincere, will naturally and necessarily take the means which God appoints. God only helps those who help themselves.   VI. 163.

Ye have not, because ye ask not. Ye ask, and receive not, because ye ask amiss. — JAMES iv. 2, 3.

NOVEMBER 26.

Once more the liberal year laughs out
  O'er richer stores than gems or gold;
Once more with harvest song and shout
  Is Nature's bloodless triumph told.

   .   .   .   .

O favors every year made new!
  O gifts with rain and sunshine sent!
The bounty overruns our due,
  The fulness shames our discontent.
WHITTIER.

FOR the blessings of freedom and self-government we ought to thank God. . . . There is not an [American] among us all who ought not to feel and to rejoice that he is a son of

"The land which freemen till,
  Which sober-suited Freedom chose;
A land where, girt with friends or foes,
A man may speak the thing he will."

We, then — perhaps more than any nation under the sun — owe this debt of thanksgiving unto God. . . . So shall we be able to hold our own against every force which can be brought against us; so shall we realize more and more the Psalmist's golden picture of national prosperity, that "truth shall flourish out of the earth, and righteousness look down from heaven. Yea, the Lord shall show loving-kindness, and our land shall give her increase. Righteousness shall go before Him, and He shall direct her going in the way."   II. 269, 270, 285.

It is a comely fashion to be glad, —
Joy is the grace we say to God.
JEAN INGELOW.

NOVEMBER 27.

Blessed are they which do hunger and thirst after righteousness; for they shall be filled.
MATT. v. 6.

ALAS! there are many in the world who seem to hunger and thirst after *nothing*. It is a type which in this age is getting more and more common, the type of those who live as though they had no souls, as though no God had made them, no Saviour died for them, no Spirit shone in the temple of their hearts. They live but little better than the beasts that perish, the life of dead, stolid, spiritless comfort, the life without purpose, without effort, without nobility, without enthusiasm, "the dull, gray life, and apathetic end." The great sea of human misery welters around them; but what is that to them, while the bread is given and the water sure? Over them, vast as the blue dome of Heaven, brood the eternal realities; before them, deeper than ever plummet sank, flows the river of death; beyond it, in gloom unutterable or in beauty that cannot be described, is either the outer darkness or the City of our God; but it seems as though they had neither mind to imagine, nor faith to realize, nor heart to understand. VI. 24.

Thanks, O Lord,
That still my heart with hunger faints!
The day will come when at Thy board
I sit, forgetting all my plaints.

If rain must come and winds must blow,
And I pore long o'er dim-seen chart,
Yet, Lord, let not the faintness go,
But keep the hunger at my heart.
GEORGE MACDONALD.

NOVEMBER 28.

Be ye also ready, for in such an hour as ye think not the Son of Man cometh. — ST. MATTHEW xxiv. 44.

"THE last day is hidden, that all days may be observed." . . . The lesson to us, the lesson to all, is, Watch. One of those old Jewish Rabbis . . . tells how once in a vision he asked the Prophet Elijah when should Messiah come. "Go and ask Him," said Elijah. "Where shall I find Him?" "He sits among the beggars at the gate of Rome." The Rabbi went and found Him, and asked when He would come. "To-day," was the answer. The Rabbi returned to Elijah the Prophet, and told him the story; but even while he was telling it, the day was over, and the sun had set. "How?" exclaimed the Rabbi; "the day is past, and He has not come! Has He then spoken falsely to me?" "No," answered the Prophet; "what He meant was, 'To-day if ye will hear His voice.'" Yes, . . . "to-day if ye will hear His voice, harden not your hearts."

I. 203.

Who shall know the Master's coming?
Whether it be at dawn or sunset,
When night dews weigh down the wheat-ears,
Or, while noon rides high in heaven,
    Sleeping lies the yellow field?
Only may Thy voice, Good Master,
Peal above the reaper's chorus
And dull sounds of sheaves slow falling, —
  "Gather all into My garner,
    For it is My harvest time."

DINA MULOCH CRAIK.

NOVEMBER 29.

CHRIST comes in many ways. In some way, we know not How, we know not When; it may be this very day; it may be (for to Him a thousand years are but as one day), it may be long æons hence, He shall return in Visible Presence on the rolling clouds of heaven, with ten thousands of His saints. But meanwhile to each of us, in one way or another, in mercy or in judgment; like the falling dew or the flaming fire; by natural retributions, or in special providences; in the events of life, or at the hour of death, Christ comes. There are for us but two lessons as regards His coming, . . . which all Scripture teaches; the first is, Be ready for Him; the second is, Be ready by the faithful performance of your duties, whatever they may be, in that state of life to which God has called you.

I. 202

Who are we to entertain,
. . . .
  Him the glory of whose train
    Makes the stainless Heavens afraid?
  Yet He comes, and sweetly waits
    Entrance to our hearts to win:
  Lift your heads on high, ye gates,
    Let the gentle Master in!

  And as we receive this day
    Joyfully our Royal Guest,
  So at length when far away
    Breaks the dawn of promised rest,
  Where the Lord His Church awaits,
    Sweetest welcome may we win:
  Lift your heads, ye golden gates,
    Let My ransomed people in!

B. M.

NOVEMBER 30.

In quietness and confidence shall be your strength.
Is. xxx. 15.

THE connection of this text with the name and life of St. Andrew is not quite meaningless or artificial. The very little that is known of him exhibits forcibly that quietness and confidence to which our text exhorts. . . . It was to that untroubled vision enjoyed by the pure in heart and hand that he owed by God's blessing the proud preëminence of being among the very earliest of our Lord's disciples; and this is why his name stands first, in immediate connection with Advent Sunday, in the bright calendar of the Apostles and Saints of God. There are two kinds of character, — the fervent and the contemplative, — and each of them is admirable. . . . But each of them is liable to a certain degeneracy, so that instead of fervor we find restlessness, and instead of quietude, lethargy. . . . To both of these characters this text offers an antidote; to the self-satisfied a confidence which is not conceit, a quietude which is that of a glassy sea, not of a stagnant and corrupting pool; to the restless and anxious, a quietude and a confidence which are nothing else than a calm and happy faith in God.
VI. 72, 73, 75.

> Serene will be our days and bright,
> And happy will our nature be,
> When love is an unerring light,
> And joy its own security.
> And they a blissful course may hold
> Even now, who, not unwisely bold,
> Live in the spirit of this creed.
> WORDSWORTH.

DECEMBER 1.

"What can we do, o'er whom the unbeholden
    Hangs in a night wherewith we dare not cope?
What but look sunward, and with faces golden
    Speak to each other softly of hope?"

NOT to one of all the unnumbered generations whose dust is blown upon the desert winds has it been permitted to breathe one syllable or letter of the dim and awful secret beyond the grave. And yet the faith of man has not been shaken, nor, for all this deep, unbroken silence, has he ever ceased to believe that He who called us into being will bless, will save, will cherish the souls which He has made. We feel sure He did not mean us merely "to be born weeping, to live complaining, and to die disappointed," and so cease to be, but that He has a new home for us in other worlds. It is the *fact* which we believe; the details are not revealed to us.   XIV. 12.

*I believe in the Communion of Saints,
In the Forgiveness of sins,
The Resurrection of the body,
And the Life everlasting. Amen.*

DECEMBER 2.

Oh, for a nearer insight into heaven,
More knowledge of the glory and the joy
Which there unto the happy souls are given,
Their intercourse, their worship, their employ;
For it is past belief that Christ hath died
Only that we unending psalms may sing;
That all the gain Death's awful curtains hide
Is this eternity of antheming!

T. LYNCH.

IN other stars, amid His countless worlds, for all we know God may have work for us to do. Who knows what radiant ministrations, what infinite activities, what never-ending progress, what immeasurable happiness, what living ecstasies of unimaginable rapture, . . . [may be ours] where all things are lovely, honorable, pure; where there is no moral ugliness; where repulsive squalor, and insane desire, and pinching selfishness shall be no more!

Oh, if this be a dull, gross, selfish, sensual conception, give us a greater and a better that we may live on it; for we can conceive of none lovelier than this, and to us *this is* Heaven.

XIV. 19, 21.

We know not: but if life be There
  The outcome and the crown of this,
  What else can make their perfect bliss
Than in the Master's work to share?

E. H. PLUMPTRE.

DECEMBER 3.

> For faith and peace and mighty love
> That from the Godhead flow,
> Showed them the life of Heaven above
> Springs from the life below.
>
> EMERSON.

IF we desire Heaven, we must seek it here; if we love Heaven, we must love it now.

Put away the love of money, and ask God to give you His true riches. Put away selfishness, and ask God to give you the Spirit of His holy love. Put away lying, and be sincere. Put away conceit, and in the ashes of your self-abasement, tie round you the sackcloth of humility. . . . So shall you begin to know what Heaven is! so shall you begin to have a foretaste of its happiness, even amid the sorrows of earth. So shall there be in your own hearts, amid all darknesses, a circle of radiant peace. Oh, you shall need the aid of no symbols, for you will think of Heaven not as of some meadow of asphodel beside the crystal waters, or golden city in the far-off blue, but as an extension, as a development, as an undisturbed continuance of righteousness, and peace, and joy in believing; you shall know that, whatever else it be or mean, Heaven means holiness; "Heaven means principle;" Heaven means to be at one with God.

XIV. 21, 25.

DECEMBER 4.

*Why art thou cast down, O my soul? . . .
Hope thou in God: for I shall yet praise Him for
the help of His countenance.* — Ps. xlii. 5.

NEVER let us despair of ourselves; never let us despair of others. There is a light which lighteth every man that cometh into the world; we may dim it as with the darkness of the mine; we may make it burn low as in the vapors of the charnel-house, — but quench it quite finally and utterly we cannot. "Our lamps are gone out," say the foolish virgins in the parable, but it is in the original, not "our lamps are gone out," but our lamps are being quenched, are going out.

I. 154.

And therefore I bid you take courage. Even if in your slothfulness the lamp has burned too low, even if in your sinfulness it has been all but smothered, yet, oh, believe that even now there is One who will not quench the smoking flax, there is a breath of God which even now, like a stream of fire, can rekindle the smouldering flame.

VI. 50.

From lamps going out, gone out; from any light that shineth not to the glory of our Heavenly Father,
From such temporal love and joy as forfeit eternal love and joy,
From earthly gain which is heavenly loss, . . .
Deliver us, deliver all men, O Lord. Amen.

CHRISTINA ROSSETTI.

Behold, the bridegroom cometh; go ye out to meet Him. — MATT. xxv. 6.

YOU who will go forth on the path of life to meet the bridegroom, beware but of one conscious, one admitted, one unresisted sin. Nothing quenches more surely the holy lamp. You may try to think of the sin as venial; you may try to hold each fresh commission thereof light; but it is even thus that, star by star, the whole heavens fade away from the human soul; even thus that one by one its excellences vanish, its virtues faint, its graces cease to shine. As when a man descends slowly into some dark mine and carries a taper in his hand, and knows that so long as the flame of that taper burns bright and clear, so long the atmosphere he breathes is safe; but as he gets lower the flame begins to contract and to grow pale, and then to waver, and at last, as the foul fog-damps surround and imprison it, . . . expires with a foul breath of sickening fume; even so it is, alas! with him who, from the sunlight of God's countenance, descends deeper and deeper — with conscious self-surrender, with willing guilt, with impotent because with unresisting will — into the deep dark underground of a besetting sin. VI. 48.

"Pure oil of love, and faith, and steadfast will,
Give us, O Lord, our failing lamps to fill!"

DECEMBER 6.

Blessed are they that hear the word of God, and keep it. — LUKE xi. 28.

WE profess to regard the Bible as the one sacred Book. We profess to derive from it, almost exclusively, the doctrines of our faith and the rules of our conduct. We turn to it in hours of temptation; we find in it the songs of our purest rejoicing; the memory of the dead . . . passes into it; the potent traditions of childhood are stereotyped in its verses; it speaks to us with a music that can never be forgotten; we read it (and it seems as if we could read nothing else) by the bedside of the dying, and over the graves of our beloved. Yet how many of us ever approximately understand it? How many of us obtain from this one Book of God the treasure, and the joy, and the peace which we might obtain from it, better and in larger measure than from all the books which fill the world?   I. 160.

> This book, this holy book, on every line
> Marked with the seal of high divinity,
> On every leaf bedewed with drops of love
> Divine, and with the eternal heraldry
> And signature of God Almighty stamped
> From first to last, — this ray of sacred light,
> This lamp from off the everlasting throne,
> Mercy took down, and in the night of time
> Stood, casting on the dark her gracious bow:
> And evermore beseeching men, with tears
> And earnest sighs, to read, believe, and live.
> POLLOK.

DECEMBER 7.

The Scripture cannot be broken. — JOHN x. 35.

SCRIPTURE contains in germ nine-tenths of all that is best and noblest in the literature of two millenniums of Christianity. . . . The hundred best books, the hundred best pictures, the hundred best pieces of music, are all in it. "The literature of Greece," says Theodore Parker, "which goes up like incense from that land of temples, has not half the influence of this book of a despised nation. The sun never sets upon its gleaming page." "What a book!" exclaimed the sceptic Heine, after a day spent in the unwonted task of reading it. "Vast and wide as the world, rooted in the abysses of creation, and towering up beyond the blue secrets of heaven! Sunrise and sunset, promise and fulfilment, birth and death, the whole drama of humanity, all are in this book." Millions loved it passionately who have cared for no other literature; and it has led them through life as with an archangel's hand. . . . The greatest men have esteemed it most; and its words speak to the ear and to the heart as no other music will, even after wild and wicked lives.

Read it teachably, read it devotionally, read it in humility and love, and then no Urim which the High-Priest wore has ever gleamed with such lessons as it will reveal to you.

VII. 154, 157.

DECEMBER 8.

Whatsoever things were written aforetime were written for our learning, that we through patience and comfort of the Scriptures might have hope. — ROM. xv. 4.

LET me entreat you . . . not to confuse mere questions of exegetical or scientific learning with the deep, awful, imperishable lessons which the Bible, and the Bible only, can bring home to your soul. Other books may fascinate the intellect; by this alone can you cleanse the heart. In other literatures may trickle here and there some shallow runnel from the "unemptiable fountain of wisdom," . . . but in this book, majestic and fathomless, flows the river of the water of life itself, proceeding out of the throne of God and of the Lamb; . . . here alone — in more infinite abundance, of more incomparable worth — are the pearls of great price, the wisdom more precious than rubies, the "Light from beyond the sun." And be sure that the hour will come not rarely to you in the destinies of life — the hour of sickness, of bereavement, of disappointment, of deathful agony — when all other knowledge and all other insight shall be as useless dross; but every text stored up in the memory, each pure lesson, each bright example from the sacred page, shall be to your stricken and fainting souls "better than gold, yea, than much fine gold; sweeter also than honey and the honeycomb."

XI. 5.

DECEMBER 9.

We have not followed cunningly devised fables.
II. PET. i. 16.

IF the lapse of centuries have dimmed for us the historic brightness of the facts of our religion, it has at least attested the permanence and the beneficence of the system which rests upon them as its base. And since, undeniably, the rock on which Christ built His Church *has* risen unshaken out of the stormiest waves of past assault, we may well feel an undaunted confidence, that even amid the decuman billows of modern scepticism it shall remain immovable as the granite bases of the world. It may be deluged again and again by the fiercely recurrent surge,—it may be hidden again and again from the eyes of the multitude by the blinding spray,—but it is there; and so long as the feet of the Church militant on earth be planted firm upon that living rock, she may indeed be desolate, she may be wounded, she may be oppressed, but so long we believe and are sure that "the gates of Hell shall not prevail against her."

XII. 4.

'Mid toil and tribulation,
  And tumult of her war,
She waits the consummation
  Of peace for evermore;
Till with the vision glorious
  Her longing eyes are blest,
And the great Church victorious
  Shall be the Church at rest.

SAMUEL JOHN STONE.

THE CROSS.

Sink in, thou blessed Sign!
  Pass all my spirit through,
And sever with thy sacred touch
  The hollow from the true.
. . . .
Through my heart's very ground
  Thy ploughshare must be driven;
Till all are better loved than self,
  And yet less loved than Heaven.

CAROLINE M. NOEL.

THE Cross is the sign of eternal conquest. Is it the sign of conquest for ourselves only? dare we so confine its significance? Is its divine power to be dwarfed into the narrowness of self-congratulation, or into the slightly expanded egotism which shall see nothing more in Christ's work than the salvation of some handful of a Church, or some fraction of a sect? Are we to eternize and deify

"The sin of self, who in the universe,
  As in a mirror, sees her fond face shown,
And crying 'I' would have the world say 'I,'
  And all things perish so but she endure"?

Not so! Christ who has left us is still with us; and He shall return again.   II. 162.

DECEMBER 11.

IF you would know how God loves even the guiltiest of His children, see Misery left alone with Mercy on the Temple floor, and hear the voice so awful in its warning, yet so solemn in its tenderness, "Neither do I condemn thee; go and sin no more." And he who thus represented God by His acts, how did He represent Him in His words? Was it not solely, essentially, exclusively as a Father? as "our Father which art in Heaven;" as the God who maketh the sun to rise on the evil and the good, and sendeth rain on the just and on the unjust; as the God of little children, whose angels behold His face in heaven; as the God of the lilies and the ravens; the God of the lost sheep; the God of the falling sparrow; the God of the Prodigal Son; the God by whom the very hairs of our head are all numbered; in one word, which comprises all, the God of love? Yes, this is the true God and Eternal Life.

> Dear God and Father of us all,
>   Forgive our faith in cruel lies,
>   Forgive the blindness that denies,
> Forgive thy creature, when he takes
>   For the all-perfect love Thou art
>   Some grim creation of his heart.
> Cast down our idols; overturn
>   Our bloody altars: let us see
>   Thyself in Thy humanity.
>
> VIII. 182.

Inasmuch as ye have done it unto one of the least of these my brethren, ye have done it unto me.

MATT. XXV. 40.

DECEMBER 12.

IF we would help to cure the world . . . of the cancer of *Greed*, it will be useless if we ourselves are basely and selfishly fond of money. We must ourselves be superior to this dull yellow fascination; we must ourselves be able to pour silent contempt on gold; to have the open hand and the liberal heart; to prove our belief in the truth that it is more blessed to give than to receive; to find our best investments in private acts of charity and public deeds of munificence; to stem, so far as we can, that creeping wave of niggardliness which, like the muddy tide on the coast of Lancashire, is "always shallow, yet always just high enough to drown." The threepenny pieces in the offertory plate must no longer be the indication of the organized hypocrisy of our charitableness, and the daring secrecy of our unbelief.

II. 74.

Better to be the man that daily strives,
  Though humbly poor, to uplift human lives,
Than he whose hand, though heaped with shining gold,
  Is reached to shield no outcast from the cold;
Who drags out life in dull and dark unrest,
  And leaves the world unblessing and unblest.

JANE GREENOUGH AVERY CARTER.

DECEMBER 13.

Judge nothing before the time, until the Lord come, who both will bring to light the hidden things of darkness, and will make manifest the counsels of the heart. — I. COR. iv. 5.

MAN'S judgment days are partial, hasty, unjust, mechanical. God's assize is silent. His retributions execute themselves. His thunder-bolts are slowly hammered by our own hands in the furnace of our iniquities, when at last they gleam with the white heat of Divine anger, and they rush down with unerring aim on the head of him who has been forging them. Meanwhile His handwritings are on every wall. And though men and churches and nations are blind to them, and go spinning round their circle of custom and compromise after the giddy flag of their popular falsehoods, they read at last by the unnatural glare of ruin that "God is the only final public opinion."

Why did [Rome] perish? because of her too glaring contrasts between shivering pauperism and colossal wealth. Because she found no men strong enough to rule, and so flung the reins of government to the noisiest and the worst.

VIII. 65.

> When the Muses nine
> With the Virtues meet;
> When the statesman ploughs
> Furrows for the wheat;
> When the Church is social worth;
> When the Statehouse is the hearth, —
> Then the perfect State is come.
>
> EMERSON.

WE cannot serve God and mammon; if we follow Christ in anything but in name, we must sit loose to the world and the world's interests; we must be content, if need be, with the beatitudes of poverty and persecution. For easy wealth and epicurean self-indulgence, though we see in them but little to reprobate, Christ had nothing but that thunder-clap of judgment, and the silence which followed it, "Thou fool, this night;" nothing but the lurid picture of one carried from purple and fine linen to burning thirst and tormenting flame. And why is this? Is it because the infinite King of heaven grudges one poor enjoyment to atoms such as we? No, but because the prosperity of fools destroys them; because these coarse luxuries of the body, these evil joys of the mind, have no happiness in them, and yet, such as they are, make the heart soft and surfeited and vulnerable, unworthy to enjoy His holiness, unfit to do His work.
XI. 47.

Who, in all this world
(Wherein we are haply set to pray and fast,
And learn what good is by its opposite),
Has never hungered? Woe to him who has found
The meal enough: if Ugolino's full,
His teeth have crunched some foul, unnatural thing;
For here satiety proves penury
More utterly irremediable.

ELIZABETH BARRETT BROWNING.

IF you would shun utter shipwreck, you must, by prayer, and penitence, and thoughtfulness, and humility, see that your spirit controls the warring lusts of the body and purifies the wandering affections of the soul. If not, yours will be one more of those wretched dual lives we see; the lives that face both ways; the lives rent by a fatal schism of disunion; the lives which are like bells jangled out of tune; the lives perfectly clear in their convictions, utterly contemptible in their actions. And oh, let me earnestly warn you against the fatal delusion that such a dual, such a divided, such a disharmonious life as this, is enough for God; that there is either virtue or religion in this miserable moral see-saw; that it is sufficient for us to do homage with our lips to what is good, while all the while our unregenerate hearts are full of worldly imagination, and our unsanctified bodies are made the instruments of unrighteousness. VI. 355.

> *Thou* to wax fierce
> In the cause of the Lord,
> To threat and to pierce
> With the heavenly sword!
>
> . . . .
>
> Thou warnest and smitest!
> Yet Christ must atone
> For a soul that thou slightest—
> Thine own!
>
> JOHN HENRY NEWMAN.

DECEMBER 16.

What will ye give me ? — MATT. xxvi. 15.

THE sin of the whole world is essentially the sin of Judas; — men do not disbelieve in Christ — they sell Him. . . . I fear that we are guilty of it in all ranks down to the poorest; guilty of it as individuals, and guilty of it as nations. The growth and habit of luxury, the multiplication of things which are falsely deemed necessary for life, the deepening cleft between capital and labor, the more and more glaring contrast between the ever-breeding thousands and boundless superfluities of the affluent rich and the cramping misery and ingrained envy of the poor; the toleration in great cities of infamous streets full of rotting and fever-causing habitations; the all but total absence of the conception that each one is the steward, and not the owner, of what we have; that wealth is a talent intrusted to us for God's service, not a gift heaped on us for our own aggrandizement; — ah, when we are content with all this, are we never afraid of that awful doom which crashed upon the confidence of sensual and self-congratulating ease? "Thou fool! this night — this night they shall require of thee thy soul!"

VIII. 227.

DECEMBER 17.

OH, if I am speaking to any who are sometimes vexed by the thought that they can only plod on in the paths of humble usefulness, to any who feel that God has given to them but the one talent, not the two or the five; I would remind them how infinitely the great are transcended by the good, I would say to them: Work on without one shadow of discouragement, without one pang of self-depreciation. Do your best, assured that God loves you as though the soul of Plato or of Shakspeare were your own; work with as manly a self-respect as though Empires would be moulded by your counsels, and Senates listen to your words; work with as calm a certainty that He will accept and will bless and will reward that work, as though the sunbeam that falls upon you were streaming down direct from His hand of fatherly blessing, held in invisible consecration over your stooping head.

VI. 69.

The lives which seem so poor, so low,
  The hearts which are so cramped, so dull,
The baffled hopes, the impulse slow,
Thou takest, touchest all, and lo!
  They blossom to the beautiful.

Susan Coolidge.

DECEMBER 18.

THE Roman Senate never did a nobler act than when, after the stupendous defeat of Cannæ, they went out to meet and thank the defeated general, because he had not despaired of the Republic. Even so should all humanity thank the humble martyrs, the obscure benefactors, the unfamous faithful, who, amid toil and obloquy, defrauded of justice, hopeless of reward, deluged with ingratitude, have yet believed in the redeemableness of their brother men. They teach us to look to humanity in its ideal, not in its degradation; in its angelhood, not in its pollution. Even in the vilest they see, as Christian saw, the living soul. They judge of manhood by its saints and heroes, not at all by its "men-slugs and human serpentry."

VII. 241.

> Give human nature reverence for the sake
> Of One who bore it, making it divine
> With the ineffable tenderness of God;
> Let common need, the brotherhood of prayer,
> The heirship of an unknown destiny,
> The unsolved mystery round about us make
> A man more precious than the gold of Ophir;
> Sacred, inviolate, unto whom all things
> Should minister, as outward types and signs
> Of the eternal beauty which fulfils
> The one great purpose of creation, Love,
> The sole necessity of Earth and Heaven!
>
> WHITTIER.

DECEMBER 19.

Am I my brother's keeper? — GEN. iv. 9.

THE spirit that tempts you to deny that you are your brother's keeper is the spirit of Cain; it is the spirit of envy, and sensualism, and selfishness; it is the spirit that draws rents from rotting houses; the spirit that fills our streets with harlots; the spirit which ruins myriads by tempting them to drink; the spirit which for gain poisons everywhere the peace and the purity of life; it is the spirit of Society, not the spirit of the Church; it is the spirit of Mammon, not the spirit of God; it is the spirit of Gain, not the spirit of Christ. In our measure, and in a very full measure, you and I are responsible for the sins of the community. Ask yourselves, search yourselves as with candles, and ask: "Directly or indirectly have I in any way condoned, encouraged, tampered with all these evils?"
IX. 8.

Later, a sweet Voice "Love thy neighbor" said;
Then first the bounds of neighborhood outspread
Beyond the confines of old ethnic dread.
Vainly the Jew might wag his covenant head:
"All men are neighbors," so the sweet Voice said.

. . . .

But oh, the poor! the poor! the poor!
That stand by the inward-opening door
Trade's hand doth ever tighten more;
And sigh their monstrous foul-air sigh
For the outside hills of liberty,
Where Nature spreads her wild blue sky.
SIDNEY LANIER.

DECEMBER 20.

Be careful for nothing. — PHIL. iv. 6.

MYRIADS may tell you of cares haunting them from sunrise to sunset — cares for our livelihood, cares for our health, cares for our prosperity, cares for our incomes; cares — more anxious than any others — about our children and our families; cares, meanest of all others, as to what people will think or say of us; cares whether we shall succeed or no; cares whether our little comforts will last or no; cares out of a haunting past; cares in a restless present, cares about an uncertain future, — oh, it is a chaos, a weltering sea of cares for him who suffers himself to be choked therein. From how many have they torn the diadem to brand in its place the festering stigma of the slave; from how many have they taken the "freshness of the meadow, the coolness of the stream;" in how many have they quenched "bright thoughts, clear deeds, the constancy, the fidelity, the bounty, the generous honesty, which are the germs of noble minds!" . . . Yet we might shake them off for ever, by sitting more loosely to the things of earth; by learning to despise the gilded dust which debases all who love it and set store by it, we might recover our manhood and be free.

XI. 95.

God often would enrich, but finds not where to place His treasure; — nor in hand nor heart a vacant space.

R. G. TRENCH.

DECEMBER 21.

We have seen the Lord. — JOHN xx. 25.

TO him [Thomas] the news seemed too good to be true. . . . Happily for us, though less happily for him, he declared with strong asseveration that nothing would convince him short of actually putting his own finger into the print of the nails. . . . Once more Jesus appeared to them, and after His usual gentle and solemn blessing, bade him stretch forth his finger, and put it into the print of the nails, and to thrust his hand into the spear-wound of His side, and to be "not faithless, but believing." "My Lord and my God!" exclaimed the incredulous Apostle, with a burst of conviction. XIII. 459.

Oh, that each one of us, . . . even if he have doubted as Thomas once doubted, even if he have denied as Peter once denied, — yet feeling that "God was in Christ, reconciling the world unto Himself," feeling that in Him his yearnings are satisfied, by Him his sins forgiven, — may be enabled to raise his eyes to heaven and exclaim from the depths of an adoring and believing heart,
"MY LORD AND MY GOD!"

XII. 88.

Grant, O Lord,
    To the faithless faith,
    To the faithful confirmation of faith. Amen.
CHRISTINA ROSSETTI.

DECEMBER 22.

NOT know the future? Nay, we know it; if we be Christians we know it; not, indeed, this little future of joys that break as the bubble breaks, or of brief afflictions which are but for a moment; not that little future of diseased egotisms and contracted selfishness which is not life; but that great future of the single in purpose and the pure in heart, that great future which blooms to infinitude beyond the marge of death, — *that*, if we be children of God, we know. For we are pressing forward to the mark of the prize of our high calling, and that mark we cannot miss, and there it shines for ever before us — a crown of life, a crown of glory, a crown that fadeth not away. The true Christian need know no fear. Be true to yourselves, be true to God, be "true to the kindred points of heaven and home," and then even . . . on the steep hill of Difficulty, in the Valley of the Shadow, amid the crash of a universe smitten into indistinguishable ruin, "Thou shalt keep him in perfect peace whose mind is stayed on Thee!"

VI. 58.

Behold, He that keepeth Israel
Shall neither slumber nor sleep.
The Lord is thy keeper:
The Lord is thy shade upon thy right hand.
The sun shall not smite thee by day,
Nor the moon by night.
The Lord shall keep thee from all evil;
He shall keep thy soul.

PS. cxxi. 4, 5, 6, 7.

DECEMBER 23.

And this shall be a sign unto you: Ye shall find the babe . . . lying in a manger.
St. Luke ii. 12.

TO the unilluminated fancy it would have seemed incredible that the most stupendous event in the world's history should have taken place without convulsions and catastrophes. . . . The inventions of man differ wholly from the dealings of God. In His designs there is no haste, no rest, no weariness, no discontinuity; all things are done in the majesty of silence, and they are seen under a light that shineth quietly in the darkness, "showing all things in the slow history of their ripening."
XIII. 6.

> The Infinite always is silent,
> It is only the Finite speaks;
> Our words are the idle wave-caps
> On a deep that never breaks,—
> We question with wand of science,
> Explain, decide, and discuss,
> But only in meditation,
> The Mystery speaks to us.
Boyle O'Reilly

DECEMBER 24.

Come unto Me, all ye that labor and are heavy-laden, and I will give you rest. — MATT. xi. 28.

MANY of you are sorrowful. Come ye also to the cradle of your Lord, for you need it most. . . . By the Christmas firesides of some of you there will be vacant chairs and vanished faces. Forget not that the joy of the Incarnation is the joy of the Resurrection also, and that there is not one single innocent joy on earth that is not a shadow of a promise of the eternal joy in heaven. The end of our journey, and the end of their journey, whom you loved, and have lost, is not here. In human life, at one time the wind blows, the rain falls, the frost is cruel; at another the sun shines, the birds sing, and all is May; but through shadow or through sunlight we are travelling onward — they have not changed the end of our journey.

IX. 40.

Glory to God, on earth good-will and peace:
 The song endures, the singers pass away,
 To sing it haply in a fairer day
Where never discords come, nor concords cease.

We sing it too, with hearts that keep the key,
 Though voices falter, — listening evermore
 For far, sweet echoes from that golden shore,
Where we, too, hope one day in peace to be.

J. L. M. W.

DECEMBER 25.

The Word was made flesh. — JOHN i. 14.

THE Nativity, that is the fact. The Incarnation, that is the doctrine and the mystery. The birth of a little babe in the stable of the humble inn, that is the event The Word became flesh — that little babe laid in the manger; He is the King of Kings — there is the mystery.

Through the fact, through the mystery, through all the life and teaching of our Lord, there is one lesson, which, if we could grasp it, would be a lifelong source of strength, of purity, of peace. It is the grandeur of that human nature which God has given us; the sacredness, the majesty, the lofty privileges, the immeasurable possibilities of man. . . . He who looks upon himself as immortal, as a child of God, as a partaker of the nature which Christ wore and Christ redeemed, will hold himself ever more and more bounden to aim at a noble and godly life. VII. 299, 301.

O Blessed Day, which giv'st the eternal lie
To self, and sense, and all the brute within;
O come to us amid this war of life;
To hall and hovel come! to all who toil
In senate, shop, or study! and to those
Ill-warned and sorely tempted —
Come to them, blest and blessing, Christmas Day!
Tell them once more the tale of Bethlehem,
The kneeling shepherds and the Babe Divine,
And keep them Men indeed, fair Christmas Day!
                                            KINGSLEY.

DECEMBER 26.

But he [St. Stephen], *being full of the Holy Ghost, looked up steadfastly into heaven, and saw the glory of God, and Jesus standing on the right hand of God.* — ACTS vii. 55.

> No golden dawn that glitters
>   On the Eastern sea,
> No burning glories of the West,
>   Which transient be,
> Can image how that light broke forth,
>   O blessed martyr, on thee!
>
> He stood transfigured there
>   In the smile of God,
> Not noting the fear and wrath that shook
>   The cruel crowd,
> Not knowing how they set him free,
> To stand with Christ in ecstasy,
>   Where the angels sang aloud.
>
> B. M.

IS not looking at such a life something like looking at a hill-top fired by the first beams of the rising sun? Such palms and such crowns are hardly for us who would "go to heaven in an easy chair." By the side of such lives and such self-denials, do not our lives look very vulgar and very selfish? Yes, but remember that such lives at the best are but a pale reflex and faint echo of His life — the life of the Son of God, by whose precepts they were guided, by whose Spirit they were inspired.

VI. 346.

DECEMBER 27.

"LITTLE children," says St. John, "keep yourselves from idols." God is Light: God is Love. With those hammers of the Word dash in pieces the Ignorance that takes itself for Infallibility, and the Hatred that forges on its phylacteries the signatures of Love.

In Himself God is Light: when His Light disperses itself in color, it is the Universe; when it passes in one unbroken ray, it is He who was the brightness of His Glory, the Eternal Son; reflected upon us, it is the self-communication of perfect love. . . . God is Light: shall we love the deeds of darkness? God is Love: shall we make no sacrifice for Him who has done so much for us? I. 488.

> For by loving, he would not feel the burden
> Because love would carry all burdens;
> And therefore those who complain of the burden,
> Show that they are but little advanced in love.
> To serve Thee from love is most pleasant,
> And a solace of labors.
> Love looks not to its own advantage,
> Nor fears to suffer inconvenience,
> But seeks Thy good pleasure in all things.
> **THOMAS À KEMPIS.**

And in their mouth was found no guile; for they are without fault before the throne of God.
                                  REV. 14. 5.

THE three days since Christmas have been sacred to martyrs — to those who for Christ's sake have been cruelly slain; first, the young man, St. Stephen, then the old man, St. John, and to-day the little innocent children whom Herod murdered when he wished to slay the child Jesus. And this is to teach us that while Christ came to make us happy, yet we must not therefore think that we shall escape trouble. It is to teach us that all Christians — young men, and old men, and even little children — must learn to deny themselves for Jesus' sake. VII. 61.

Humanity at every period of its brief life is sacred, for it is Humanity redeemed and consecrated from the cradle to the grave. The valley of its utmost weakness, no less than its valley of the shadow of death, has been illuminated by the footsteps of its heavenly King. I. 80.

Hath He gone up to glory? so have they. Their grace is eternized, their lustre eternized; their feet rank with wings, their speech has become song:

Unspotted lambs to follow the one Lamb,
  Unspotted doves to follow the one Dove;
To whom Love saith, "Be with Me where I a'
  And lo! their answer unto Love is love._{JETTI.}
                          CHRISTINA I

DECEMBER 29.

But this, I say, brethren, the time is short.
I. COR. vii. 29.

ONCE, when a king was being conducted in a splendid triumphal procession, in all the intoxication of human pride and glory, one of his flattering courtiers asked him, "What is wanting here?" And with a sigh answered the magnificent monarch, "Continuance!" Yes, "for ever and ever." That belongs only to what is divine in man. Continuance, permanence, is the stamp of the eternal life; evanescence, momentariness, the blight of this.

Even if the things for which men toil and moil, and weary themselves in the very fire, could last, they could not satisfy the noblest nature for a day; they could not satisfy even the meanest for a year. . . . Why, it would be even worse for us if such things did last! Of their own selves they would dwarf us into vileness and insignificance. Believe me,

> "The worst of miseries
> Is when a nature, framed for nobler things,
> Condemns itself in life to petty joys,
> And, sore athirst for air, breathes scanty life
> Gasping from out the shallows."

Ought not, then, our one prayer to be the prayer of St. Thomas of Aquino, "Give me, O Lord, a noble heart, which no earthly affections can drag down"?

IV. 251, 252.

DECEMBER 30.

Forgetting those things which are behind, and reaching forth unto those things which are before. — PHIL. iii. 13.

THE river is the same, but the wave is different, — different in its constituent elements, though identical in its continuity of life. This very fact preaches to us to-day; it bids us forget those things which are behind and reach forth to those which are before. . . . Forecast, meditation, retrospect — these are what it demands. *Aspice*, it seems to say, *Prospice, Respice;* look thoughtfully at the present, look forward to the future, look backward at the past; at the present with firm and holy resolution, at the past with humble and penitent gratitude, to the future with calm and earnest hope.

For all of us alike, with the end of this [year], will be shut and ended another volume, wherein is written by Time, the great transcriber, the history of ourselves. In *one* more day the last page will have been turned, the solemn *finis* written.

"Whose hands shall dare to open and explore
Those volumes, closed and clasped for evermore?
Not mine. With reverential feet I pass,
I hear a voice that cries 'Alas! Alas!'
Whatever hath been written shall remain,
Nor be erased, nor written o'er again;
The unwritten only still belongs to thee,
Take heed, and ponder well, what that shall be."

VI. 52, 54.

DECEMBER 31.

Finally, brethren, farewell. — II. COR. xiii. 11.

THERE must be something sad and solemn in partings. They remind us that there is nothing in this world which we can call our own; that all which God gives us is His, not ours; lent, not given. . . . At the best, we, like our fathers, are only dwellers in tents. Here and there — by some sweet well, under some spreading tree, on some green spot — we linger for a time; but the evening comes at last, the stars come out, the encampment is broken up, and we must move away. And very soon we shall have made our last stay of all; the sky will flush with the crimson of its last sunset; the last long shadows of the twilight will lengthen round us; the last farewell will be sighed forth from weary lips. After that our tent will be moved no longer; for then we hope that it will be pitched, for the last time, under the walls of the heavenly city, and the sun shall go down on us no more. VI. 389.

And the city had no need of the sun, neither of the moon, to shine in it: for the glory of God did lighten it, and the Lamb is the light thereof. — REV. xxi. 23.

> O fields that know no sorrow!
> O state that knows no strife!
> O princely bowers! O land of flowers!
> O Realm and Home of Life!
> THE CELESTIAL COUNTRY.

www.ingramcontent.com/pod-product-compliance
Lightning Source LLC
Chambersburg PA
CBHW020312240426
43673CB00039B/785